BABBITTS AND BOHEMIANS

BABBITTS AND BOHEMIANS

The American 1920s

ELIZABETH STEVENSON

The Macmillan Company, NEW YORK
Collier-Macmillan Limited, LONDON

Library of Congress Catalog Card Number: 67-15709

FIRST PRINTING

The Macmillan Company, New York
Collier-Macmillan Canada Ltd., Toronto, Ontario

Printed in the United States of America

To JOHN F. KENNEDY—
who made the American 1960s a good time to be alive—
this book about the American 1920s

ACKNOWLEDGMENTS

My thanks are due:

to William C. Archie, of the Mary Reynolds Babcock Foundation, for sustained belief,

to the Emory University Research Fund, for a grant supporting research, travel, and a summer's leave;

to John C. Stephens, Jr., Dean of Emory College, for understanding and encouragement;

to the Emory community, for patience;

to the New York Public Library, for the use of the Wertheim Room;

to the Prints and Photographs Division of the Library of Congress, for permission to reproduce fourteen photographs;

to Underwood and Underwood, for permission to use five photographs from that firm's collection housed in the Library of Congress;

to Mrs. Esther C. Goddard, for permission to use a photograph of Robert H. Goddard;

to Peter A. Juley & Son of New York, for permission to use a photograph of Stuart Davis;

to New Directions Publishing Corporation, for permission to use quotations from William Carlos Williams: three passages from *The Autobiography of William Carlos Williams;* two passages from *In the American Grain;* and lines from "To A Poor Old Woman" and "The Red Wheelbarrow" (complete poem), from *The Collected Earlier Poems of William Carlos Williams;*

to Joseph Wood Krutch, for a phrase, "the Libertarians," and a quotation from his book, *More Lives Than One,* and for other insights;

to Holt, Rinehart and Winston, Inc., for permission to use Robert Frost's phrase, "America is hard to see," from *In the Clearing;*

to Harcourt, Brace & World, Inc., for permission to use lines from Carl Sandburg's "Jazz Fantasia" from *Smoke and Steel* collected in *Harvest Poems, 1910–1960,* and lines from T. S. Eliot's "The Waste Land" in *Collected Poems;*

to the New Yorker Magazine, Inc., for permission to quote an untitled poem by P. G. Wylie, from the January 2, 1926, issue of *The New Yorker;*

to the Liveright Publishing Corporation, for lines from Hart Crane's "The Bridge" in *Collected Poems of Hart Crane;*

to Alfred A. Knopf, Inc., for permission to use two quotations from Langston Hughes' *The Weary Blues,* and for a phrase, "hard heart of a child" from Elinor Wylie's poem, "Beauty," in *Collected Poems of Elinor Wylie;*

to Grove Press, Inc., for permission to use quotations from two poems of Federico García Lorca, *Poet in New York* (Ben Belitt translation);

to The Viking Press, Inc., for permission to use lines from "The Evening Land" by D. H. Lawrence in *Complete Poems of D. H. Lawrence.*

I appreciate the opportunity to view the special twenties exhibit of the Gallery of Modern Art of New York; and I am thankful for the help I received from the following: Elmira Bier, Assistant to the Director, The Phillips Collection of Washington; Dorothy C. Miller, Curator of the Museum Collections of The Museum of Modern Art of New York; Margaret McKellar, Executive Secretary of the Whitney Museum of American Art of New York.

Living for short periods in Reid Hall in Paris and Crosby Hall in London—both affiliated at the time with the International University Women—enabled me to understand better the world of the expatriates of the 1920s.

My particular thanks are due to Cecil Scott, Editor in Chief of The Macmillan Company, for providing an opportunity for this study of the 1920s—and for imagination and patience during the years of writing.

My gratitude is due my mother, Bernice Upshaw Stevenson, for intelligent sympathy and practical help.

E.S.
Atlanta

CONTENTS

ILLUSTRATIONS

In the eyes of posterity, the success
of the United States as a civilized
society will be largely judged by the
creative activities of its citizens . . .

THE PRESIDENT'S COMMISSION
ON NATIONAL GOALS (1960)

BABBITTS AND BOHEMIANS

I

IDENTITY
OF A DECADE

"America is hard to see."[1] R. Frost

THE RELATIONSHIP BETWEEN THEN AND NOW, between past and present, is always shifting. To a people hungry for depth of history, the American past is a fresh discovery for each generation. As an instance, consider the 1920s. It is a time we thought we knew, but its meaning is changing as we look. Having rounded a radical corner further on in the twentieth century, we find not only the future unknown and the present uncertain ground, but the past strange territory that must be made again to support a groping for the moon and the stars, the uncharted territory of automation, and new kinds of wars.

It is especially hard to see the day before yesterday, the recent past with which we have live connections and which has become mythology before it has become history—"The twilight zone that lies between living memory and written history is one of the favorite breeding places of mythology."[2] The twenties have lent themselves to extravagant foreshortening since they are years set off sharply on one side by the first of the world wars and on the other by the greatest of American depressions. The decade has seemed a sort of accidental pause in history, much of it remembered as if it were a willful, elegant sport of time.

It has become a blurred montage of gangsters terrorizing great cities and of heedless flappers dancing the Charleston upon the tabletops of speakeasies about to be raided by lively but ineffectual cops; of, on the other hand and most unaccountably, great dull stretches of small-town space labeled Main Street or Middletown where the generation just older than the flappers, the cops, and the gangsters are occupying the foreground and doing a respectable fox-trot at a conformable country club. It is reported that there were then also, filling in the hinterland, great numbers of sweating, underpaid farmers and their dowdy wives, clothed out of Sears Roebuck and Montgomery Ward catalogues, living without electricity and waterworks, unable to get their creaking Fords or rusty wagons out to the highway when rains mired up the country roads. But this known fact has been set aside and what has been made to count for memory are the other, more fortunate folk: the townspeople with radios and automobiles, with new washing machines and toasters and vacuum cleaners, caught up in the life of installment buying and the emulation of the heroes and heroines of the advertisements in the *Saturday Evening Post*. The strenuous complacency of such citizens seems to have been matched by the furious denials of the vagrant and extreme few who would have none of this kind of bliss. Bohemians in Greenwich Village and expatriates in Paris were apparently as fervent in saying no to the good life of the twenties as the solid majority of citizens were in a massive, dumb affirmation.

It is only now beginning to be possible to look at the contradictions objectively and to find out perhaps how much of the myth is true, how much of the truth is different or even more entertaining than the myth, and to see the real life of people below the catch phrases "The Golden Twenties," "The Roaring Twenties," "The Jazz Era," "Prosperity Decade," "Normalcy," "After the Great Crusade," "The Boom," "The Crash." Perhaps it will be possible to see the twenties growing out of a rich immediate past and growing into and becoming part of a complex and disturbed future. Accepting the twenties as a pathway of years connected to time before and time after, an age involved in a real way with the outside world it tried to deny, the viewer discovers that the short episode remains distinct, poignant, and perhaps significant. Those who deplore and those who delight in the twenties would agree that it was a fountain of life that rose into the light of a universe that had not seen its like before, that it displayed itself in some style, a new American style, and then willfully and tragically descended out of light into darkness. A whole people partook of drama, did things foolishly or brilliantly, and in doing so created a recognizable mode. A careless running to extremes, a contradiction of license and oppression, of stuffiness and gaiety: the whole somehow hung together as the expression of a young people at a certain stage of their development.

To understand, it is necessary to imagine those years as well as to analyze them. But to create a picture for imagination to work on, it is needful to shove aside a great deal of mental furniture, not only the overruling ideas under which we live, but a hundred small occupations of the emotions. Many modest, indispensable things of our time have to be set aside before we can begin where the twenties began. To be flippant, January 1, 1920, was a day that did not know zippers. It was also a time before television and stereo, before nylon stockings and Scotch Tape, before electric-eye doors, before quick-frozen foods in sterile paper. Such *things* make a pattern of life that is only superficially trivial. Upon consideration, it is not overstating a fact to say that red and green traffic stoplights have influenced us in our deepest imaginations. And such traffic lights began to be used only in the middle of the twenties.

It is not that the twenties existed without gadgets; it is rather that the invention of gadgets accelerated sharply in that decade; it was the fountainhead of our present infatuation with clever little aids and accompaniments to life. But in the twenties, gadgetry was still a romance. In the twenties there were cellophane and rayon, toasters and washing machines, vacuum cleaners and electric bathroom heaters, and automobiles in the millions: shiny, new, delightful. For a few years these toys were pleasant to play with. It is touching to look back upon that romance, knowing where it all came out, in the maniacal outpouring of such tricks and aids in the 1940s, the 1950s, and the 1960s and in the tyranny of the advertising that has accompanied them.

Again, to understand, it is helpful to underline the fact that the decade of the twenties was a time before bulldozers and throughways, before antibiotics and antihistamines, before computers and programmed learning, before such sinister accouterments of mid-twentieth century life as satellites, missiles, rocket motors, and atomic-powered submarines, before the popular presence of deep space, before the popular acknowledgment of such a problem as the population explosion. It was a time that had not experienced—going backward from now to then—the shock of the detonation of the first atomic bomb, the atrocities of World War II and the Nazi occupation of Europe, and the grinding humiliations of the depression of the 1930s. But it was a time and a generation that had recently known the excitements of Wilson reform, had just participated in World War I, and was filled with a push-pull of hope and fear, poised ready to become all things that it had not been before. Built into its attitudes and capabilities were the opportunities and denials of the previous hundred years, the division of the Civil War, the growth of the industrial element, and the corruptions and reforms of the years before World War I.

In 1920 the continental stretch of land had been overspread and filled, but thinly and irregularly. The wild was vivid, but many safely ignored it. Farm life and town life masked the hunter's landscape that still existed for those who might want to stray into it, but the education of most farm boys—even those who completed themselves by moving to the cities—included at least some slight acquaintance with fields and woods, swamps and seacoast and mountains. The differences in the geography of 1920 and the geography of 1930, or of 1960 or 1970, were quantitative. The spaces between the towns in 1920, and even between those larger ones of 1930, were wider than they were to be in 1960. There was a sharper break between what was town and what was country. There were, practically speaking, no suburbs. There was not then, at least at the beginning of the twenties, the rapidity of movement that we know today between the scattered towns and cities—except in the magnificent trains that pursued straight, shining rails from one side of the continent to the other, ignoring vast empty spaces on each side. The roads across the spaces between the little towns, and even between the cities, were mostly narrow, muddy, tentative, designed originally for coaches, buggies, farmers' wagons, serving still a variety of horse-drawn vehicles as well as the occasional brave, high-bodied automobile.

There were no daily, hourly flights of airplanes overland, not even the imagination of the sight, only the hearsay of the Wright brothers' cranky invention, which had, however, figured recently in the war in France—a long way from home. The accustomed sight of the biplane, the monoplane, the clipper ship, and the others to come lay beyond the horizon.

The riches on the surface of the ground and underneath had been ravaged unsystematically wherever found—in the oil fields of Pennsylvania, the copper deposits of Michigan and Arizona, the deep rich hills of Butte, and in diggings for silver, gold, coal, and iron. Cropland, ill used, had been allowed to erode, streams to run foul, whole species of wild things to be destroyed, and the people who worked these riches to be degraded. Yet there seemed much left to waste or use. The original, typical destroying impulse still worked powerfully; in the twenties it would become more terrible in being made thoughtful, thorough, and respectable. The assumption held innocently by inhabitants of the great, plentiful, generous continent was that the wild, the natural, the nonhuman was created only for man to use. This was the logical end of one track of Western thought, applied with careless fervor to a new land. On this continent, until the conservation movement began in the 1870s, the destruction of the natural environment had not been tempered by either the traditional or class forms of propriety as in Europe or the religious sense of the sacredness of all life as in the East.

Americans of the twenties were rarely conscious of how unique a society they lived in, although they boasted that it was the best. The simplicity of this faith and its ignorance were to be special qualities of the American society in the first decade of their prominence in world history. The naïveté was in outlook, not in organization. By 1920, American society was already complex and sophisticated in its functioning, old beyond its accumulation of years. The groupings and regroupings of the population by new functions was to be one of the creative achievements of the decade. The gain in total numbers did not compare with the leap that came after World War II. It was so unremarkable that it seemed like a remission, and there was some worry in the twenties about a loss of growth rate and a decline of birth rate. Before the beginning of the decade, the count of Americans was 100 million; in 1920, 106 million; in 1930, 123 million. It was in habits of work, thought, and play, in transactions of love and hate, of gain and loss, that the decade was to be original.

What came to an adolescent fullness after the 1917 war was a new civilization—thin, uneasy, volatile, oppressive, boastful, unsure of itself, and yet variously accomplished. Provincials pouring into the great cities brought news of backgrounds and attitudes not known before to the whole, and they sent back to the counties and main streets word of sophistications not heard of in those little places. America began to be self-conscious, and the whole world was witness. Some of the fruits of this new American self-consciousness were to have vitality and to carry an American way across all the oceans.

The circumstances for this special creativity have occurred only once. The conditions were partly geographical. The population that had loosely filled the continent had arrived in an irregular flowing and ebbing of immigrations. In 1920 the immigration stopped. Heretofore, communication and transportation between the thickly settled parts of the continent had been chancy, slow, and lagging. After 1920, new methods of transportation and communication linked all the parts together. This helped to consolidate the population into a national whole although continental geography was never a national unity. The historic conditions were also unique. The decade was a pause between two upheavals, a war and a depression. It was a brief adolescence preceded by a promising youth and followed by a richer maturity. It was a time that assumed that it possessed security when it was in fact menaced by several economic and political forces. It was a time that imagined that it could live alone.

Did American isolation from foreign affairs exist as a fact in the twenties? If it did not exist, was not the passionate belief as important as fact? To begin again: the decade usually thought of as one wrapped in isolation was in reality the time of the end of American isolation. This separateness had started crumbling in the years of the Spanish-American War, when the people of the United States acquired offhandedly some of the colonies of Spain. Isolation was finished in 1917, when American troops went to France. The interesting reaction of almost the whole American people—intellectuals and comic-paper readers alike—was to deny the fact and to pretend and to assert and to insist that isolation was possible, necessary, and true. The oceans seemed much wider in 1920 than they were to seem a little later—and much more protective. The European and South American landmasses were so far away as to have interest only for tourists and salesmen. There was no belief in any connection between events happening in Asia or Africa and those happening in the United States. That these assumptions were shaky did not float to the top of the national consciousness for a long time. Citizens who agreed about nothing else agreed that the United States in its differentness was exempt from the rules of international consequences. The belief was what was important. It was a blanket of comfort that made a special climate for the freedoms and the oppressions of the time. The new, the original, the creative, had to burst out of this cocoon of self-deception and containment with an almost violent force. This caused a counterpoint of tension that stretched the fabric of society many times to breaking and tearing points.

While foreign and alien influences were in fact invading the breached national consciousness, American modes were becoming highly visible to the outside world and spreading an American influence far beyond the ocean boundaries. The growth of the United States to a certain fullness and the relationship of the newly grown civilization to the outside combined to give the twenties its special flavor. It was the definition of a new American national character—the arrival of a youthful, unsure maturity and at the same time a shrinking away from the variety and complexity of experience. This juncture did not come off smoothly, but violently, out of a disequilibrium of the parts. Yet even with the elements of a civilization out of balance, often mutually destructive, there was sufficient freedom for creativity to manifest itself in many corners of life.

The word "creativity" must be taken to mean an extra quality or dimension, a spontaneity added onto the necessary in the functioning of many aspects of the national life: automobiles moving in musical sequence along an assembly line; a jazz band caught in an ecstasy of strict agreement, with the bass beating a steady rhythm to improvisation; the ordered confusion of the floor of the stock market on a busy day; a writer of fiction such as Scott Fitzgerald marshaling words to catch the reality of 1925; the profusion of possibilities in a kindergarten functioning upon the principle of progressive education; the style of Clarence Darrow defending Leopold and Loeb; Congressman La Guardia of New York claiming fervent support from a heterogeneous constituency through the seduction of wit, gusto, and hope; George Norris appealing in picturesque integrity for the saving of Muscle Shoals; Charles Lindbergh hushing a crowd to quiet reverence for simple cleanness of purpose; H. L. Mencken touching irresistibly the ribald truth underlying pretense.

In the workings of this flimsy, juvenile, and doomed age, it is the creativity that survives. But distinction could be recognized then only with difficulty. It was surrounded by and swam in an ocean of dross. There was a wide and high level of mediocrity that had an enthusiastic allegiance from millions. It was this discouragement of sameness against which talent rebelled.

This chronicle of the American twenties takes off from the assumption that the past means something to the present, the meaning not hortatory but esthetic; that the particular past of the twenties had some coherence in its unrolling; that the elements of the time were out of gear in some large way, business on top, politics and culture allowed on sufferance; but that an American style, unified and tied together all the characteristics of the age, those destructive and those creative; and that the period was a youthful definition of the American mode.

II

THE YEARS BEFORE

HOW DOES ONE ANALYZE A PERIOD over which a haze of well-being has settled? A time that coasted along on the euphoria of Paul Dresser's "On the Banks of the Wabash" (1896), Sousa's "Stars and Stripes Forever" (1897), and the unhurtful exploit of Theodore Roosevelt's charge up San Juan Hill (1898) seems an era too fortunate to have a history.[1] Even protest was naïvely hopeful. It was thought that nearly everything could be done. Everything was tried. Greed was as straightforward as reform. An emphatic and giant "No" had not appeared on the national horizon. Even in 1914, with the war spreading over Europe, Americans did not believe in the same kind of trouble for themselves. It was to take 1917, 1918, and 1919 to shake some of the confidence of this people.

Facts do not explain the good nature of the period that followed the worst depression, in the 1890s, that the United States had yet known. There were recessions also in 1907 and in 1913–14. In spite of a comparative recovery from the sharp downward skid of the 1890s, it was a time of widespread, unrelieved, and almost unremarked poverty. There were acres of tenements in every quickly grown city, slums within slums. There was a heartless gap between the lives of the rich and the lives of the poor, the rich exhibiting their riches and the poor, their poverty, as if for the sake of drama. There was no general conviction that public ills could be cured in spite of much energetic crusading for this or that cause. The emotion that greeted the passage of the Income Tax Amendment to the Constitution (1913) was as much astonishment as outrage.

At a distance, it seems a cheerful, perhaps innocent, time; but its cheerfulness was that of the hardhearted child who refuses, or is unable, to feel the ills of others. In addition to the visible chasm between the rich and the poor, who dressed differently and talked differently, there was a gaping difference between the well and ill schooled. Speech, dress, and manners divided a free and loose society into two clearly discernible levels if not classes, the privileged and the underprivileged, who were expected to lead quite different lives. The distinctions between the native-born and the naturalized were decisive. Jokes at the expense of minorities were a stock-in-trade of the theater and an element of everyday talk. This casual cruelty was a habit perhaps handed down from the frontier, where isolated settlers were frankly amazed at variations from themselves. Another lapse in this good-natured, open, changing, opportunity-full society was its taking for granted a great deal of violence. There was much tolerance of, or at least overlooking of, local and sporadic outbursts of sadism, killing and harrying of those who seemed different. The "good years" before the war had many more lynchings than the more famously violent period after.[2] And in 1915, the Ku Klux Klan, new in everything but name, was reconstituted.

What then was the character of this period, with its innocence and its hope, living in the midst of its poverty and violence? What inheritance did the twenties have from it? What in it did the twenties reject? It will take the whole story of the twenties to arrive at answers. But a sketch of prewar energies prepares the way for the story of the postwar twenties. The greatest difference was in politics.

The public sphere was creative in the years before the war; it was inept or supine in the years afterward. There was one dominant figure in American life in the years before the war, and he

was a political figure. Wilson stood athwart the prewar and war
years, cajoling, leading, commanding, making his presence felt in
every sphere of national life, giving it a tone. His firm, fine pro-
nouncing of such words as the ones he enunciated to the graduating class of the Naval Academy in June, 1914—"The idea of
America is to serve humanity . . ."[3]—raised aspiration for a dazzling moment into official policy. He said to another audience in
Independence Hall in July, 1914, "I am glad to say that there
are some simple things in the world. One of the simple things
is principle. Honesty is a perfectly simple thing. It is hard for
me to believe that in most circumstances when a man has a
choice of ways, he does not know which is the right way and
which is the wrong way."[4] For a time, before complications
tangled Wilson's way, many thousands stepped to the tune of his
words as if mesmerized. In his simple and passionate appeal he
caught the imagination of diverse layers of society and pushed
and pulled them into tremendous, moving, and important acts,
sudden changes, immediate breakups of crushing inequities.

He operated with equal power on sophisticated and on un-
formed minds. The profoundest experience of Bernard Baruch's
life was his turning from private to public interests under Wilson's influence.

The laws Wilson caused to be passed, the executive acts he
authored, the appointments he made (such as placing Louis
Brandeis on the Supreme Court on January 28, 1916) exerted
force in the twenties, when the charm of his leadership was gone.
Specific acts changed whole areas of life. The Federal Reserve
Board (1913) and the Federal Trade Commission (1915) were
new organizations of federal power. The Federal Highways Act
(1916) brought about a new design of the national landscape,
new ways for the parts to be in touch with each other. Production
for war, anticipated by a council of national defense (August 29,
1916), changed business and government relationships permanently. All the revulsions felt toward these changes during the
decade following the war could not prevent multiple consequences operating with great effect throughout the national
framework. While reacting against Wilson, Americans in the
twenties lived in the aftermath of Wilson's acts, words, and tone.

Yet the sum of Wilson's qualities held contradictions, even in the years before the war. He enlarged governmental powers more effectively than any president before him. He was also a gentlemanly Virginia democrat with modest and definite aims for democracy, defending many liberties effectively. What made him remarkable was the tone of the man. He was able to funnel aspiration toward act as if hope were a tool in his hand. Wilson's style was the high achievement of "the years before," never possible again in the same combination. He belonged to the age that he helped to make and brought to climax in his years of reform.

There was any amount of aspiration lying about ready for use, firewood to his kindling. It was an age of unaccentuated striving, of individual efforts in all directions at once, of a vast range of ambitions aiming at several kinds of fruition in a period that had no goad from disaster, no belief in cataclysms to come. The age was given a shape not by differences among its parts, but by a vague hopefulness that permeated all its elements. All of its kinds and qualities of life grew slowly, almost unconsciously, toward the vivid accomplishments, coordinations, and expressions of vitality that Wilson and the war called into being when, for a historical moment, the political voice of the president unified the purposes and focused the energies of a diffuse people.

That Wilson vivified and coordinated this loose energy was an achievement. Lacking major disasters or disturbances since the Civil War, this people sincerely modeled itself on a bland goodness and asked few questions about the evil edges and depths of society. It was a society that had a marked settledness of outlook and habit, caused in part by the rarity of visible change. Rural American life—American life was mostly of the country in 1914— was bounded by the experience of the farm family. Nothing was much read but the Bible and the local newspaper. Crossroads preachers, lawyers, politicians, and schoolmasters furnished the only wit and wisdom. Away from the disturbing influence of the growing cities, there was a simple, coherent, known way of doing things. It was an effortless skill, a way of greeting every eventuality, knowledge accumulated through slow generations of hacking and then smoothing the wilderness. It was a vastly ignorant as well as a secure civilization, one that knew little of the outside world, and it sent its more forceful individuals to the cities. Here, rural Americans were changed quickly into many kinds of urban Americans, sharp-elbowed, quick-talking, often corrupt, very rich or very poor, and not at all content. Yet the slow-moving country life was the norm.

Wilson carried these Americans, of the country and of the city, through reform and into war. After the war, his generous, idealistic, ignorant followers, who had not been tested before in such a crisis and who found they did not want to be tested, turned on him. There was to be a sharp reaction in 1919. The twenties were to try to stand for everything opposite to the generation of the years before. The citizens of the twenties threw over the actions, ideas, and style of Wilson's time and yet carried along with them much baggage and impedimenta from that period. So it is needful to suggest a few of the energies and occupations of the time before, energies the war shook like a kaleidoscope but did not disperse.

Each hope of the time had its shadow in a limitation. For a few years political life seemed the means to many freedoms and enlargements for great segments of the population. Yet this was also the accession time of a generation of city and state bosses whose "reigns" were coincidental with Wilson's governorship and presidency and extended triumphantly into the twenties. After his years as president of Princeton University, when he tilted (unsuccessfully, it was forgotten) against the dining clubs of that institution, Woodrow Wilson was elected governor of New Jersey in November, 1910, and president of the United States in November, 1912. There are rich incongruities to be noted in other elections. Frank Hague became one of five city commissioners of Jersey City in 1913; he became mayor of the city in May, 1917. James Michael Curley was mayor of Boston for the first time in the years 1914–17. In Texas the joint careers of Mr. and Mrs. James E. Ferguson began with "Pa's" election to the governorship in 1914; he was reelected in 1916; impeachment in 1917 was only a halt to a career that was to have its full flowering in the decade to follow. William Hale Thompson served his first term as mayor of Chicago in 1915. Theodore G. Bilbo of Mississippi began his first term as governor in 1916.

The bosses were not merely a reprehensible opposite of Wilson's political idealism. They were an energetic functioning of political power in places where there was an absence of power equipped with restraints. The bosses were not only symptoms of the tenacity of greed and the eagerness to corrupt and to be corrupted, they were symptoms of the void of moderate power in places where such rational power was needed: the cities, with their unassimilated new populations, and the rural spaces of the South and West. The ignorant, fecund, new people of the cities found comfort in the bosses' ministrations, the personal doling out of jobs and welfare, as well as the opportunity to function as part of a "machine." They enriched the bosses with extravagant gratitude.

It was a chance conjunction between boss control and an educated, high-minded view of public life that gave "the new freedom" its scope. The bosses fixed upon Wilson, the university president, as a man they thought they could use. They created the circumstances for him to become governor of New Jersey and then president of the United States. When he nimbly took hold of the power they had conveniently put in his way, they were left disconsolate, amazed, admiring, and helpless—in the wake of his superior talents.

"This is not a day of triumph; it is a day of dedication," said the new president on March 14, 1913.[5] On the eighth of the next month he called a joint session of Congress, delivered an address in person (returning to the practice of Washington and Adams), and asked for tariff revision. Thus began the acts of the new president. Wilson, in causing his domestic program to be enacted (a lowering of tariffs, a new national banking system, federal action against trusts, regulation of large businesses, the initiation of a system of federal highways), had in mind the good of small, independent businessmen and farmers such as he had known in his years of growing up in the Shenandoah Valley. He was also generous to helpless new Americans. He returned to the House without approval H. R. 6060, an act to regulate immigration, saying:

In two particulars of vital consequence this bill embodies a radical departure from the traditional and long-established policy of this country . . . It seeks to all but close entirely the gates of asylum which have always been open to those who could find nowhere else the right and opportunity of constitutional agitation for what they conceived to be the natural and inalienable rights of men; and it excludes those to whom the opportunities of elementary education have been denied . . .[6]

1. A late photograph of Woodrow Wilson, whose presidency ended at noon, March 4, 1921, and who died February 3, 1924. His shadow lay across the decade. The measure of his achievement was the violence of the twenties' reaction against him.

2. President Warren G. Harding. A good-natured, likable, and ordinary man; a bad president. His friends exploited the influence surrounding the office of the president. Yet Harding induced industry to accept the eight-hour day; he pardoned Eugene Debs—and invited him to the White House; and he instituted the Bureau of the Budget.

Yet Wilson lessened opportunities for Negroes in the federal civil service. He was a moderate segregationist from Virginia and blind in this respect. Other contradictions existed. The big laws he caused to be passed, aimed at the control of big business for the sake of small individuals, in the long run brought about a closer and more efficient meshing and functioning of big business and government in a relationship of cooperation. Later presidents with other sympathies used these laws to allow business to enrich itself at the expense of other elements in the shadow of governmental protection and regulation.

As in Wilson's career as a domestic reformer, so in other aspects and acts of other men in this hopeful period, there seemed to be infinite possibilities; not all of them turned out as expected. The basic ground of national energy was the presence of unassimilated immigrants. It was not known that this was to be the final period of their flowing in in unrestricted numbers. It was thought that they would continue to come in forever. Meanwhile, these unabsorbed, eager, anxious people made different kinds of opportunities—for a boss such as Thompson in Chicago, for a reformer such as Fiorello La Guardia in New York. They were the objects of careful attention for humanitarians like Jane Addams and instances of hopeful pride to someone like Mary Antin, who had been an immigrant herself and wrote, as if in a letter to all the complacent, native-born citizens: "What if the cross-legged tailor is supporting a boy in college who is one day going to mend your state constitution for you? What if the rag-picker's daughters are hastening over the ocean to teach your children in the public schools?"[7] The immigrants were beings to be loathed by the racial theorists of the time. Madison Grant, chairman of the New York Zoological Society, linked into one vague menace the presence of both internal and external immigrants, his assumption being that an original purity of stock was being threatened:

Speaking English, wearing good clothes, and going to school and to church, does not transform a negro into a white man. Nor was a Syrian or Egyptian freedman transformed into a Roman. . . . We shall have a similar experience with the Polish Jew, whose dwarf nature, peculiar mentality, and ruthless concentration on self-interest are being engrafted upon the stock of the nation.[8]

While those who came from Europe and those who moved from the country to the city or from one region to another supplied continual new energy for the comfortable layers on the summit of society, the new members wanted to have what the others wanted to keep: a *share*. The share was not definable and was to be obtained in many different ways, but every individual assumed that there existed somewhere, in circumstances he had not yet fallen into, in conditions he had not yet divined, at some conjunction of himself and an American situation, his *share*. This was the new thing in a new country. It was the assumption of the right to occupy space, to have importance, to be somebody; it was infinitely unsettling, sometimes destructive, occasionally creative.

The transformation of the circumstances of one's life was assumed to be a matter of emotion and will. The farmers' sons and daughters who came to town for good wages and the stir and movement of street corners had hope.[9] Young men tinkering with the engines and binding together the makeshift bodies of the new automobiles were filled with confidence. The younger J. P. Morgan, coming into his inheritance of money and position in 1913, felt his spirit glow with aspiration for what he could do and be. Even the Wobblies were optimistic.

These most militant, individualistic, disunited labor agitators were authentic examples of American aspiration. Related vaguely to the more logical European anarchists, they renounced physical violence and were only violent in the extremity of their ideas. The leaders of the IWW (International Workers of the World) were often men of great gentleness, self-educated, comradely, angular only in relation to the plentiful injustices of the loose, generous, grossly unfair society in which they lived. They had only what they called their "preamble" for a creed, only their "little red songbook" as their hymnal, only their bindlestiff guitar music for communion as they twanged away in hobo jungle campgrounds by all the train lines of the country. They spent much of their time proudly and clandestinely putting slogan-stickers on boxcars and barns, like little boys, mischievous with bad words. Farmers and city folks shivered in their beds at an unnamable threat and, when they caught the Wobblies, locked them up, beat them, and ran them out of town, afraid of their words: "anarchism," "one big union," "direct action."

The IWW organized themselves obscurely in meetings in 1903, 1904, and 1906, and had more members (70,000) from 1912 to 1914 than at any other time. Their influence was startling but ephemeral. For a very few years just before the war, they drew large, irregular numbers into a following, gaining an ebbing and flowing loyalty from the depths of the American deprived, from those so badly treated or situated as to feel that they were falling out of reach of the promise that seemed tangible to everyone else.

Having no gift or desire for slow gains, they squandered their energies upon drives, campaigns, crusades (the key methods, also, of American welfare, politics, and police protection). They frightened the copper camps, lumberyards, and waterfronts of the Northwest and made some forays into the industrial east. Their greatest victory was in 1912 in the Lawrence, Massachusetts, strike; at its end, wages were raised, hours of work reduced. For a moment it seemed that this feared and hated organization might change the balance between employers and employees.

The IWW set up an almost respectable office in Chicago, with typists and a receptionist. Its newspaper, *Solidarity,* gained a considerable circulation. However, the basic fecklessness of the organization is seen in a member's recollection of the routine of press day, when the paper was printed on "an obsolescent flatbed press":

Folding, addressing, and mailing were done by a group of fellow-workers willing to donate time after work. They were young, lively, witty, and pugnacious, the same group that formed the nucleus at the Wobbly hall and the open-air meetings. We made press day a gala occasion by singing I. W. W. songs as we folded the papers. By midnight the mailbags would be full, and we would carry them on our backs to the post office. Afterward we stopped at the corner saloon for a sandwich and a glass of beer.[10]

The movement had a folk hero in Joe Hill and folk leader in Big Bill Haywood. Hill was the troubadour of the movement, a songwriter who moved about from strike to strike, who wrote the songs of the Wobblies, and who was trapped in Utah by a trumped-up murder charge and executed by a firing squad on

November 19, 1915. The funeral in Chicago of this obscure Swedish immigrant whose real name was Joseph Hillstrom was a demonstration, a pageant, and a celebration of the movement.

In Chicago the Wobblies rented the West Side Auditorium, occupying the top floor of a building.

Long before the services on Thanksgiving Day crowds gathered at the street intersection until traffic was blocked in all directions. An estimated twenty-five to thirty thousand were there. They were of every race, creed, and color. They waited stoically for hours. The police couldn't move them. When the services started, many looked up at the open windows with tears streaming down their faces. The casket was placed on the flower-laden, black-and-red draped stage. . . . The funeral ceremony opened with the singing of Joe Hill's song, "Workers of the World, Awaken," . . . Bill Haywood spoke a few sentences, introducing Judge Hilton, chief counsel in Joe's court appeal. (He recounted the events of the trial and the argument for Joe's innocence.) . . . After Judge Hilton's address, the crowd in the hall marched out slowly, while Rudolph Liebich and the orchestra played Chopin's "Funeral March."[11]

If Joe Hill was the folk hero, William D. Haywood was the almost legendary leader of the movement, a man of rough and magnetic presence, cheerful, blustery, emotional, and somewhat gullible. He led the movement in its trappings of innocence and color and vitality into a blind alley, where it foundered during the war years. He was blind to the serious kind of opposition the movement faced from a public turning all its available loyalties to the pull and drama of the war. Then his uncompromising pacifism ran head on into a new patriotism he did not understand. When there was not fear, there was complacency on the part of the top level of society about the depressed conditions below, where desperation occasionally aroused a sporadic loyalty to such a movement as the IWW or flared up in hopeless and violent outbreaks of shooting, destroying, striking—the striking not well organized or sustained.

Such was the spontaneous movement among the Kanawha miners in 1911 and 1912, who fought the mineowners and their own union, the UMW, which had accepted a contract that the workers refused. There were massacres and shootings with machine guns into the tent camps of evicted miners. In retaliation, the miners took up their rifles and through the thin winter woods stalked the paid gunmen of the owners in cold blood. An armored train brought in ammunition for the owners; the men attacked the train. Among the leaders of this strike and involved in others of the period was "Mother" Jones, an elderly woman always dressed in dark, prim clothes and bonnet, a fearless virago of the labor movement whose husband had been killed years before in another strike. During one period of the Kanawha violence, the state militia captured her and other leaders of the movement and locked her up in the upper floor of a store building. A witness to the scene said that the old woman "leaned out of the window shaking her fist at a squad of militiamen bringing in a group of prisoners. 'Give those sons-of-bitches hell, boys,' she shouted. 'They can't keep us down!' "[12]

These years of the lurid activities of Mother Jones were the same years in which a gush of sentiment propelled cities (Philadelphia was first), then states, and, at last, the national Congress into making an official and recognized national holiday out of something to be known henceforth as "Mother's Day." Sunday, May 10, 1913, was first set aside by congressional edict for this purpose. Mother Jones and Mother's Day: such were the contrasts possible in what was already an infinitely amusing and infinitely terrible country.

Far removed from Mother Jones' world, tolerant of the middle-class fervor of Mother's Day, the very well off floated upon the assumption that they deserved their riches. They lived in unrepentant luxury, in houses with countless servants and many rooms (the third floor of which, where the servants lived, was rarely heated); guests ate and drank extravagantly, and daughters often married English lords.

Below those who had were those who wanted, the sweating, busily cheerful money-makers, the organizers of Rotary Clubs and Chambers of Commerce. The first national Rotary Club was created out of sixteen local groups in 1910; the American Chamber of Commerce came into existence in 1912.

Below the levels of those who had and those who strove to acquire were those who worked for wages. The aristocracy of labor, the craft-union men, came to be tolerated; they came to seem an addition to those in agreement as to the way things should go. Slowly, these proud, conservative workmen had gained solid benefits, in part through the effect of the individualistic efforts of such wild men as the Wobblies. However, any suggestions of amelioration of the lot of the rank and file of laboring men, whether from the AFL's Samuel Gompers or from Socialist Eugene Debs, could go too far very quickly. Not demands but a change in the conditions of work brought new things both to capital and labor. The men who employed and the men who were employed were bound together in these changes.

Many individuals had a share in bringing about the new conditions of work; one name symbolized the change: Henry Ford. His new plant at Highland Park in Detroit speeded up and brought quickly to a climax the methods of work that became a new way of life.

This moment in industrial creativeness shared the happy mood of many activities of the prewar years. There was excitement and emulation in the Highland Park plant as men vied with each other, from top to bottom, some ideas coming down from the top, others rising from the bottom, to make a process work.[13] The immediate excitement of drastic change was felt, but the remote consequences could not be foreseen. The new rhythm of work in the perfected assembly line, the shortened and standardized workday, and the higher daily wage were to change the workmen more radically than anyone could know. Just as drastically, the pressure upon the employer to organize work in rational units and progressions, to organize supply, distribution, selling, advertising, and personnel management so that these elements would be as predictable as materials, all these necessities led toward a new mold of life. And the spare, elegant angularity of the new *thing* rolling away at the end of the line in Highland Park, the Model T automobile, which enchanted its creators as they worked feverishly for the best conditions for it, was to mesmerize in incalculable and unimaginable ways a whole people.[14]

The very ground of all the hopeful activity of these years was an adequate supply of land to farm, water to drink, air to breathe, oil or coal or waterfall to provide power for industry. This people had few thoughts about a continuing relationship to the natural setting that supported them and their activities. They felt free to use, waste, destroy as they pleased because it never occurred to them that the material of life itself might give out.

One of the new ideas of the time was the conservation of natural resources, the striking notion of saving and managing the land that had been so ill used. The hero of the new idea was Gifford Pinchot, whose family belonged to the privileged top layer of society. With the encouragement of an imaginative father, Pinchot, after graduating from Yale in 1889, determined to make himself not a lawyer or a minister, as he might have done, but a forester, a career that did not as yet exist in the United States, where there were millions of acres of timber but no forest management. The young man went to Europe to learn. Something in his radiant good faith caused the great men of the old European profession of forestry to give him advice. Sir William Schlich, head of the British Forest School at Cooper's Hill, and Sir Dietrich Brandis, who had founded the practice of forestry in India for the British, were his mentors. Almost by chance, he was directed to the French forestry school at Nancy and spent a year studying there. He came back to the United States, aching to put his newfound knowledge to work, but at first he found no outlet except in making talks or writing articles. Chance helped him again and put him in the way of the landscape architect Frederick Law Olmsted, adviser to George Vanderbilt in the planning of the Biltmore Estate in western North Carolina near Asheville. Olmsted had persuaded the millionaire-owner to make his land an example of scientific management. He now suggested that Vanderbilt put Pinchot in charge of his forest lands, both the acres surrounding Biltmore House and the higher land near Mount Pisgah, where Vanderbilt planned a hunting preserve.

Thus, in the southern highlands, American forestry was born in the 1890s and early 1900s. Eventually the highlands around Pisgah became a national rather than a private forest. For, having begun by demonstrating what could be done on private lands, Pinchot moved on irresistibly to a public career in forestry. Under President Cleveland, he saw the first national forest preserves set aside. Under Theodore Roosevelt, whose progressivism was congenial to him, Pinchot came into a magnificent public opportunity.

The various scattered governmental bureaus that were concerned with forests were consolidated and Pinchot became the first Chief Forester of the nation. Under him, the first national forests were surveyed and set aside; conservation was instituted in the national parks and Indian reservations; the conservation of national waterways was initiated. In the Bureau of Forestry (to become the Forest Service) Pinchot enlisted and trained a devoted corps of professionals. Tirelessly these men worked to preserve what existed and to improve its quality by creative forestry. Pinchot did not flinch in calling public attention to the pillage of the people's resources, a process that had long gone unnoticed.

Yet as soon as a sympathetic president stepped down, the whole program was in trouble. When he succeeded Roosevelt, President Taft appointed Richard A. Ballinger as Secretary of the Interior. The new secretary could not have cared less for conservation or the activities of the Forest Service. He was engaged privately in a barely legal attempt to gain personal control of the governmental coal reserves in Alaska. With confidence and a fatal verve, Pinchot went about the country making speeches and writing articles denouncing the activities of the Secretary of the Interior. Some of Pinchot's Forest Service colleagues did the same thing. On January 7, 1910, Taft dismissed Pinchot. The warm public support Pinchot had gained melted away. There were expressions of outrage and then silence. A whole generation had to pass before the fight was taken up again. Yet Gifford Pinchot had laid the groundwork for rational governmental conservation and his men remained in the Forest Service. Things were never as bad again as they had been. It was a typical American progression: a dramatic campaign for the good; disorder and retreat; finally a starting again under new leaders. The exhilarating effort and letdown took no account of the limited quantity of resources available for this careless people to play with. However, Pinchot had had his say, and his words reverberated: "The Conservation of natural resources is the key to the safety and prosperity of the American people, and all the people of the world, for all time to come. The very existence of our Nation, and of all the rest, depends on conserving the resources which are the foundations of life. That is why Conservation is the greatest material question of all."[15]

The ground of life being natural resources, the flowering of life was in the arts. But while all the other ends of life had received their due in ambition and desire, the arts had not flourished in the decades leading to the years before the "great" war. The reorganization of life after the Civil War, the great growth of the population, the addition of immigrants to the fermenting whole, the swelling of new kinds of power and wealth, the coming into being of heavy and complex industry, the stretching out cross-country of the routes of roads and railroads, the burgeoning of cities: all this change was at first mentally and emotionally indigestible. The older culture of New England no longer spoke to the conditions of life under Theodore Roosevelt, William Howard Taft, and Woodrow Wilson. The people of the United States had no way of knowing what they had become, for there was no mirror of art to reflect unflinching truth. Creators were exceptional or isolated, often denied or ignored, with no company or support in colleagues, patrons, or audience.

Yet suddenly in the years before the war this was no longer altogether true. There began to be a tentative, spontaneous outpouring from many unexpected sources, of poems, stories, pictures, photographs, works of architecture, systems of thought, new modes of expression. This outburst was a sign that the American social order was forming a new unity out of confusion and energy and vitality.

The new creation was lonely and sporadic. The public read *The Winning of Barbara Worth*, by Harold Bell Wright (1912); *Pollyanna*, by Eleanor H. Porter (1913); and *Lone Star Ranger*, by Zane Grey (1915). In popular nonfiction, it desired a reflection of its own easy ideas: a comforting picture of immigrants fulfilled in Mary Antin's *The Promised Land* (1912), or a promise that men could learn to get along with machines through applied psychology in Hugo Münsterberg's *Psychology and Industrial Efficiency* (1913). In public lectures, it liked the crude assurance of John B. Watson that people could not only be easily understood but manipulated.[16]

In the last three decades of the nineteenth century and the early years of the twentieth century, isolated careers and works pointed toward the new. But these appearances seemed to be without issue. In the visual arts, the distinction of men like John La Farge in decoration, Thomas Eakins and Winslow Homer in illustration and in oil and watercolor, Augustus Saint-Gaudens in sculpture, Henry Hobson Richardson and Louis Sullivan in architecture had not been succeeded by anything but the work of smooth academicians and insipid popularizers. In 1908, Maxfield Parrish's illustrations for Edith Wharton's *Italian Villas* were an excellent example of the good bad taste of the time.

In the 1890s and early 1900s, the following figures were visible in the high relief of originality: Frederick Jackson Turner in history; Thorstein Veblen in sociology and economics; Stephen Crane, Theodore Dreiser, and Henry James (continuing a long career but coming to a late climax) in fiction; Henry Adams in speculative history and autobiography; Robert Henri in art teaching and informal esthetics. Perhaps not growing directly out of these men and their work, but playing comfortably with new forms and ideas against the background of this older creativity, younger artists of a new age began to appear as if at random.

A protected daughter of a Baltimore Jewish family studied at Radcliffe and fell under the influence of William James, moved on to Johns Hopkins, and went a certain distance in the study of medicine. Giving up this sequence of formal study, she settled in comfortable exile in Paris, where shortly she published a volume of stories. Gertrude Stein's *Three Lives* (1909) was filled with the homely details of a Baltimore adolescence and was yet disturbingly original in its use of language. The writer made words follow the very movement of thought itself, hesitant, repetitive, yet supple. In the most original of the stories, "Melanctha," she seemed to be inside the skin of a sensitive, lost Negro girl, using monotonous, hypnotic phrases of half-conscious thought to express every errant up-and-down of mood.

The colors, shapes, and contrasts of light and dark in American life met in a striking way the eyes of a group of painters who exhibited together in 1908 for the first time and were called "the Eight." They went their individual ways afterward; some of them seemed fulfilled in styles of the time before the war; others grew into the future. The original eight were Robert Henri, Everett Shinn, John Sloan, William Glackens, George Luks, Arthur B. Davies, Ernest Lawson, and Maurice Prendergast. John Marin, who sometimes exhibited with them, Sloan, Davies, and Prendergast sustained a survival in tune with the nerves, mood, and sensual temper of the years to come. They were all lumped together as "the Ashcan School" although there were many differences among them. They shared only gusto and stubbornness and the strength to go about their business, ignoring praise, abuse, and neglect.

In Chicago in 1914, a magazine that its unencouraged founder, Margaret Anderson, called *The Little Review* began asking the best writers in England and the United States to write for it for nothing. Margaret Anderson was a young woman of astonishing good looks who had nothing but enthusiasm and ambition to equip her to produce her magazine. In her youthfully arrogant way she commanded greatness to appear and it did. She was joined soon by another penniless and self-possessed young woman, Jane Heap. Together, these two kept the magazine going, supporting the appearance of much good writing (the first American publishing of *Ulysses*) as well as much that was merely eccentric and amusing. A businessman who had walked out of job and marriage to become a writer proclaimed "The New Note" in the first issue. Sherwood Anderson wrote that this note was "the voice of the new man, come into a new world."[17]

The Little Review was only the best of the many new "little" magazines. It lasted longer than many. *The Seven Arts* announced itself in New York in November, 1916, with a manifesto: "It is our faith and the faith of many, that we are living in the first days of a renascent period, a time which means for America the coming of that national self-consciousness which is the beginning of greatness."[18] James Oppenheim was editor; Waldo Frank, associate editor; on the advisory board were Van Wyck Brooks, Robert Edmond Jones, Louis Untermeyer, and Robert Frost, who, after a sojourn in England, where he had published his first book of poems and met other writers, had returned to New Hampshire and the raising of chickens to supplement an almost nonexistent writer's income. *The Seven Arts* soon offended by being against the war, and after one year suspended publication. In its bouncy proclamations, its careless attitude to fashion, its gathering together of people who were talented but unknown, the magazine was typical of the writing and publishing of the period.

Movies made by Charles Chaplin and Mack Sennett were typical also. Sennett threw together a robust slapstick product whose action went freewheeling in the new angular automobiles along all the ordinary streets and around all the corners of everybody's hometowns. In 1915 alone Chaplin made fifteen movies, one short film after another, crowding into months all the characteristic images, symbols, and sequences that he would never surpass in later years. In 1916, in Provincetown, Massachusetts, an amateur theatrical group put on a plotless short play, *Bound East for Cardiff*, by one of its members, Eugene O'Neill, a vagabond, half-educated son of an actor.

What was happening in so many directions, going on unnoticed or unrecognized, was called for imperially in 1915 by Van Wyck Brooks in *America's Coming of Age:*

Dessicated culture at one end and stark utility at the other have created a deadlock in the American mind, and all our life drifts chaotically between the two extremes. . . .

It is true that under the glassy, brassy surface of American jocosity and business there is a pulp and a quick, and this pulpy quick, this nervous and acutely self-critical vitality, is in our day in a strange ferment. A fresh and more sensitive emotion seems to be running up and down even the old Yankee backbone—that unblossoming stalk.[19]

The yeasty working of "cultural" history on "general" history was bringing about change in the temperament of a people without their noticing that it was happening. People of "good taste" continued to buy Maxfield Parrish for their living rooms and the millions continued to read Harold Bell Wright and Zane Grey. But Theodore Dreiser published *Jennie Gerhardt* in 1911 after the discouragement of a number of years of silence and even of menial labor. Not only contemporary writers said new things; some old writers seemed to say new things. Six years after his death, in 1916, a new Mark Twain appeared in the posthumous publishing of his story *The Mysterious Stranger*. In 1905, John Sloan asked his friend Maurice Prendergast, "Who is this fellow Cézanne?"[20] In 1913, the Armory Show in New York shattered old certainties, and many people asked Sloan's question. The secret life of American small towns, "the pulpy quick," was treated in verse by Edgar Lee Masters in *The Spoon River Anthology* (1915), and the quickening energy of cities in Carl Sandburg's *Chicago Poems* (1916).

It was a world of loose, unassorted activity. Yet scholarly

thought was beginning to take account of it. There was a beginning of rational criticism and appreciation of the phenomena of American life. In 1913, *An Economic Interpretation of the Constitution* by Charles Beard broke the habit of treating early American history as a sacred text. By analogy he made his readers aware that contemporary government in its functioning was also subject to material pressures. Another aspect of the same "revolt against formalism"[21] was expressed by Justice Holmes when he said that "the life of the law is not logic."[22] John Dewey destroyed an old concept of the public school and created another, saying that the school was "to be made a genuine form of active community life, instead of a place set apart in which to learn lessons."[23] Henry Adams' *Rule of Phase* (1909) and *Letter to Teachers of History* (1910) exhibited an ambiguous concern for the dynamic forces that were expanding and exploding culture, destroying old balances, definitions, and limits. Brooks Adams, more logical than his brother, less tethered by irony, attempted to explain history as a series of cycles of contraction and expansion.

Brooks Adams' theory might be applied at least as metaphor to his time. Two motives worked in the new American civilization: one, toward suppleness, change, the multiplication of freedoms; the other, toward organization, the dovetailing of loose ends into large, closely cooperating enterprises. The accelerating career of Woodrow Wilson may be taken as an epitome of the time. In him, both tendencies worked. He harnessed inchoate energies and abilities by appealing to aspirations toward freedom, spontaneity, and generosity. Yet the end toward which he drove himself and the nation was to be the complex, detailed, inhuman organization of a people into a process.

After 1914, Wilson could not keep his own attention or the nation's focused at home. On February 10, 1915, the President warned the German Government of the consequences if German submarines continued to destroy American ships on international waters. His warning was exact in its promise. Meanwhile, Wilson demanded an impossible and contradictory tone at home:

The example of America must be a special example. The example of America must be the example not merely of peace because it will not fight, but of peace because peace is the healing and elevating influence of the world and strife is not. There is such a thing as a man being too proud to fight. There is such a thing as a nation being so right that it does not need to convince others by force that it is right.[24]

Into preparations for war, Wilson carried the nation on the breath of the same intensity, the same sense of rightness, the same exultation. The mood did not prevent his being practical. On August 29, 1916, the President, through an appropriation act that Congress passed that day, saw to it that a council of national defense was created; the bill named the Secretaries of War, Navy, Interior, Agriculture, Commerce, and Labor as members. Before his country was in the war, Wilson sent his glance beyond the immediate to the far consequences and addressed his imagination, firm and powerful, as well as idealistic, to the terms of peace: "There must be, not a balance of power, but a community of power . . . It must be a peace without victory."[25]

The words remembered from his war speech were to be dulled through repetition and tarnished by derision, but the thought was endurable. He looked beyond the immediate situation in April, 1917, to a possible human community after the war. But then, in the actual situation of the war, other forces in the man and in the American people nullified many high aspirations. On May 1, 1917, Congress, over Wilson's veto, restricted immigration. On June 15, 1917, apparently with the President's blessing, an espionage act was passed, which, with subsequent revisions, was to be as restrictive of variety, spontaneity, and freedom in the national life as any law ever passed in the United States. In July, 1917, the War Industries Board was created, and in March, 1918, it was given executive power. On January 8, 1918, when Wilson enumerated his fourteen points for peace before Congress, the United States had been tightened for deadly effort as it never had been before.

III

THE EXPERIENCE
OF THE WAR

MORE THAN FORTY YEARS AFTER THE EVENT, Bernard Baruch remembered vividly how America went to war in 1917. He had sat in the Senate Gallery to hear the President pronounce the words that would change his life and the lives of all Americans. Below the distinguished audience in the gallery, many of these sophisticated listeners carrying flags in their hands, were those about to be called on to act: the two houses of Congress, assembled in an extraordinary joint night session. Looking back to that night, April 2, 1917, Baruch recalled both the freshness of the rain-washed spring air outside and the tense human density inside the beautiful room. He remembered how quickly he was caught up in the general expectancy when the President entered the room to speak; and how, when Wilson stood at the rostrum with his impressive, stressful bearing, they all leaned forward to listen; and how affecting, then, was "the husky voice sounding the evangelical call that struck deep into the heart of everyone in that crowded chamber."[1]

With a profound sense of the solemn and even tragical character of the step I am taking and of the grave responsibilities which it involves, but in unhesitating obedience to what I deem my constitutional duty, I advise that the Congress declare the recent course of the Imperial German Government to be in fact nothing less than war against the government and people of the United States; that it formally accept the status of belligerent which has thus been thrust upon it; and that it take immediate steps not only to put the country in a more thorough state of defense but also to exert all its power and employ all its resources to bring the Government of the German Empire to terms and end the war.

With rare gifts, Wilson lifted the sights of his audience beyond the immediate situation.

We are glad, now that we see the facts with no veil of false pretense about them, to fight thus for the ultimate peace of the world and for the liberation of its peoples, the German peoples included: for the rights of nations great and small and the privilege of men everywhere to choose their way of life and of obedience. The world must be made safe for democracy. Its peace must be planted upon the tested foundations of political liberty.[2]

The Senate passed the war proclamation two days after Wilson asked for it. The House passed a similar resolution four days after. The President, with a fatal gift for words, began in this way a movement of his country not only into international war but into a future deflected and quickened in its tempo from the hopeful, aimless, lethargic, and yet richly creative course it had taken for a number of years.

Two days after Wilson spoke, two days before the final House vote, another passionately sincere man spoke. On April 4, George Norris of Nebraska asked his fellow senators not to put their country in the war. What he said was very like what many of his countrymen might have said. He spoke out of a deep immersion in the moods, beliefs, and prejudices of millions of citizens. They (and he) felt that they were safely isolated from Europe and that this was good; they (and he) thought that Wilson's neutrality had been a sham; they (and he) saw that profit for some would result in misery and death for many sons of American fathers and mothers. Out of safety, animal skepticism, and the kind of idealism that had been prevalent for the generation of "progress" and the "new freedom," George Norris said No. Surprisingly, Norris seemed to stand almost alone. Only five others in the Senate voted with him against the war proclamation. Some others, he wrote later in his autobiography, expressed private agreement but voted for Wilson's proclamation.

Both the President and the senator used phrases that condensed much into little. Wilson said, "The present German submarine warfare against commerce is a warfare against mankind. . . . Neutrality is no longer feasible."[3] Norris said, "We are going to war upon the command of gold. . . . The troubles of Europe ought to be settled by Europe."[4] A long series of events had led to this confrontation of ideas, but the push of Wilson's words toward the act of war was at this moment immeasurably more forceful.

Wilson had talked neutrality; he had been reelected president on the basis of his neutrality. The difference was made by the resumption of German submarine warfare—the sinking of American ships, the drowning of American civilians—in the months preceding the April, 1917, declaration of war. By solemn proclamation the policy of neutrality was abandoned, the posture of war was taken on. Yet the break was more apparent than real. George Norris had been partially right. Wilson and the United States had not ever been really neutral. After some early difficulties with Great Britain, the United States, as Norris pointed out with withering clarity, had accepted the defined British war zones and refrained from sending American ships into them. On the other hand, American ships had insisted on steaming into German war zones and so into German torpedoes.

To the seventy-nine-year-old Henry Adams, who had always been immune to the President's charm, Wilson seemed close to being a hypocrite. In June, 1917, Adams wrote to an English friend, Charles Milnes Gaskell, "Never could I have conceived that in a short three months we could have gone into a great war and adopted a conscription not unworthy of Germany, at the bidding of a President who was elected only a few months ago on the express ground that he had kept us at peace."[5]

Wilson's reasons seemed eloquent to those who did not have Henry Adams' distaste for the President's style or an analyzing habit. A propulsion of sentiment swayed the voting Congressmen and probably a majority of the people the way Wilson indicated.

In spite of a supposed official neutrality, the President's constituents, Democrats and Republicans, were not neutral in their feelings. They wanted the British and the French to win; they feared the Kaiser. When he sank American ships in his logical pursuit of victory, they ranged themselves solidly behind the President. Loyalty to European ancestors near or remote counted for less than a present sense of continental American nationality. It was a cohesiveness that had grown unnoticed in the increment of opportunities that had come to the immigrants who had poured into the United States during the decades succeeding the Civil War. When Wilson presented an opportunity for complex action to this American nationality, it responded with a willingness that was naïve, whole, and capable of effort and endurance, thus astonishing the world, which had not before seen the American people perform upon an international stage.

Feeling and interest had put the United States in the war on the Allied side. However, President Wilson was one of the first men to see that a new objective condition had made the going to war almost inevitable. Wherever there was war, the United States was likely to be involved. The corollary: only a whole and seamless peace, a peace for the entire world, would ensure peace for the United States in the future.

For the American people the war broke in upon creativities and lethargies alike. The war was a process of large transformations and startling reorganizations. Some learners were the soldiers. They came from backgrounds as diverse as the county courthouse seat of Mississippi, the town split by the railroad in Nebraska, the crowded settlement-house neighborhood of Chicago. Upon these representatives of scattered corners of the country the whole heavy system of the army descended. The arithmetic of the draft picked them up and gathered them together. The camps trained and shaped them. Then the ponderous operation, after reducing the wild, the meek, the rebellious, the frightened into some kind of unity, transported them still farther from home. Overseas, the uprooted mountain boys from the coves of East Tennessee, the upstate New Yorkers, the farm boys from Iowa cast a swift, unhappy glance at strange peoples and immediately in self-protection invented a slang of derision to express what they learned in that quick look: frog, limey, eye-talian. This quickly-put-together knowledge filtered home, to confirm there fears of the alien and the strange. A few were steady-eyed; their insights would tell in a reaction much delayed.

The war was an education for civilians too. It was as if a giant hand had stirred the population. It moved the conscripted soldiers from one extremity of the country to another. It drew countrymen to shipyards and city factories; it took women away from housewife's work and into scenes of movement and noise and company; it brought southerners, white and black, out of the South and drew northerners south to army camps.

Every kind of activity, public and private, was organized. In charity, cities and towns tried out a new plan of giving. A "war chest" fund was collected all at one time for many different causes. The method proved itself first in Cleveland and Detroit and Dayton. It had not as yet been tried in New York City by September, 1918, but it was expected to be initiated there soon.[6] The plan had proved successful and gave a kind of exhilaration to the organizer and organized alike.

In the privacy of the kitchen, the housewife hung up Herbert Hoover's new chart of "household economies" to study and abide by, or ignore. As United States Food Commissioner, he told them:

Save the wheat—One wheatless meal a day. . . .
Save the milk—The children must have milk. Use every drop. Use buttermilk and sour milk for cooking . . .
Save the meat—Beef, mutton, or pork not more than once daily. . . .
Save the fats—Use butter on the table as usual, but [not] in cooking . . . Make your own washing soap at home out of saved fats.
Save the sugar. . . .
Save the fuel. As a Nation we eat too little green stuffs. Double their use and improve your health. . . .[7]

There was no real sacrifice involved, only an organization of attention and effort. The early effect of the war was a quickening of energies. As the war went on, individuals and communities expressed these energies with marked differences in temperament.

Atlanta, which had been out of the mainstream of American life since the Civil War, with only a shy commercial brightening in the years before the war, reacted with freshness and naïveté. It gave up its cherished season of Metropolitan Opera (Atlanta was the only city to which at the time of Caruso's greatness the company traveled out of New York); it cheered the flag on Peachtree Street; it stood at attention. Relatively untouched by this new war (one of the few American cities that had ever suffered heavily in any war) until the late heavy casualty lists came in, Atlanta also remained relatively tolerant. It had no spy scares and explosions. It was a city that did not gain a great deal financially from the war, for its business firms were awarded no very large war contracts. What touched Atlanta was the new superficial bright street life of wartime. That it welcomed. A city much given during its long warm season to living out of doors, it displayed its own life and welcomed new life in the open air, as if the city itself were a sort of operatic stage.

It has always been worth watching, this Peachtree parade on a sunny afternoon, for Atlanta women and Atlanta girls are surely as easy on the eyes as those of any other city, and their reputation for taste and elegance in dress has spread far and wide. But nowadays the parade is worth traveling many a mile to see, for beside the girls are the officers and men from the camps, especially on Saturdays, when leaves of absence are plentiful. They swing down the street in pairs and quartets and sextets, spreading across the sidewalks and unwittingly crowding such unimportant persons as middle-aged married folk into the street. They fill the soda water emporiums to overflowing, and stand three deep before the candy counters, and when the lights are turned on in the movies the rows are seen to be filled with olive drab.[8]

The war stirred crowds. It stirred individuals too. It twisted the vitals of an old man like Henry James, who had lived in England forty years. He had not thought of becoming a British citizen till the war came. But he made his own declaration of war before Woodrow Wilson made his. He had to hunt up "four honorable householders," as he said, "to testify to their knowledge of me as a respectable person, 'speaking and writing English decently,'" so that he could throw the fervor of his loyalty into the cause.[9]

The people at home were at first in love with war. They thought war was the spectacle and sensation of people giving up things (without pain), working together long, hard, purposeful hours (at good wages), sacrificing (without suffering much). The war was a public drama in which many eagerly took part and lost their private selves in the performance of public functions. There were many parades. People other than soldiers put on uniforms: YMCA workers, Red Cross men and women. The buying of government bonds was a spectacle of the street corners. Entertainers performed on platforms in Times Square; Charles Chaplin mimed; Mary Pickford made speeches; Elsie Janis sang. Slogans ruled many minds. Bonds to support the war were "liberty bonds"; objectors to the draft, concientious or otherwise, were "slackers"; "our boys" became a sacred phrase. Sugarless coffee, days without meat, became rituals. The most effective drama of all was that which introduced the draft, the blindfolded high officer of government fishing in a goldfish bowl for a number that would send a certain random set of men to army camps. The workers who had been without work, the old people who had been slack and neglected, the women who had been bored, escaped out of the routine of their lives to run streetcars or to make munitions or sweep up shops. All private lives became public. Because this was a young society, the whole effort was exaggerated.

Forces let loose by so much uninformed goodwill tightened pincerlike upon the national and individual character. "Chicago is calm," wrote Ben Hecht in August, 1918. "It is seemingly indifferent. It does not cheer. It keeps forgetting to take its hat off when the flag goes by. Its features are composed, its voice contained. . . . This curious mask of silence and indifference distinguishes Chicago today. It is the expression of a people inspired by loyalty rather than idealism. It is the Indian face of the silent Middle West."[10]

If one can credit the hindsight of two newspapermen, Wilson expected the ugliness.

I think I know what war means. It would mean that we would lose our heads along with the rest and stop weighing right and wrong. . . . Once lead this people into war and they'll forget there ever was such a thing as tolerance. To fight you must be brutal and ruthless, and the spirit of ruthless brutality will enter into the very fibre of our national life, infecting Congress, the courts, the policeman on the beat, the man in the street. . . . Conformity would be the only virtue, and every man who refused to conform would have to pay the penalty.[11]

Upon a people whose emotions might lead them anywhere, pressures closed down. The two great pressures for those at home were the forcing of the manufacturing and moving of goods, and the forcing and moving of thought. The two succeeding ways that goods were procured for the war were quite different. In 1914 the House of Morgan had used the Allied need for supplies to enlarge the scope of an already powerful institution. George Norris feared a vague entity, "the bankers." The reality of the monopoly the Morgan firm enjoyed in the early years of the war was far more complete than the suspicious, bank-hating Norris could have imagined. All of England's and all of France's war orders in the United States were handled by the one firm. "These orders exceeded $3 billion. . . . Bethlehem Steel received within three months two orders for ammunition totaling, respectively, $83 million and $64 million."[12] The Government stood on the sidelines in 1914, 1915, and 1916. After April, 1917, there was a shift from private to public control of war production.

But it was not until the spring of 1918 that the War Industries Board became effective. Meanwhile, it had to be found out that government and industry did not work together smoothly out of patriotism alone. By January, 1918, such a snarl had been reached in transport, especially in the transport of coal, that Fuel Administrator Garfield shut down every industrial plant (except those producing food) east of the Mississippi for a period of five days, and thereafter for nine consecutive Mondays.[13]

It was curious that the person who was to organize the chaos of war production should be Bernard M. Baruch. He had been a Wall Street speculator who had enjoyed the exercise of his frivolous, glittering talents. He had easily, with energy to spare, made a name for himself in the heartless world of Wall Street. But Baruch, for all the sophistication of his specialized talents, was a person of grand and spacious simplicity. His father was a Jewish surgeon who had served in the Confederate Army. He had grown up in a small town in South Carolina where he had lived the classic, barefoot boyhood of rural America. His family had inculcated generous, simple notions within its warmhearted and happy circle. President Wilson had touched him to the core. He was ready to throw away—for a time—a career that had been joyful and easy and to try his abilities in something infinitely more complex and entertaining, the service of the President and of the nation.

In September, 1915, Baruch had some ideas on mobilizing business resources and took them to Secretary of the Treasury McAdoo, who passed them on to President Wilson. Baruch was made a member of an advisory commission of the Council of National Defense. The council made immense and detailed plans but accomplished little. Baruch's ruthless intelligence would not rest. He went to the President in May, 1917, and urged him "to create a centralized purchasing agency with authority over prices and the closing of defense contracts." When the waste and break-down of control moved the President to reconstitute the War Industries Board, he asked Baruch for a memorandum and on March 4, 1918, summoned him to the White House to hand him his appointment. Baruch was made to understand that "the President himself was the only court of appeal" and "that the raising of armies and navies alone was not adequate to the demands of modern war."[14]

The practical energy Baruch put at the service of the job was fueled by personal admiration for Woodrow Wilson. "He took me out of Wall Street and gave me my first opportunity for public service. His political philosophy helped shape my own. His practical idealism, ability, and conduct still provide the standard by which I measure public men."[15] The way Baruch used his gifts to channel American goods toward Europe was a spectacle in itself. It was also illustrative of the kind of response many men made when called to war jobs and touched in their deepest imaginations by the opportunity to direct large administrative processes the success of which seemed vastly important.

The way he persuaded the manufacturers of automobiles to go into war production was characteristic. Sitting with them at a long, hot session around a table and making no progress, he suddenly seized a phone and called McAdoo of the Railroad Administration: "Mac, I want you to take down the names of the following factories, and I want you to stop every wheel going in and out." Next he called Secretary of War Newton Baker: "Mr. Secretary, I would like you to issue an order to commandeer all the steel in the following yards." Then he called Fuel Administrator Harry Garfield. The men sitting around the table, paying rapt attention to his calls, were to have no more coal. William C. Durant, of General Motors, at this juncture said amicably, "I quit." The others gave in immediately. Only Henry Ford, who was not in the room, held out longer and had to be persuaded further.[16]

Not only material production was organized, but an attempt was made to line up thought and emotion and will. Three laws authorized federal criminal jurisdiction not only over disloyal acts, but over disloyal thoughts. These laws were the Espionage Act of June 15, 1917, the Trading with the Enemy Act of October 6, 1917, and the Sedition Act of May 16, 1918. The third act strengthened the two previous ones and "extended the power of the United States over speech and printed opinion, regardless of consequences."[17] It "defined as seditious and punishable all disloyal language and attacks on the government, the army, and the navy, or the cause of the United States in the War."[18] If the laws had been interpreted narrowly, they might have been argued against as an infringement of freedom. However, they were interpreted broadly. Punishment was excessive and harsh. To put the matter in perspective, no such prosecution took place during World War II, except in the treatment of the Nisei, and nothing as excessive as this was known during the 1914–18 war in Great Britain—much nearer the enemy. "It puzzles me," wrote Sir Frederick Pollock to his American friend Associate Justice Holmes, "that a special Act of Congress should be necessary to make seditious denunciation of the Government and incitements to rebellion in time of war, offenses of the same kind. But, as a matter of policy, I believe there were many leaflets of much the same kind distributed in this country on which it was not thought useful to prosecute any one."[19]

Denial of the use of the mails was an effective, if capricious, method of censorship. Postmaster General A. S. Burleson denied circulation altogether to the Socialist *Leader* of Milwaukee and to *The Masses* of Greenwich Village—a typical product of the years before the war, small in circulation, wildly individualistic in its old-fashioned radicalism, irreplaceable in the cartoons of Art Young. Burleson also denied the use of the mails to the September 14, 1918, issue of *The Nation*. The editor, Oswald Garrison Villard, who had continued to say that participation in the war was wrong, searched the issue to find the offending article. He thought he had it in the lead editorial, which, following the example of the New York *Tribune,* criticized the Justice Department for arresting 75,000 men in two days to find out if they were draft dodgers, only to discover that less than 3 per cent were. His astonishment was great when he was told that the offending article was not this, but another, one criticizing the choice of Samuel Gompers of the AFL to be the Government's emissary to investigate labor conditions in Europe. Villard was told he could circulate the magazine if he tore out the page about Gompers; Villard refused; he went raging to J. P. Tumulty, Wilson's secretary; Tumulty told Wilson; Wilson rescinded the order. The September 14, 1918, issue of *The Nation* was in the mails, no pages torn out, one week late.[20]

Individuals suspected of dangerous thoughts had as short shrift as publications. Thousands of German-speaking Americans fell under suspicion and suffered imprisonment or harassment by officious fellow citizens or neighbors who assumed that they had government support for this endeavor. H. L. Mencken, of an old German family of Baltimore, was permanently embittered by this stupid cruelty—embittered and sharpened: out of this reaction came an outpouring of invective and satire against a wide range of national stupidities.

The war years saw a new use of the word "hyphen." The form "hyphenated" was applied to Americans who kept a vestige of the identity of their ancestors, and it was not tolerated. As early as October, 1915, Theodore Roosevelt had shouted to a crowd, "There is no room in this country for hyphenated Americans."[21] The war was also an excuse to cut down on the untidy democracy of free immigration.

The bundle of restrictions upon free thought and free movement had a grave general effect:

The extreme penalties provided in the law and the militant activities of the enforcement agencies thwarted all rational consideration of public questions. There could be no free discussion of fiscal policies with respect to taxation, bond issues, or war loans to the allies; or of the relative merits of conscription and volunteer enlistments; of mistaken administration policies touching upon neutrality; of the economic and imperialistic basis of Allied war aims; of profiteering and official corruption; or of many other issues about which there are always honest differences of opinion and which can be approached intelligently only after free interchange of opinions."[22]

The general effect was not to be perceived for many years; the individual and personal effects were felt intensely by the "hyphenated" victims. German-Americans could not bring themselves quickly enough and strongly enough to hate their original countrymen; the Irish-Americans could by no means be brought to love the British; those ordinary mulish citizens who could not or did not want to hate at all were vilified. There were arrests and an officially encouraged ostracism that ruined businesses and friendships. State legislatures passed laws against the teaching of the German language in the public schools. Even Governor James M. Cox of Ohio saw to it that his state banned the teaching of German, thinking in all seriousness that he was combating a dangerous influence in German clubs and organizations. Popular fervor stopped the performance in concerts or on popular occasions of German music by symphonies and bands and opera companies. German foods were renamed. Sauerkraut was transformed into "liberty cabbage" in the kind of act that, without the accompanying emotion, would have been ridiculous, but that, in the context of feeling, was shrugged off as excessive but acceptable. Except for skeptics sitting on the sidelines preserving the private habit of criticism, such actions seemed no longer remarkable. Even outrageous jail sentences for expressions of opinion were slurred over in discussion; all of this strange frenzy of patriotism was seen as necessary to preserve an ideal of American thought and attitude from what was conceived as dangerous and foreign.

Entirely native radicalism fell under the same ban of emotion and suffered heavy penalties under law without any protest being made upon the part of the ordinary citizen. Using its war powers, the Government put an end to the functioning of the IWW. In any case, the Wobblies had already lost their influence. The interest of the public was turned outward and away from domestic troubles toward foreign ones. The urgency of the IWW could not function in this atmosphere, but lost its impetus and became somewhat ridiculous and futile. Yet the fear the IWW had inspired remained. The heavy weight of the new laws was laid upon the dying organization to exterminate it. In November,

1916, the Wobblies had met in convention to condemn war. In April, 1917, the United States went to war. In September of that year, the Justice Department raided the headquarters and the homes of the officers of the IWW in several cities. All the leaders were arrested, all papers relevant or irrelevant were seized. No search warrants were issued. In Chicago 166 men were indicted on September 28. "Each of us," one of them wrote, "was charged specifically with having committed 'ten thousand crimes.'" They were confined in the Cook County Jail, where they amazed the jailers by their energy and high morale. "The cells and bull pen were vile with the accumulated filth of decades. It took much persuasion, and not a few threats of adverse publicity, to induce Head Jailer Davies to accede to demands for soap and scrub brushes." In addition to cleanliness, the jailed Wobblies busied themselves with calisthenics, educational meetings, and entertainments on Sundays. But the small, impractical, high-minded, isolated world in which they lived was now airtight. The Wobblies were completely out of touch with the large general effort on which the public spent its energy and imagination. Judge Kenesaw Mountain Landis sentenced them on August, 1918, after they had spent almost a year in jail, "consigning almost a hundred men to prison for a total of over eight hundred years."[23]

Two other well-known radical leaders with very different styles were also arrested and jailed: Emma Goldman, of the romantic, personal and ineffectual call to anarchism; and Eugene Debs, of the steady sweet temper, the mild and seraphic apostle of socialism. It was not in either case act but opinion that frightened and excited the gesture of repression. Yet none of these people—not Emma Goldman, nor Eugene Debs, nor all the Wobblies—had had any determining effect upon the general course of events. The process of the war thus turned irrelevant powers upon conspicuous persons and harmed the health and welfare of the country as much as it harmed its obvious victims.

It was perhaps immaturity, inexperience, the not-having-been-through-this-kind-of-thing-before, and the authority and unanimity of all the voices of propaganda that caused safe citizens to tolerate such actions. Very few opposed the oppression of native freedoms. The victims always seemed to be aliens. It was assumed that the laws were necessary and could be ignored by those not affected. There was only opposition by those suspect. In this matter, President Wilson's absorption in winning the war—and a certain intrinsic narrowness and righteousness—let him be blind. His urgency made him tolerant of tyrannies that were cruel and unnecessary.

The free interchange of opinion had in fact become impossible. Goodwill, self-sacrifice, honest support were not considered enough. For the first time, the United States resorted to an official organization for national publicity. George Creel, a newspaperman who suggested the idea to Wilson, became executive secretary of the Committee on Public Information. He guaranteed to mold a suitable public opinion, suborned or persuaded scholars into writing pamphlets, and hired movie producers, directors, and actors to sell the idea of the war. The quality of effort that resulted may be seen in the postwar justification he wrote. The war was "a plain publicity proposition, a vast enterprise in salesmanship, the world's greatest adventure in advertising." What he saw as his task was "to weld the people of the United States into one white-hot mass instinct with fraternity, devotion, courage, and deathless determination."[24] Creel's energy was large. He accomplished his purpose and vulgarly manipulated the genuine love of country that was in plentiful supply. After the war, patriotism, real or false, seemed to leave a bad taste in the mouth.

A vein of criticism ran through the assent, not to mention layers of indifference. There was, refreshingly, a good deal of healthy self-criticism in Wilson's speeches and other papers, but the response to him from inflamed citizens was a tame assent. Out of touch with the tone of the time entirely were a number of thinkers and journalists. One of the most interesting of these critics of governmental war policy was Randolph Bourne. At the time he wrote, there seemed not much connection between his attitude and what happened; yet his vital criticism survived and helped shape the next generation.

Crippled from birth, dwarfed in growth, but luminous of mind, Bourne grew up in Bloomfield, New Jersey, a quiet town in which his family had a modest but secure place of importance. When he reached the age to enter college, his family lost its money and Bourne was thrown into the working world, which treated him roughly. At one time he found a job doing piecework for a musician, who taught him to operate a machine that perforated the paper music rolls for player pianos. He was paid five cents a foot of paper during his apprenticeship (his employer received fifteen cents from the manufacturer). Increased deftness and speed caused the musician to reduce his employee to four and a half cents a foot of paper. From this time on, Bourne pondered bitterly and deeply systems of labor and of employment. During the rest of his brief life he had the benefit both of his good family background, which gave him an insight into "normal" and middle-class ideas, and of the rough life he had lived among the underprivileged.

In 1909, at the end of six years of drifting from one mean job to another, Bourne at twenty-three was able to enroll at Columbia University on a generous scholarship. Under professors like John Dewey, James Harvey Robinson, and Franz Boas, he made his mark as a graceful, fluent writer on literary and cultural topics (before he left Columbia, he was published in the *Atlantic Monthly*). But he was also remembered as a student who wrote to the college paper denouncing the low wages the university paid her scrubwomen.

After a brief respite and ease (a trip to Europe, a national reputation as the reporter who praised progressive education), the war brought Bourne's thought and ability to a crisis. If he had avoided controversy, he could have been a popular writer, perhaps; he was already an influential one. Settled in an apartment in Greenwich Village, hospitable and generous to other writers, he lived in the midst of conversation, music, the coming and going of friends. In his characteristic black cloak, Bourne, the hunchback, frightened people on first sight and then warmed them by his emotional and intellectual force. The essays in which he questioned the war diminished his influence and his income. He became too unpopular for both the *Atlantic* and *The New Republic*, for which he had written regularly for a number of years. His only outlet was a magazine of small circulation, *The Seven Arts*. His writing, as well as that of a few others, caused the magazine to lose its financial support, and he had at last no regular place to publish. He suffered in his own person, too, moving from poorer to poorer lodgings. What Bourne believed seemed, for a time, irrelevant.[25]

Bourne believed that the experience of the war had damaged the inventive, spontaneous, humane, and progressive variety of American life. The United States might have had more influence upon Europe if it had remained neutral. The young men of his own generation, who were the generation educated in the pragmatism of William James, the last and most creative development of American thought, had thrown all their cleverness into the war organization to make it work and had not once considered proper aims and ends. His own teacher and mentor John Dewey had given his fine intelligence to the war without asking any questions. In effect Bourne said, Where does this worship of process get one except into a dilemma if process alone is thought to be enough? "The American, in living out this philosophy, has habitually confused results with product, and been content with getting somewhere without asking too closely whether it was the desirable place to get."[26]

Bourne was technically loyal, but he thought it was his duty to resist turning over his thoughts, emotions, and critical abilities to the irresistible current. His opposition was not much noticed at the time. In retrospect, it can be seen as an unusual mixture of social progressivism and personal estheticism. He was concerned with political and economic arrangements—he always kept them in view—but only incidentally and for the sake of what he phrased as "art and all the desires for more impassioned living."[27] After he died (at the age of thirty-three, in the influenza epidemic of 1918), his words seemed mottos for the succeeding generation, who, luckily or unluckily, did not have his real dilemma to solve. He wrote, as if for them, "The conservation of American promise is the present task for this generation of malcontents and aloof men and women. . . . Our insulation will not be against any great creative ideas or forms that Europe brings. It will be a turning within in order that we may have something to give without."[28]

In Bourne was the imaginative side of the isolationism that plagued Wilson. This is to undertake a reversal of assumptions. Wilson, in this context, was the everyday man who grasped immediate, unavoidable dangers besides making sensible arrangements to get around them. The creative isolationist like Bourne was the dreamer, the idealist aware of distant, deep, and undeniable truths, discounting and misapprehending the needs of the moment, and thus terribly impatient of Wilson's ways and means. Fruitful cross-purposes at play in wartime created the frustrated richness of the succeeding decade. Bourne faced toward the time he did not live to see, outlining a program for malcontents:

All they want is a new orientation of the spirit that shall be modern, an orientation to accompany that technical orientation which is fast coming, and which the war accelerates. They will be harsh and often bad-tempered, and they will feel that the break-up of things is no time for mellowness. They will have a taste for spiritual adventure, and for sinister, imaginative excursions. It will not be Puritanism so much as complacency that they will fight. A tang, a bitterness, an intellectual fibre, a verve, they will look for in literature, and their most virulent enemies will be those unaccountable radicals who are still morally servile, and are now trying to suppress all free speculation in the interests of nationalism. Something more mocking, more irreverent, they will constantly want. They will take institutions very lightly, indeed will never fail to be surprised at the seriousness with which good radicals take the stated offices and systems. Their own contempt will be scarcely veiled, and they will be glad if they can tease, provoke, irritate thought on any subject. . . . They will give offense to their elders who cannot see what all the concern is about, and they will hurt the more middle-aged sense of adventure upon which the better integrated minds of the younger generation will have compromised. Optimism is often compensatory, and the optimistic mood in American thought may mean merely that American life is too terrible to face. A more skeptical, malicious, desperate, ironical mood may actually be the sign of more vivid and more stirring life fermenting in America today.[29]

Neither the people left at home nor the soldiers sent abroad understood the war or the changes it was going to make in American life. Yet the sending of American troops to Europe was the beginning of a permanent breach in the national experience. It was not perceived as such at the time. The soldier transported to France was to perform certain curative acts; he was then to return home, and the door open to the alien world was to be shut. But the door was never closed again. Ideas as well as men traveled back and forth through the breach.

What the war came to mean day by day to the soldier was

something not to be conveyed in letters written home. It was an experience of cold, hunger, heat, wet, cold, pain, death—an experience to be expressed at this time only in a vivid shorthand language of slang and obscenity, an experience that could not be shared in any plainness. The numbness had to wait to find words. The words found would be part of the expressiveness of the next decade. Much of the tone of the twenties would come from the straining of words to load themselves with the experience of the war.

Meantime, during the months of fighting, the gap widened between those who fought and those who stayed home. Some among the soldiers were pickets in an unknown land out beyond the unseeing, uncaring majority, whether of their own companions or their relatives and friends at home, gorged upon the slogans of war. What these pickets of new experience were feeling, in addition to their own discomfort, terror, and dislocation, was, all round them, the destruction of populations and terrain, want, disease, corruption, death in meaningless quantities and in forms without shame, a total irrationality of life.

The end came like a sharp crack to those fighting and to those at home. Peace arrived precisely and melodramatically at eleven o'clock on November 11, 1918, cutting off and delimiting an experience that had seemed endless. The men in the dugouts and trenches and shattered woods could only wonder, shocked rather than rejoiced. At home it was easier to throw up one's cap, get drunk, and dance in the streets. An eternity of distance stretched between the one whom peace had caught in the shell hole and his brother or friend back home who clasped arms with the nearest passerby in a sudden geniality. For some, the distance would never be bridged. For others, it would be crossed shakily and war pushed out of mind, out of sight. When the war ended, more than two million Americans had been shipped to Europe and 116,500 would stay: 53,000 in battle, the rest from accident or sickness. More than 205,000 had suffered wounds. All of this had happened in nineteen fierce, swift months, an interval that determined that the United States of America would never again be as it had been.

3. Sinclair Lewis. During the 1920s he wrote *Main Street, Babbitt, Arrowsmith, Elmer Gantry, The Man Who Knew Coolidge,* and *Dodsworth.* He taught a generation to apply names, or at least labels, to new conditions of existence.

4. Andrew Mellon, Secretary of the Treasury (with Assistant Secretary
Lincoln C. Andrews after a routine White House conference, on
April 29, 1925). Under three presidents, Mellon was the cool director
of the continuity of politics during this age of business.

IV

THE UNRESOLVED
PEACE

Month after month, long into 1919, the port of New York was crowded with ships returning from the war. In the utmost haste, the great organization of the war brought back and turned loose upon the land the men it had gathered out of the ordinary affairs of their lives and shipped to France. The city was choked with the soldiers and sailors who had not had time to put the war out of their minds and who were not yet prepared for peace. They came home and were immediately dispersed into the society in which haphazardly they found or did not find a place.

One man among the others recorded his homecoming. The son of a clergyman who had gone to France to drive an ambulance and had been held in a detention camp through a malevolent mistake was moved by the sight of the harbor of New York as much as the most ignorant fellow soldier or newly arrived immigrant. He turned away from the dull horrors he had experienced and seized upon an impossible hope in the scene:

The tall, impossibly tall, incomparably tall, city shoulderingly upward into hard sunlight leaned a little through the octaves of its parallel edges, leaningly strode into firm hard snowy sunlight; the noises of America nearingly throbbed with smokes and hurrying dots which are men and which are women and which are things new and curious and hard and strange and vibrant and immense, lifting with a great ondulous stride firmly into immortal sunlight.[1]

The pressure of yearning poured out upon the physical place was unfair to actuality, but actuality strained to live up to expectation. Reality became as overwrought as expectation. This was a hectic people released for a few years into exemptions that did not seem to incur penalties.

Many dismissed from the war found they had no place to go back to, and the dead did not return at all. Many, maimed in body or in mind, stopped short of the harbor. Two sisters, returning on a ship full of Red Cross workers like themselves, jumped overboard, one in silence, the other with a cry, and were swirled away beyond the reach of help. "I believe that everyone of us on that boat might have done the same. The business of turning around psychologically and facing towards our old life again was difficult enough in all conscience."[2] Some who had stayed at home had suffered in their imaginations and were in as great a revulsion as those who had gone overseas. One wrote, "Too much war! I swear if there's another war on top of this one I shall refuse to know anything about it. I have ordered all my papers and magazines discontinued after July 4, 1919. . . . What fun we'll have when we can get back to poetry."[3]

The war became a myth almost as soon as it was over, both to those who had stayed at home and to those who had gone abroad. Only President Wilson, on his way to Europe on December 4, 1918, breasting the irresistible movement of those returning home, tried to keep the war and its consequences in the public mind. He was unable to do so. Thirty-one months after his voyage to the Peace Conference, a separate American peace was concluded by Congress in a joint resolution of House and Senate. This piece of paper, promulgated on July 2, 1921, did not make peace. It did set a seal upon the past and signified that the American people were looking the other way. The time between the two dates December 4, 1918, and July 2, 1921, was an uneasy interval between two strongly defined and differing periods. As the war moved toward an end, patriotism passed all reasonable bounds, and opposition to Wilson's aims grew ugly and irrational. *The New York Times* of October 20, 1918, carried an advertisement for a theatrical presentation called *The Yellow Dog.* "A wonderful dramatic story that is making 100 per cent Americans of everyone who sees it." The mood of the opposition to Wilson was typified by headlines on November 2, 1918:

TAFT SEES WILSON IN AUTOCRATIC ROLE
DECLARES PRESIDENT DEMANDS POWER
EQUAL TO THAT OF THE HOHENZOLLERNS
DENOUNCES PEACE POINTS

After the war ended, the nation found itself with a good deal of whipped-up feeling yawing about, dangerous in potential. For some, it was going to be possible to hold tightly on to hate and fear and transfer the attention of these emotions to local and domestic objects. Such haters and fearers were a minority, but they made much noise and unfortunately for a time had highly placed allies. The general, undistinguished, goodwilled majority, ready to descend into apathy, not ever having been whipped up into frenzy, held for a time a friendly and kindly regard for the President's aims. They might have gone along with him; in silence they followed; but their dispersed, low-keyed support was no match for the sharp, fierce, dedicated opposition. Wilson, with his need for delicate negotiation and adjustment in the postwar world, was to be blasted by a sudden concentration of hate turned on him as a scapegoat. He was not tactful or particularly careful in shoring his defenses at home when he turned away to do his work abroad.

Wilson's great enemy was ignorance. The American people, educated and uneducated, came out of the experience of 1917–18 believing that the end of the fighting was the end of the war. To ignorance was added a bumptious arrogance. We won the war, these citizens said to each other and to themselves; we won the war for them; see how the Allies are tearing at Germany and at each other; let us forget them; let us enjoy the cleaner air of our own good fortune and superior virtue.

With his country changing fluidly behind his back, the President, not very conscious of this change, went to Europe to represent the United States in the inter-Allied negotiations that were to decide what kind of terms to impose upon Germany and the other Central European powers. He had lost majority support in Congress in 1918. He might have mended this lack of Congressional support by taking well-picked Republicans with him to match his Democratic advisers. This he did not do. He might also have accomplished more by staying in the United States in close touch with opinion, adjusting himself to it, swaying it to his aims. But he did not do this. He was pushed by a sense of personal duty. Hindsight might forget another fact very present to him at the time. Wilson had accumulated a great quantity of goodwill abroad. When the Peace Conference opened in Paris on January 18, 1919, Wilson knew that in his own person he represented a new kind of world. He hoped to use that concentration of hope. It was Wilson's strength that he moved people by the mesmeric expression of general ideas; it was his weakness that he was in part possessed by ideas rather than was the possessor of them. He horrified a rational man such as Felix Frankfurter, who recalled that he heard the President say in Paris in a talk to a group of delegates, "If I didn't feel that I was the personal instrument of God, I couldn't carry on."[4]

It was the extrapersonal quality in Wilson that moved groups of people. At the late-starting conference, he spoke over the heads of those assembled to an international body of opinion that he had found and touched in his tour of European countries in the weeks before the opening of the conference. On January 25, 1919, he said to the assembled diplomats and to those listening beyond:

There are many complicated questions connected with the present settlements which perhaps cannot be successfully worked out to an ultimate issue by the decisions we arrive at here. I can easily conceive that many of these settlements will need subsequent reconsideration.

.   .   .

We are assembled under very peculiar conditions of world opinion. I may say without straining the point that we are not representatives of Governments, but representatives of peoples. It will not suffice to satisfy governmental circles anywhere. It is necessary that we should satisfy the opinion of mankind. The burdens of this war have fallen in an unusual degree upon the whole population of the countries involved. . . . We are bidden by these people to make a peace which will make them secure.

.   .   .

It is a solemn obligation on our part, therefore, to make permanent arrangements that justice shall be rendered and peace maintained. . . . We can set up permanent processes.

. . .

Therefore the United States should feel that its part in this war had been played in vain if there ensued upon it merely a body of European settlements.

. . .

Therefore, it seems to me that we must concern our best judgment in order to make this league of nations a vital thing—not merely a formal thing, not an occasional thing, not a thing sometimes called into life to meet an exigency, but always functioning in watchful attendance upon the interests of the nations—and that its continuity should be a vital continuity . . .[5]

Wilson's large view was impeccable, but he worked as a negotiator within personal limitations of intelligence and patience. He accomplished more than his contemporaries in the throes of an irresistible disillusionment were able to recognize. It was necessary to blame Wilson because Wilson was the one who had made them hope so extravagantly. If he did not accomplish everything, he accomplished nothing. If he compromised at all, he was wicked. The attitude was a particularly American idealism that refused to cope with particulars.

As Gerald Johnson has put it:

The truth was that the average man himself was the romantic, because he could not realize how profoundly the world had changed since 1776, and Wilson was the stern realist, seeking to adapt American theory to the facts of life. . . . His greatness lay not in the fact that he was high, holy, and all-wise from the beginning, for he was nothing of the sort, but in the fact that he set himself to learn, and having learned, did not shrink, trembling and appalled, from the Herculean labor that was thrust upon him, but rose to meet it, grappled with it, flung health, strength, life itself into the struggle and went down, defeated, but unsubdued. . . . [His fate] was sealed even before Lodge sat at Theodore Roosevelt's bedside and concocted schemes to kill any possible treaty that Wilson might negotiate. It was sealed at the moment when he devoted himself heart and soul to an idea too vast to be comprehended by a nation not yet sufficiently disciplined to look a generation ahead.[6]

Gerald Johnson's view is the large one the future was to take. The close-hand view may be seen in memoirs of the Peace Conference. Harold Nicolson, in 1919 a minor member of the British mission, was disappointed because the President did not press his principles, did not use the power he had to make Europe do better:

I knew that the President possessed unlimited physical power to enforce his views. We were all, at that date, dependent upon America, not only for the sinews of war, but for the sinews of peace. Our food supplies, our finances, were entirely subservient to the dictates of Washington. The force of compulsion possessed by Woodrow Wilson in those early months of 1919 was overwhelming. It never occurred to us that, if need arose, he would hesitate to use it. 'Never,' writes Mr. Keynes, 'had a philosopher held such weapons wherewith to bind the Princes of the world.' He did not use these weapons. He was not (and the slow realisation of this was painful to us) a philosopher. He was only a prophet.[7]

The other side of the alleged prophet was a little democrat, in the self-respecting, self-limiting sense. In his daily negotiating in Paris, Wilson was not a prophet but a functioning politician—reasonable, just, compromising when he had to be, although not particularly happy in doing so, courteous, and patient. His lesser experience of the world and something provincial and small in his background that was part of Wilson even in his late days caused him to seem somewhat stiff and slow in the confrontations of the diplomatic table. He suffered the full reward of overconfidence. He used his advisers only when he felt himself ignorant. He failed to use the press to push his point of view, particularly at home, where his enemies were zealous and busy.

Delayed too long while the people of Germany suffered needlessly from a blockade, the conference began its work without a clear-cut agenda. Unimportant and peripheral concerns leaped into the center of attention. Perhaps the conference should have been limited to the immediate conditions of peace and the details left to be ironed out after an agreement on main points. It would have worked better if the war could have ended in an atmosphere of reality. Germany might have been helped and the aura of revenge dissipated, particularly if war reparations could have been set at a definite and reasonable figure. But this was not to be. The conference ended on June 28, 1919. Its conclusion was taken as a reversion to old European methods, a betrayal of the hopes that Wilson had stirred. It did not seem to be a new world at all, but the same old one.[8]

Behind Wilson's back, the economy of the United States veered up and down in roller-coaster plunges. Men were thrown out of work by the abrupt ending of the war. Returning veterans for whom no provision had been made competed with those already out of work. Clerks and stenographers in government jobs were cut off with little advance notice and had to borrow train fare to go home to numberless small towns. There was no tapering off, only a sudden cessation of effort. Many men and women scrambled for a decreasing number of jobs at the end of 1918 and into 1919. Then, before 1919 was half over, an intemperate boom caused rising prices, which hurt many. In February, 1919, a strike of building-trade workers in New York City affected 125,000 men. In the same month there was a general strike in Seattle. In August the railway-shop workers' strike began, with 250,000 men taking part. On September 9 the policemen of Boston struck and by their act caused the later election of a President of the United States. On September 22 the steel strike began—long, desperate, degrading. In 1920 the coal miners' strike brought 435,000 men up from the ground.

The steel strike of 1919 was the most painful and the most interesting of the strikes because it contained much of the past and the future in its three-month duration. It began when Judge E. H. Gary, chairman of the board of U.S. Steel, refused to deal with any organization that said it spoke for the men. From May to September various attempts were made by labor to communicate with Gary. He answered typically to one early attempt, "As you know, we do not confer, negotiate with, or combat labor unions as such. We stand for the open shop, which permits a man to engage in the different lines of employment, whether he belongs to a labor union or not."[9] To this intransigence, the unions, unified by hard times and strengthened by the leadership of some remarkable men, presented an equal hardness in insisting that they must and would strike.

Conditions in steel were archaic. For the most part, the workers were immigrants, cheated out of hope for their children by the conditions in which they worked and lived. Half of them (69,000), said an objective report, worked a twelve-hour day; one-fourth, a seven-day week.[10] Those who worked the seven-day week worked a shift every two weeks that lasted twenty-four unbroken work hours. The wages of one-third were below the level which the Government considered to be subsistence for families of five. No union had been allowed to establish itself. In some industries unionism had gained during the war; in other industries, particularly in steel in England, the eight-hour day was becoming standard. On the other hand, U.S. Steel had increased its undivided surplus of profits from $135 million in 1914 to $493 million in 1919.

The demands of the union leaders included the right of collective bargaining, the eight-hour day, one day's rest in seven, abolition of the twenty-four-hour shift, reinstatement of men discharged for union activities, and "increases in wages sufficient to guarantee an American standard of living."[11] The demands met silence. The workers struck.

The thing visible now is how like in aims and methods the strikers were to all other parts of the population, not how different they were. William Z. Foster, the strike organizer, was proud of his orderly methods, even calling them businesslike. (He had a curious career. Genuine in his feeling for social injustice, naïve in his thinking, he passed from the IWW to the AFL, and ended, after conversion by Lenin's writings in 1923, in the Communist Party of the United States.) The thousands of steelmen who struck had little interest in revolutionary ideology. They were possessed of a great yearning toward the aims and conditions of the American majority. They asked only to belong to that majority.

This was not seen. The press for the most part supported the steel company and condemned the strikers, presenting a picture of them as dangerous aliens and radicals. Preachers preached against them. The general public just across the tracks did not understand or sympathize. Only a few radical magazines with tiny circulation told a sympathetic story. An article by Mary Heaton Vorse presented the strike from the viewpoint of a workman. She had him say about the long day's work:

'You see, twelve hours, that's too long for a man to work,' said
Mike. 'A man can't work so long and be anything but tired out like a
beast. You see my boys—I got four. By and by they goin' to grow up.
Maybe they goin' to go and work in the mills, like me. Well, I want
those boys to have a chance to learn more than I had a chance. I want
they shouldn't have to work fourteen hours night and ten hours
light.'[12]

Mary Heaton Vorse described the cleanliness and industrious-
ness in the bare house of her exemplary worker; she described,
too, the beauty of the mills at dawn with the fiery stacks like
organ pipes against the sky. But she wrote too late for too few
readers to affect the outcome. Her mood of passionate sympathy
for the strikers was out of date. It belonged either to the years
before the twenties or the years after. Something that had once
united all the layers of society in their varieties of experience into
one striving society had been sundered. The parts were now separated from each other and saw and heard news from the other
parts as if from a different people.

Vorse's Mike was defeated after hanging on to his strike for
three months. He went back to work, back to "fourteen hours
night and ten hours light." It seemed that Judge Gary had won.
William Z. Foster was not discouraged. He was as much interested, perhaps more interested, in the technique of striking than
in any one particular strike. He believed that the strike of 1919
had taught his men how to strike and that later they would use
these methods with success. So he wrote in his white-hot book,
The Great Steel Strike, in 1920.

What was to happen to labor in the twenties was not what
either Judge Gary or Foster expected. Industry was persuaded to
accept the principle of the eight-hour day. So much for Judge
Gary's expectations. On the other hand, Foster's expected labor
boom did not take place. Union membership declined during the
twenties. Mike did not gain his full share of the twenties' good
times. From 1919 to 1929 he expected to move up and, therefore,
neglected to cultivate his union organization. The prosperity of
the twenties, which was to be a false prosperity for those at the
bottom, held off protest and made protest doubly fierce at the
end of the decade.

Even beyond the real needs and sufferings of people in such trouble as those on strike, in this transition period the temper of the country was unsettled. There was a conflict of impulse, toward relaxation and toward control. The men coming home from the war, for the most part, melted back into the sections and levels from which they had been combed, unusually quiet men, having no words to express what they had seen. Others, however, seemed to want to move about swaggeringly, to assert themselves in groups. They formed a veterans' organization of strident patriotism, which many veterans quietly dropped out of when they discovered the tone in which it was to be carried on. Instances occurred again and again in 1919 and 1920 of sailors entering a Socialist publication office and smashing the machinery, of soldiers breaking up a meeting in Madison Square, of veterans "cleaning out" buildings known to be occupied by various kinds of radicals.

Anarchic impulses were indulged in. Contrarily, among other changes that seemed to come of themselves was a giant one for control: the national prohibition law. People watched wonderingly as this thing seemed to come irresistibly upon them. There was one setback only, President Wilson's veto of the implementing act, the Volstead Act, on October 27, 1919. But Wilson's interposition was only momentary. The movement by which state after state ratified the constitutional amendment had gone on steadily, although without much thought of the consequences. The instigators were efficient and well organized and had a long history of agitation to support their present words. That there had been a transformation of the original movement from one kind into another was not at first grasped. What had started as a movement toward temperance became one for prohibition. The fulfillment was suddenly a fact on the hour of midnight, January 16, 1920. It was an enormity of good or bad according to the eye of the beholder. *The New York Times* editorialized on January 17: "With what dizzying swiftness have the Legislatures competed with one another in the race to add this Article to the Constitution? Has this contagion or consensus of emotion and politics been accompanied with an equal conviction among the people?"

With feeling, the liquor people advertised before the event:

Before Prohibition is Effective
Your Home Should be Supplied with
B A C A R D I[13]

Meantime, an act of vivid fanaticism of a small number of genuine political radicals distracted public attention from the issues of the hour. In New York City a postal clerk named Charles Caplan was on the way home by subway at 2 A.M. on April 30, 1919. He had finished his day's work and was tired, but a story in his newspaper caught his attention and caused him to get off the train and go back downtown. The story was about a bomb's exploding in Senator Hardwick's house in Atlanta, a bomb that took off the hands of the maid who had opened a package addressed to the senator. The description of the parcel sent his mind racing back to the parcel room in the main post office building, where he worked. He was at once convinced that he had set aside for insufficient postage upon a certain shelf sixteen packages identical to the one described in the story.

Back in the parcel room, he stared at the sixteen packages, all of them labeled "Novelties," all stamped with a label from Gimbel's just like the one in the newspaper. The packages sitting in a neat row were addressed to the Postmaster, the Attorney General, Justice Wendell Holmes, John D. Rockefeller, and others. Caplan notified his superiors of his suspicions. A bomb expert was called in who with ticklish care worked one package open. It was indeed a bomb and highly explosive. The post office department began a search for other bombs; thirty-six in all were found, some on the way to the West Coast. All had been mailed in the New York post office after having been put together, wrapped, addressed, labeled with the false Gimbel labels, and posted by one person or one group of persons in a highly ingenious and murderous fashion. They were all stopped except the one delivered in Atlanta. The sender or senders were never found, but conclusions were immediately jumped to. "A nationwide bomb conspiracy, which the police authorities say has every earmark of I.W.W.-Bolshevik origin . . . has been discovered." Such was *The New York Times* conclusion in an article on May 1, 1919.

There was a second bomb scare in early June, 1919. One bomb, tossed into the doorway of the Attorney General, A. Mitchell Palmer, scattered into bits and pieces the unfortunate bomb thrower, whose identity was never learned. The mailed bombs of late April and the tossed ones of June, incendiary and insane, had no consequences of insurrection, or even of continued bombings. But there were intense emotional consequences. Some of them were spontaneous; others were organized. The principal organizer was the new Attorney General, Palmer.

President Wilson had appointed a valuable Democratic Party campaigner, A. Mitchell Palmer, to the office of Attorney General in March, 1919. Palmer came into office when the President's attention was steadfastly concentrated overseas. In the vacuum left at home, Palmer became a figure of authority. If Wilson noticed, he gave no evidence of disapproval; there had grown in him a harshness and even repressiveness toward what he took for treachery quite unlike his generosity and idealism in other areas. Palmer had real zeal against radicals. He had been frightened by the bomb thrown into his own doorway. He had the spur of ambition. He intended to be a presidential candidate in 1920. He wanted to be famous, he wanted a cause, and he found one in the "Red scare" that existed—amorphous, diffuse, vague—on which he concentrated.

On August 1, 1919, Palmer organized a new force within the Attorney General's department, the General Intelligence Division, the function of which was the listing and locating of aliens. He then proceeded to prosecute alien radicals, imprisoning and then deporting them by the thousands. This campaign against domestic danger was spoiled by its vagueness, the use of hearsay and gossip as evidence, the willingness to throw a wide net and make a big splashy story. The Attorney General's official agents were willing to accept information turned in by private patriotic clubs and even used the services of these groups in conducting raids. Zeal spread rapidly. Four hundred soldiers and sailors devastated the New York office of the Socialist daily *Call*, on May Day, 1919. This loose, vague, public confidence that anyone and everyone knew who was radical and who was dangerous was encouraged instead of discouraged by the responsible federal officer, the Attorney General of the United States.

There was some highly placed public opposition. Senator Thomas J. Walsh was sarcastically calm about the evidence collected by Palmer. "Nothing, so far as the evidence here has described, has evinced anything in the nature of preparation for a military uprising."[14] A military uprising was what Palmer loosely predicted. There was an almost official encouragement of the belief that the many splintered radical groups were conspiring with Bolshevik *and* German aid to collect arms, drill, form an army, and take over. On July 2, William J. Flynn, one of Palmer's top investigators, stated categorically that the recent bombings were "connected with Russian Bolshevism, aided by Hun money."[15] Palmer and his men, among them Francis P. Garvan, William J. Flynn, Frank Burke, J. Edgar Hoover, the new head of the GID (later the Federal Bureau of Investigation), were sincerely infected with the fear of a general uprising, and they spread this fear among the uncritical members of the general public.

The radicals at this time aided the investigators by being noisy and triumphant, celebrating the recent Bolshevik victory in Russia, which they little understood. The dedicated leaders of these tiny parties and associations often dramatically withdrew from the United States at this time to visit Russia. Meantime, a contagion of emotion—the radicals' of coming success, the public's of alarm—grew. An overt move was expected on Independence Day, 1919. All the police in New York City were ordered to be on duty. Nothing happened. Yet by fall, Palmer was generally criticized, by *The New York Times,* by many civic organizations, and by officials of various states and of the Federal Government, for holding back his hand. When Palmer acted, it was the act of a shrewd, ambitious, shortsighted man who had a great deal of administrative ability.

Palmer first tried to use Section 6 of the criminal code against those he conceived to be enemy aliens. This was a law passed to handle dangerous men during the Civil War. But cases brought to trial under this ruling were thrown out. Federal Judge John Raymond Hazel found that those arrested had not attempted "overthrow of our institutions by violent means" and that "Congress in passing it did not have in mind, in my judgment, the overthrow of the Government . . . by the use of propaganda."[16]

What Palmer now found usable, vague enough to cover any case he might prepare, was the Immigration Act of 1917, as amended in 1918. Under it, as Coben in his full treatment of Palmer's character and acts has said: "Any alien anarchist, no matter how pacific his beliefs, was deportable. So was any alien advocating use of violence against property, public officials, or the government; or who belonged to an organization which advocated the use of violence."[17] Under this act, the Justice Department had no authority except to arrest. Palmer and his men had to turn over the men they had arrested to the Labor Department's Bureau of Immigration to complete legal action. It seemed at first that all would go like clockwork. The first joint raid of the two departments took place on November 7, 1919, against the Union of Russian Workers, an organization of 4,000 Russian immigrants.

In twelve cities, arresting officers invaded the headquarters of the organization. They carried warrants signed ahead of time by Anthony Caminetti, the Commissioner General of Immigration. The warrants were without names, for the names were to be filled in *after* the arrests. There were not even enough of the blank warrants. In the enthusiasm of achievement, many men and women were held without warrants until warrants could be secured or manufactured. People on this first day of raids were knocked about, picked up because they happened to be in the building raided, and held for long periods without access to counsel. This was the beginning of three months of such actions.

On January 1 and 2, 1920, Department of Justice men, helped by local police in thirty-three cities, arrested in homes and public places more than 3,000 persons assumed to be members of two Communist parties. A reporter for *The Nation* magazine wrote a description of the conditions of detention in Detroit, where a raid had been made against a building called the House of Masses:

As a result [of the raid] 800 men were imprisoned for 3 to 6 days in a dark, windowless, narrow corridor running around the big central areaway of the city's antiquated Federal Building; they slept on the bare stone floor at night, in the heavy heat that welled sickeningly up to the low roof, just over their heads; they were shoved and jostled about by heavy-handed policemen; they were forbidden even the chance to perform a makeshift shave; they were compelled to stand in long lines for access to the solitary drinking fountain and the one toilet, they were denied all food for 20 hours, and after that they were fed on what their families brought in; and they were refused all communication with relatives or with attorneys.[18]

Some of those arrested happened to be in the House of Masses only because they were attending geography classes or taking part in a dance, attracted as lonely men to light and noise and activity; one at least had merely delivered a parcel to the building. A particular example of the hit-or-miss method of arrest was noted in *The Nation:*

One young man who [was arrested] was getting his dinner in the cooperative restaurant run by the Workers' Educational Society, which controls the House of Masses. "He quit the Communist Party because he didn't believe in force," his sister said. "But the restaurant has better meals at cheap prices than any place around there, and he always ate there. They've had him 10 days now."[19]

It took some time, and many injustices endured, for the general opinion of the country to perceive the enormity of what Palmer was doing. The press and a robust, indiscriminate public at first supported the Attorney General's vigorous actions. The series of strikes of 1919 had caused alarm and anger against the working classes. As recently as November 1 the coal workers had struck, 435,000 strong, and this act was taken not as a demand for justice due but as a sign of radical activity. On November 11 there had been a genuine battle in the streets in Centralia, Washington, between IWW workers and American Legionnaires, which had turned into a nightmare of killings. In April, 1920, the New York State Legislature had expelled five duly elected Socialist members from its body rather than allow them to sit in their midst. And on May 5, 1920, two anarchists named Sacco and Vanzetti were arrested for a payroll murder.

The warming spring of 1920 saw an accident deliver authority in the immigration cases into the hands of a man who applied the brakes of skepticism to the whole process. Louis F. Post, Assistant Secretary of Labor, Acting Secretary during the illness of Secretary of Labor William B. Wilson, found under his jurisdiction the mountainous pile of cases assembled for prosecution by Attorney General Palmer.

What happened was unexpected, the kind of event that seemed the deliberate thrusting of a spike into the mindless progress of history. At this particular point, one crotchety, stubborn man over seventy years old said no. Post simply sat down and read the cases, staying up nights to do so and meanwhile halting all legal processes in these matters. Then he simply threw out most of the cases and freed the men imprisoned. He found the letter of the law did not apply and reversed the whole swift procedure which Palmer had initiated.

Post was a small man, jaunty and dandiacal in appearance. He did not mind a fight when the powers of Congressional investigation were turned upon him. It was in the publicity of the hearings, in which he was threatened with impeachment, that he made his point. With reason, wit, coolness, and the flavor of a pungent, unafraid mind he tempered the atmosphere. His defense of his conduct was a detailed presentation of cases. His best illustration was that of a Presbyterian "Communist" accused in one of the dossiers on his desk. He persuaded a good many of the Congressmen and some of the public beyond that what had been going on was absurd.[20] Post's testimony made the public realize that it had grown tired of Palmer's crusade. Some of the hysteria of the Palmer raids perpetuated itself across the twenties, but never again did such feeling spread so widely and rouse the whole population.

It is helpful to remember that Wilson brought back his unresolved peace to an unresolved domestic situation, to a people distracted from paying full attention to what he was saying. There were many modest, quiet men who supported him still, who thought: Woodrow Wilson is right; the League is necessary. But such supporters were to be ineffectual in the noise and frenzy of organized opposition. They too were tired of effort. They assumed that they could not make much difference individually. The war had been efficient in curbing political idealism and effort, the kind of individual sally into public life for this or that cause that had been so marked a part of the national scene in the years before the war.

The Peace Conference ended and the Treaty of Versailles was signed on June 28, 1919. The scene was stage-managed in a way that repelled sensitive viewers. There was an unsavory atmosphere of victor and vanquished, the German signers being held back and then herded in before the others in a kind of demonstration of humiliation. Many members of the press and many lesser diplomats expressed disgust with the display of implied vengeance out of keeping with the magnanimity of Wilson's Fourteen Points, on the basis of which the Germans had asked for an armistice.[21]

Wilson came home with a fixed and brilliant idea, the connection between domestic happiness and foreign arrangements. The majority of the American people had arrived at different conclusions. We were strong. Had not the war proved it? Those people over there, while to be pitied, were not to be helped. Suffering from their picturesque and inconceivable revolutions, famines, bombings, executions, they were of another kind from us. They must take the consequences of being what they were. Hadn't we gone over and attempted to straightened them out? Let them persist in their errors; there were new things to do over here. The public was suffering from a variety of delusions, among them the belief that there was no connection between foreign troubles and domestic tranquillity. Therefore, Wilson's fixed idea could make no strong impression when separated from the magnetic presence of the man himself.

Wilson was conscious of the hypnotic powers he possessed and was reconciled to using these gifts to supplement reason. In February, 1919, he had interrupted his Paris negotiations to come home to Washington for a visit to consult with Congressional leaders. During the extended sessions of the Peace Conference he had struggled in detail with one problem after another, wisely or unwisely, but with full attention, patience, and every personal persuasion that he could use. In exchange for these sacrifices, he had pushed through the awkward American idea of the right of a nation to withdraw from a solemn "covenant." He had accepted various European claims and made compromises again and again in order to save his League of Nations. When he came home after the conference ended, he brought with him, he thought, a positive minimum good that his country must accept for the future peace of the world. The wrongs of Paris could be mended within the framework of the League. He was aware of the opposition he faced, but not perhaps its strength or the indifference of those

who were not even his opponents. He faced the task of getting his
Treaty and his League through the Senate, the members of which
were armed with their grand right to advise and consent.

The enemies of the League within and without the Government were a varied lot. They did not like each other. Senator
William E. Borah was an honest, simple isolationist, shocked by
the new internationalism because it seemed wicked. "Clemenceau
and Lloyd George and others like them were willing to make any
reasonable sacrifice which would draw America away from her
isolation and into the internal affairs and concerns of Europe. . . .
Once having surrendered and become a part of European concerns, where, my friends are you going to stop?" so Borah argued.[22] The very ground of Borah's attitude was confidence. He
did not fear the future.

Henry Cabot Lodge, who belonged to the revisionists—that is,
those who claimed that they supported a League but must revise
it—had more complex objections than Borah. To Lodge the
League seemed an impudence designed to throttle the American
power that he had helped nurture under Theodore Roosevelt and
Taft. "Are we ready to abandon the Monroe Doctrine and leave it
to other nations to say how American questions shall be settled
and what steps we shall be permitted to take in order to guard
our own safety or to protect the Panama Canal? Are we ready to
have other nations tell us by a majority vote what attitude we
must assume in regard to immigration or in regard to our tariffs?"[23] Lodge believed in the victory that had just been won.

Wilson had also gained enemies among the liberals. These were
allies in old causes who had defected from his leadership, men
like Oswald Garrison Villard, editor of *The Nation,* and John
Dewey, who wrote in *The New Republic,* "We are not holier than
other nations, but there is an obligation upon us not to engage too
much or too readily with them until there is assurance that we
shall not make themselves and ourselves worse, rather than better, by what is called sharing the common burdens of the world,
whether it be through the means of a League of Nations or some
special alliance."[24] Wilson's own acts had caused many liberals to
switch allegiance: the abrogation of civil liberties, the management of news, the jailing of Eugene Debs. In Paris at the Peace
Conference, he seemed to have trimmed and compromised, and
to have turned subject peoples over to tyrants. What none of the

opponents saw was the one central idea that was almost the only one now that the stained, compromised, egotistical, and obsessed President could see: that the future peace of the world, including America, depended upon conserving what had been signed into treaty in Europe, giving it loyalty in principle, changing details perhaps, but holding on to it to prevent future and more terrible wars.

To all those who did not share Wilson's vision, he seemed to have become a tired old man, shaky in his health, shaky perhaps in judgment, talking in large phrases, living in a time that had already passed. He seemed intolerable, a being stuffed full of errors and egotism.

On July 10, 1919, the President presented the Treaty and the League to the Senate. On September 10, Lodge, speaking for the Foreign Relations Committee, in irony it seemed, recommended ratification, with *forty-two* amendments and reservations. Meanwhile, on September 3 Wilson had taken his fight very late to the people. In twenty-two days he was to make forty-five speeches, for the most part without preparation, yet in doing so uttering some of his finest sayings. The recollection of Wilson's journey was to have a historical resonance; the immediate effect was of something infinitely moving but with little practical result. Yet to those taking part, to the speaker, to the listeners, it seemed that something important was happening.

Through city after city along the railroad tracks cleared for the presidential train, Wilson spoke from the back of the train itself or in hastily scheduled public meetings, never pausing to rest. He traveled against the warnings of his physician and his wife. Columbus, Ohio, was his first stop. Pueblo, Colorado, was his last. The audiences were at first uncertain as to what he required of them, but as the story of his journey preceded him, at each stop they were more and more ready to follow his argument and to enter into the urgency of his entreaties. They sensed the drama of his effort; they became a part of it.

The Pueblo speech was a mixture of the worst and the best of Wilson. Like many of his countrymen, he was possessed of a fear of divided loyalty in the American society:

I find . . . that there is an organized propaganda against the League of Nations and against the Treaty proceeding from exactly the same sources that the organized propaganda proceeded from which threatened this country here and there with disloyalty, and I want to say—I cannot say too often—any man who carries a hyphen about with him carries a dagger that he is ready to plunge into the vitals of this Republic whenever he gets ready. If I can catch any man with a hyphen in this great contest I will know that I have got an enemy of the Republic.[25]

Through bitterness at nationalistic opposition such as that of the Irish-Americans or the Italian-Americans because he had failed to espouse Ireland for the Irish or Fiume for the Italians, Wilson in such words encouraged antiforeign hysteria. But he deceived himself if he believed that this was the important opposition to the League. The real inertia against the League was native: the innocent, ignorant isolationism of Borah of the western hinterland; the ingrown pride and suspicion of Lodge, the New Englander; the homegrown individualism of the liberals who had been disillusioned by Palmer at home and hungry nationalists at the peace table; the ordinary, self-respecting citizen who was tired and wanted to live his middling private life unworried by world affairs.

But reaching toward them, pulling at them, another almost irresistible Wilson spoke too:

War will be pushed out of that foreground of terror in which it has kept the world for generation after generation, and men will know that there will be a calm time of deliberate counsel.

. . .

There is no middle course. You cannot go in on a special-privilege basis of your own. I take it that you are too proud to ask to be exempted from responsibilities which the other members of the league will carry. We go in upon equal terms or we do not go in at all; and if we do not go in, my fellow citizens, think of the tragedy of that result—the only sufficient guaranty to the peace of the world withheld! Ourselves drawn apart with that dangerous pride which means that we shall be ready to take care of ourselves, and that means that we shall maintain great standing armies and an irresistible navy . . . It always seems to make it difficult for me to say anything, my fellow citizens, when I think of my clients in this case. My clients are the children; my clients are the next generation. They do not know what promises and bonds I undertook when I ordered the armies of the United States to the soil of France, but I know, and I intend to redress my pledges to the children; they shall not be sent upon a similar errand.

. . .

There is one thing that the American people always rise to and extend their hand to, and that is the truth of justice and of liberty and of peace. We have accepted that truth and we are going to be led by it, and it is going to lead us, and through us the world, out into pastures of quietness and peace such as the world never dreamed of before.[26]

The crowd wept; even its most critical members, the newspapermen, were with him. Wilson had done all that he could do. After the talk, during a passage eastward on the train, the President's headache, from which he had been suffering for weeks, grew fearful and unbearable. He did not sleep till morning; and his wife, his doctor, and his secretary held a conference, agreeing at last and persuading the President to agree, that he could go on no more. The train started back to Washington that morning, September 26, and arrived on Sunday, September 28. Wilson walked to the automobile that carried him to the White House. Mrs. Wilson recalled:

All the rest of that day, my husband wandered like a ghost between the study at one end of the hall and my room at the other. The awful pain in his head that drove him restlessly back and forth was too acute to permit work, or even reading. Late in the afternoon we went for a short motor ride; but still the demon of pain pursued him.

On the third night after his return from his speaking tour, Mrs. Wilson continued her watchfulness:

I had been sleeping fitfully, getting up every hour or so to see how my husband was. It was so on this night. At five or six in the morning I found him still sleeping normally, as it appeared. Relieved, I dozed off again until after eight. This time I found him sitting on the side of the bed trying to reach a water bottle. As I handed it to him I noticed that his left hand hung loosely. "I have no feeling in that hand," he said, "Will you rub it? But first help me to the bathroom."

He moved with great difficulty, and every move brought spasms of pain; but with my help he gained the bathroom. This so alarmed me that I asked if I could leave him long enough to telephone the Doctor. He said yes, and hurrying into my room I reached Dr. Grayson at his home. While at the 'phone I heard a slight noise, and rushing into my husband's apartment, found him on the bathroom floor unconscious.[27]

For the next few months the United States was without a directing President. The Constitution provided for succession in the case of the President's death or disability, but disability was hard to define. Wilson was dangerously ill for only a short time, but continued disabled. His mind was not destroyed, but it was said that his temper was affected by the stroke. In any case, during the period of his helplessness, Mrs. Wilson and Dr. Grayson shielded the man they wanted to save. No disturbing and, therefore, no vital problems were brought to him. The making of decisions was dispersed throughout the Government. For a time Attorney General Palmer was the busiest and most effective administrator in the capital. With this exception, the Government drifted.

The accident of Wilson's illness allowed certain events to take place and prevented others, but the large outline of things probably remained unchanged. What it did was to intensify a special emotional tone of the time. After the openness and frankness of the "years before," in which individual and generous things were done freely and the doing of them seemed no threat to anyone, with a suddenness that surprised, there now came a time of suspecting, probing, investigating, a condemning of acts and thoughts that seemed dangerous. There was one curious, concomitant fact: no urgency was felt toward trying to control alien happenings in a rational way by treaty agreement or by a permanent international organization such as Wilson had proposed. There was something inherently irrational in the set of public opinion.

In his illness certain traits in the President hardened. He refused to pardon Eugene Debs. Even Palmer asked for this pardon; the President refused more than once.

In the pulse of new time, Palmer soon grew ridiculous. His intensities and the intensities of Wilson seemed irrelevant. The fall of 1920, the year that began with Palmer's Red raids, was the year of the publication of Sinclair Lewis' novel *Main Street*. The book held up a mirror of satire and longing to a whole people, and Americans suddenly were in the mood to be looked at and laughed at. They were hungry to find out about themselves. Lewis was not hounded out of the country for being funny at the expense of his fellow citizens. He became popular and rich instead. After clenching themselves into a fist, Americans let go.

The railroads were given back to their owners; women received the vote. Yet the results of the previous mood continued to act and react; prohibition became constitutional law; Sacco and Vanzetti were arrested and tried; immigration was cut down to a trickle and the proportions fixed in monstrous lopsidedness. Differing national impulses or strains raveled out into separate skeins in disorder and contradiction.

The end of one era and the beginning of another was marked by the inauguration of a new president. Woodrow Wilson, able to be on his feet with the aid of a stick, was present. Senator Henry Cabot Lodge announced formally to President Wilson the end of his term. The place was the President's room in the Capitol. Wilson sat signing bills in the final minutes before noon. Tumulty, the President's secretary, witnessed and described the scene:

Presently there appeared at the door a gray-haired man of imperious manner. Addressing the President in a sharp, dry tone of voice, he said: "Mr. President, we have come as a committee of the Senate to notify you that the Senate and House are about to adjourn and await your pleasure."

.   .   .

It was an interesting study to watch the face and manner of Woodrow Wilson as he met the gaze of Senator Lodge. . . . It appeared for a second as if Woodrow Wilson was about to give full sway to the passionate resentment he felt toward the man who, he believed, had unfairly treated him throughout the famous Treaty fight. But quickly the shadow of resentment passed. A ghost of a smile flitted across the firm mouth, and steadying himself in his chair, he said in a low voice: "Senator Lodge, I have no further communication to make. I thank you. Good morning."[28]

V

SYMPTOMS
OF THE NEW

IT IS A PUZZLE WHERE DISTINCTION COMES FROM, especially in a great, scattered, various society such as the United States of America at the end of President Wilson's war. But in 1918, 1919, 1920, and 1921, new kinds of distinction were appearing in isolated works of various kinds. Common living and popular thinking made no allowances for distinction and offered no excuse or explanation.

Superficially the activities of most Americans immediately after the war seemed to revert to what they had been before the upheaval. In business, small enterprises were passed from father to son; in politics, patronage was personal and tyrannical. Amusements were what they had been: church socials and revivals, drives in buggies or buggylike automobiles, plays put on by stock companies or the new "movies" in made-over store buildings. Men attended ball games without their wives or went around the corner to the saloon. Women were said to be "advanced," but this was not much seen in vast isolated stretches of small towns and farms. Popular reading was in the easily turned pages of Zane Grey, Gene Stratton Porter, Peter B. Kyne, and Edgar A. Guest. Approved literature was bland: the comfortable parts of Emerson, Longfellow, Whittier, Bryant, early Twain, non-Socialist Howells—not Henry James at all, who seemed alien and overstrained.

Still, the smoothness was breaking up and the tempo was changing. There were disturbances underneath that now began to show in eruptions upon the surface. The experience of the war could not be forgotten, although there were no words at hand to describe it. Dumb show alone could portray it. In late 1918, just around the corner from the war-preaching propaganda play *The Yellow Dog*, Charlie Chaplin's new movie *Shoulder Arms* drew crowds who laughed at this satire of war. It celebrated what could not be done by organized effort. It celebrated backward humanity, which looked ridiculous dressed in soldier clothes, which stumbled over its own feet and its own gun, and which winked a brotherly, conspiratorial wink at the audience, who in turn laughed and felt renewed.

The war had pushed and pulled at people, rounding the edges off them, making them efficient in their public lives. It had ignored their human and individual qualities in achievements best reported in statistics. Since this was the first such American war outside the continent, there had been no guide to go by and many of the incidentals had been extreme and unnecessary. The propaganda version of the war, played out in drives, pageants, songs, parades, and in the distorted reports of the press, at last sickened the public. This public-relations version of the war was more pervasive than in the other great English-speaking country, which suffered more and contributed more over a longer period and yet recovered mentally, if not physically, more readily. The effect of forced patriotism on the United States was long-lasting. A strain of hysteria continued after the war; there was a hunting down of radicals and aliens; a hating of the new and the startling; a hugging of the false, a preventing of healthful innovation and spontaneity. On the other hand, the strong, opposite reaction to hysteria was a general letting go, sometimes in spree, sometimes in lethargy. The baseball scandal of 1919, when the World Series was "fixed," was a symptom of the extremity of the mood of the moment.[1] The private life became the all in all. Public life was considered tainted; when proven so, there was no surprise and no effort to cleanse it. Fulfillment took every form other than the political, and luxuriated and ramified and multiplied curiously. The most diverse Americans of the twenties agreed in detestation of the public life. They all united in the assumption that their private interests could take care of themselves without the frame and protection of public organization. The illusion sustained itself for almost ten years. This in itself makes the twenties an exception to every other decade before or after. No warning was taken from the fact that the abdication of responsibility in the public sphere coincided with the growth and the display of much energy and individuality and power that might possibly need some direction or control.

The election of Harding to the presidency, although it was worked by a small number of men, was acquiesced in by millions. It was not merely the end of the movement to repudiate Wilson; it was the beginning of an era. The large vote that a mediocre candidate received was the sign of exasperation among the people. The other candidates for nomination in the Republican Party were abler, stronger, more colorful men. The Democratic Party's candidate was clearly a better choice in competency and forthrightness. Yet the public seconded the choice put forward. They did so with an astounding vote. The public was so weary of being managed for great causes, organized, moved about, sloganized, its feelings whipped to passion pitch, that it was willing, at this moment, to be organized for this one vote if, as the implicit promise seemed to say, it would then be let alone.

The going back to private life was for the most part the return to making a living or to finding new and fascinating ways to do so. Making a living was not conceived in the European fashion, as filling a certain role and living within a proper place in society. Nor was it conceived of forty years later in the United States as the means for complicated consuming. Making a living was conceived as an adventure with an excessive aim, that of making money and being a success. The general belief allowed an ambition to everyone. It was a terribly serious thing, innocent, spontaneous, humorless. And yet, the possibility of "success" was real for only a small number. After a pause, hard times set in just after the war. People in the country lost at once the war prosperity they had had. Others in the cities suffered from inflation and sudden unemployment. The widespread material poverty in the

South, which had lasted since the Civil War, was further aggravated. People moved about restlessly looking for work. Many Negroes of the bone-poor rural South moved north to the cities. Yet everywhere there was a hope of more than a job, hope of getting out of dead circumstances, of changing one's luck, of striking out into a future different from one's parents'.

A certain type of popular magazine fed the voracious hunger for news about success in business. It did not signify how crude the matter was, or how monotonous; it was received with enthusiasm month after month by subscribers whose appetites were frank and not fine in taste. In the January, 1920, issue of *The American Magazine* three articles crowded each other: "The Salaries That Are Paid in Various Lines," "Are You Making Money or Losing It?" and "Interesting People: A Great Executive." The advertisements appealed as nakedly to the same motive and were little dramas of success. An advertisement of the International Correspondence Schools was headlined: "He Deposits $500 a Month!" And under a drawing the story was swiftly told: "See that man at the Receiving Teller's window? That's Billy King, Manager for Browning Company. Every month he comes in and deposits $500. I've been watching Billy for a long time." And the banker, while beaming on Billy from afar, advises the neophyte to take a course and stop working for fifteen dollars a week all his life. In the *Literary Digest* of October 9, 1920, an advertisement for Dr. Eliot's Five-Foot Shelf of Books headed "Which Will Succeed?" showed one man in handsome bathrobe, finger to chin, studious, sober, reading a book; the other, careless, yawning, reading a daily paper. Another advertisement in the same issue of the *Digest* played upon the same word which never seemed to bore:

FLEISCHMANN'S YEAST
HELPS SUCCESS

The 'Pep' creators, who breed enthusiasm and confidence in their subordinates . . . The virile chaps who send their deal over with a snap that takes your breath away . . . These are *healthy chaps.*

Fleischmann's Yeast is tuning up a lot of good
fellows to concert pitch and making them *stick*.

Lots of fellows are taking the 'Fleischmann Yeast'
road to 100% Health and Success.

This urgency to make money existed in a world where new
fortunes had been made in the war and where top money-makers
were admiringly publicized, but where also the average federal
employee made $1,375 a year; the average construction worker,
$1,924; the average agricultural worker, $830; the average public
school teacher, $936; and the average minister, $1,428.[2] It was a
grim, everyday world for many when a want ad on November 2,
1919 in the New York *World* read:

> WOMEN. $12 start
> Light factory work
> Experience unnecessary
> Can make $15–$18
> *Leo H. Hirsch & Co.*

But it was believed that there were discrepancies in bad luck.
Everyone felt qualified to win, or at least that his children were
going to. It made for an air of extremity: extreme hope, extreme despair, a teetering upon possibilities. If it was to be success, what fun; if failure, how black and unimaginable. This was
the mood of the beginning of the postwar period. For some this
pitch was maintained for the decade. The success fever infected
every kind of endeavor. Some writers talked of writing a certain
kind of successful book—"the great American novel,"—as if it
were a shady deal to be pulled off.

Yet in the midst of this engaging vulgarity an absolutely other
impulse flourished too. Farmers tended their potato patches and
lived modestly at the mercy of the weather and only hoped for
decent crops. Some businessmen and some professional people
were uninfected by the success disease. Painters painted and writers wrote what it was their fierce private business to do. For them
to be free of the contagious fever was most difficult. It was their
occupation to be aware of national moods and emotions, to make
artistic matter of them. To be aware of these energies and even to
make use of them, at the same time maintaining integrity, in-

volved strain. Creating of any kind was becoming for an American a battle with desperate terms, not just a low-keyed, patient craft. Sherwood Anderson, a businessman who had become a short-story writer, likened himself to a cunning animal. He wrote to a friend in the summer of 1919, "These are gaudy days. If you do not hear from me for some time, bear in mind that I am a prairie dog and am busy hiding corn in a hole in a field."[3] H. L. Mencken, not content with being a well-rewarded reporter and editor of the daily happenings of Baltimore, spent his time away from his job sorting his patiently gathered examples of American pronunciation, spelling, speech, slang; carried on a lively correspondence about these matters with both amateurs and scholars; and made himself into an expert in an unexplored area of scholarship, "a recreation," as he called it, "from other and far different labor."[4] Sinclair Lewis, before *Main Street* was published in the fall of 1920, scribbled on the kitchen drainboard at 6 A.M. and wrote rudely in the face of his seat-mates on the train to New York City—time stolen from a job and from his own rest. Robert Frost made a living as a part-time teacher and part-time farmer and wrestled with how to live and how to write, yet being proud of his closeness to necessities, said, "The rich are too vague from their remoteness from things ever to come to grips with things daily."[5]

Anderson, Lewis, Frost, Mencken, each in his own busyness, was an isolated and separated example of a new American consciousness. It was not that other Americans in 1920—farmers, factory workers, salesmen, businessmen even—did not also have intimations of a new consciousness. But they were inarticulate. It was these bright, strange, egotistic, or indifferent "creators" who perceived the *new* and translated it into terms that all could eventually recognize and say in the wonder of recognition: This is what I feel, this is what I know, this is what everything means. Recognition and assimilation did not come at once, except occasionally to someone like Sinclair Lewis, whose communication was striking and immediate.

In 1920 this new sense of self and sense of the world produced variously and as if at hazard the slight and charming *A Few Figs from Thistles,* of Edna St. Vincent Millay; the sensuous scholarliness of Pound's *Hugh Selwyn Mauberley;* Eliot's creative conservatism in the essays of *The Sacred Wood;* the youthful charm of Fitzgerald's novel *This Side of Paradise;* the raucous satire and yearning of Lewis' *Main Street;* the theatrical experiment and vision of O'Neill's *Beyond the Horizon* and *The Emperor Jones.* The names are samples. An example from any level might serve to illustrate what was happening, that a new American consciousness was coming into being. There was triviality in this newness and some mediocrity, as well as occasionally a sharp, never-before-seen distinction. While the magazines of mass circulation printed article after article about business opportunity, Sherwood Anderson wrote *Winesburg, Ohio,* a book about "failures," and John Marin sat down to paint a view of New York harbor.

Marin's harbor was a radically new view, made up of private feeling but shattered and shaped by light and air. It seemed to belong to a different world from the work of "the Eight" who had painted a surface of color, action, and scene a few years before. Marin dived into his personal consciousness to say something in paint and shape about the bath of atmosphere in which Americans lived, about tall buildings, water, ships, and seabirds. Sherwood Anderson dived into the hidden lives of everyone around him. What drove him was, as he said, "the hunger to see beneath the surface of lives."[6] The stories in *Winesburg, Ohio* (1919) were an expanse of tenderness and passion upon the secret, twisted motives of small-town people. Some of his readers were touched in their imaginations, others were shocked. In his work was a sensation of walls falling down, windows blowing out, roofs flying up from dingy houses and from around hidden lives. The great popularity of *Main Street,* which thousands read eagerly, was due in part to recognition. It gave them the physical world they lived in:

The buildings were as ill-assorted, as temporary-looking, as a mining-camp street in the motion pictures.

The Ford Garage and the Buick Garage, competent one-story brick and cement buildings opposite each other. Old and new cars on grease-blackened concrete floors. Tire advertisements. The roaring of a tested motor; a racket which beat at the nerves. Surly young men in khaki Union-overalls. The most energetic and vital places in the town.

Lewis' solutions were shallow; his alternatives were callow socialism and callow estheticism; but his descriptions and epithets struck home. He had also a native's feeling for the transient beauty of the land lying beyond each main street: "The sunshine was dizzy on open stubble; shadows from immense cumulus clouds were forever sliding across low mounds; and the sky was wider and loftier and more resolutely blue than the sky of cities . . ."[7]

Both Anderson and Lewis helped furnish attitudes for a lonely, busy country. This had nothing to do with the intrinsic artistic value of their books. Readers were struck by a sensation of recognition in reading these tales of small-town life, such life as they had once known or knew now. In characters, in actions, in images, both men put words to American situations that had been wordless before, gave names to American lives that had been lived but not described, gave epithets to conflicts that had been without verbal issue before. Thus, in Carol and Doc Kennicott, the inarticulate, hard-working doctor and his yearning, dissatisfied wife, and in the other various, shallow, vivid members of the population of his Gopher Prairie, Lewis enriched the vision of themselves that Americans might have from this time on. What he had done constituted a part of a national recognition of selfhood in new circumstances, of self among the Ford cars, the unpaved, rutted roads, the booming cities, the growing towns, the still lonely villages and farms of the twenties. The undramatic inhabitants of that country began in a measure imitating that vision, making themselves more defined, more idiosyncratic, more interesting. Sherwood Anderson gave comfort to rebellion and discontent, and inner differentness, to which the surface of American life offered little tolerance. His young man walking the main street of Winesburg, seeing secret meanings in secret lives, was prototype for many young men and women who were to hold themselves singular, blessed or cursed, by self-knowledge and self-consciousness, in many tightly-centered small towns of the continent, a place too large to be summarized under one style, except that of loneliness.

To feel at home in the present, there was need for support from the past. The old past would not do. It was necessary to find a new past. The blandness of authorized literature was rejected. New ancestors were found. A darker and more sardonic Twain came to light in 1916 in *The Mysterious Stranger*. Henry Adams became available all at once and was gratefully accepted into full ancestordom to the new time. His *Education* was published in 1918, after being circulated before only in a private printing. *Mont-St.-Michel and Chartres* was reprinted in 1919 and was read widely for the first time. In 1920 two volumes of Henry James' *Letters* appeared, and the publishing of two editions of his works, the New York edition (1907–17) and the London edition (1921–23), made him fully visible and influential to a new generation. James began to be seen in a contemporary light. Ezra Pound did not long stand alone in championing the writer who seemed now to be full of meaning.[8] Twain, Adams, and James were all to belong to the twenties.

Support for the new in America came at this moment from the new in Europe. Oddly, it was as if the old world were the younger. Its writers and painters had cleared away the debris of the nineteenth century and were living mentally and emotionally in a twentieth-century world. Jacques Rivière had written in 1913:

We are a people for whom the novelty of living has been reborn. A sharp little wind has blown suddenly through the darkness and boredom of the dying nineteenth century, dispersing the dreams that made us groggy. We have found ourselves outside, standing firmly, very clearheaded, happy to be here still. We are now living in a present cleansed of its past, won over by the future. Once more it is morning. Everything is beginning again; we have been mysteriously reborn; we no longer touch the world through our habits; our hands no longer slide along that smooth, worn surface of things about us without our even noticing them.[9]

Through the breach made by the war, the new Europe flowed, in images and ideas to dazzle, puzzle, alarm, and enchant. The color of the Impressionists was seen, the line of the Fauves, the disintegration of human and animal forms in cubes, cylinders, all kinds of geometries. Yeats, Joyce, Lawrence, Proust taught not one new style but several. They taught also craftsmanship and the courage to attempt any kind of subject matter.

If *The Dial* of New York, one of the "little" magazines of small circulation, may be taken as a weathercock, it seemed that European and native American originality appealed in equal degrees

5. Henry Ford and Harvey Firestone at a picnic. Folk-heroes of the time, these makers of automobiles and tires. Henry Ford's pronouncements on all topics were eagerly received. As car-maker, factory-builder, and systems-organizer, Ford was a phenomenon who changed a nation's way of living.

6. Calvin Coolidge was the perfect president for the time, one who diminished the office. His qualities—narrow integrity, shrewdness, and a kind of meager wit—made him admired by a people who preferred to enjoy a president rather than take him seriously.

to its audience. In July, 1920, a section of Rimbaud's *Season in Hell* was published and a drawing by Derain; in August "Six Poems" of William Carlos Williams appeared; in September, the story "Adolf" by D. H. Lawrence; in November "Possibilities of Poetic Drama," an article by T. S. Eliot, "Ten Poems" by Yeats, and Ezra Pound's essay "Island of Paris." In small compass for a small audience were riches: fertilizer for a dry and sterile hinterland.

The same magazine in 1921 saw an undiminished flow: in July a painting by Picasso and drawings by Lachaise, "Two Poems" by Marianne Moore, a review of Fry's *Vision and Design;* in August "Three Cantos" of Pound, the "London Letter" of T. S. Eliot, a serious review of the Ziegfeld Follies, a still life of Weber, drawings by Gropper. In November appeared a Dehn drawing and a highbrow article on Al Jolson; in December Paul Rosenfeld on "American Painting," presenting names and works that had not been known a few years before, and to continue enrichment from abroad, a picture by de Chirico.

The Dial was a remarkable magazine. It had a small number of readers. It did not reach far out from New York City into the United States in geographical distribution. However, it was a sign. In the twenties, along with much indifference, hostility, and derision, a creative ferment in many of the arts was to be possible. New York was to be the largest center of concentration in all forms of art, but there were to be other smaller centers in other cities. Artists found that they were to live in a world partly hostile, but, for the most part, magnificently indifferent. They communicated almost like political conspirators; they helped each other like relatives; they existed and turned upon the larger indifference a jaunty indifference of their own.

Unlike the "years before," in the twenties art was to separate itself from a climate of persuasion or conviction. It was to be cleaner in effort, sharper in loyalty to strictly esthetic goals. It was to be defined by style rather than ethics. This was not without connection to the general situation of society. The assumption on which all sorts of endeavors stirred, organized, conflicted, or harmonized was that life somehow had broken free from responsibility and consequences. (There was an obvious source for this mood in the rejection of Wilson's imperative involvement in international responsibilities and consequences.) Freedom without known bounds induced ugly excesses in the indulgence of personal appetites: appetite for money, show, success. For the discriminating, who shared the same blinding assumption as the others, freedom without bounds induced a care only for self-chosen boundaries for style.

In the life of all its citizens, the United States embarked on a new career. The war had generated great power to do things. Now, unabashed in business, pleasure, and the various ranges of art, this people believed itself free of the consequences of the tragic kind that seemed to afflict other peoples. It believed with naïve and deadly seriousness in the slogans of democracy as applied to personal worth, talent, importance. Private energies burst out of bounds because bounds were not believed in. This society moved, stirred, vibrated in every prosaic or exceptional activity. Sporadic works of art showed that a new time had arrived. There were new things to see, new things to hear, to feel and to think about. Carl Sandburg put some of the new words in "Jazz Fantasia":

Drum on your drums, batter on your banjos, sob on the long cool winding saxophones. Go to it, O jazzmen.
Sling your knuckles on the bottoms of the happy tin pans, let your trombones ooze, and go husha-husha-hush with the slippery sandpaper.
Moan like an autumn wind high in the lonesome treetops, moan soft like you wanted somebody terrible, cry like a racing car slipping away from a motorcycle cop . . .[10]

The poets were not alone. Scholars were beginning to give this people strands of thought with which to bind some meaning about the present moment. H. L. Mencken, in the first edition (1919) of his work of many years, *The American Language*, presented America with the gift of pride in the tool of everyday common speech, telling his fellow countrymen that they were all creators: "Nothing could exceed the brilliancy of such inventions as joy-ride, high-brow, road-louse, sob-sister, frame-up, loan-shark, nature-faker, stand-patter, lounge-lizard, hash-foundry, buzz-wagon, has-been, end-seat-hog, shoot-the-chutes, and grape-juice diplomacy. They are bold; they are vivid; they have humor; they meet genuine needs."[11]

VI

HARDING'S TIME

LIKE A GREEDY CHILD, the people of the United States turned to the rewards of peace. It seemed that friendly, ordinary, good-natured Warren Harding would help them gain these good things, and they wanted to like and approve him. The newspapermen who followed the campaign, like everyone else, wanted to like him too. He was easier to talk to than Wilson had been, almost like one of themselves, having occupied years of his life running a small-town paper. He spent much of the time just before the election in his home town, Marion, Ohio, imitating the front-porch campaign of his conservative predecessor, William McKinley, and very wisely, for he was not unattractive in a good-fellow sort of way on the common level but was soon over his depth in a formal speech. The newspapermen camped out in a bungalow in the back yard of a neighbor, and Harding came over nightly to visit them. One member of the group remembered that "Usually he seated himself on the rail of the porch and after lighting a stogie or cigarette . . . or 'bumming' a chew of fine cut, he'd say: 'Shoot!' Then in a jolly, intimate, confidential fashion, he answered without evasion any question that might be fired at him."[1]

In spite of being a nonthinker and a nonspeaker, Harding sometimes said something that touched the voter to the quick. In the month before his nomination he prescribed, "Not heroism but

healing, not nostrums but normalcy, not revolution but restoration, not agitation but adjustment, not surgery but serenity, not
the dramatic but the dispassionate, not experiment but equipoise,
not submergence in internationality but sustainment in triumphant nationality."[2] He conveyed that he was both for and
against the League of Nations; the public shared his woolly-
mindedness; they did not want to wear any attitude that would
pinch. The voters responded out of their depths. Harding promised a good future at no cost. It seemed a bargain worth buying.
Toward the end of the campaign the mesmerized press gave him
a dinner. Since he was a notorious joiner of lodges, they invented
a new one for him to belong to, the Order of the Elephant, Local
1, Marion, Ohio. A spokesman for the group said to him that
night, "There isn't a man here who is not impressed with your
character. . . . If you don't make a fine President, our judgment is
no good and we are in the wrong trade."[3]

The Democrats' candidate was James M. Cox. He was somewhat a liberal and had had more experience than Harding in the
newspaper business. He was from the same state, Ohio. His
running-mate was Franklin D. Roosevelt, of New York, Under-
secretary of the Navy. From out of his prison cell in Atlanta,
Eugene Debs appealed to what was left of the militant left, in his
person moving the prisoners, guards, and the warden of the federal penitentiary to be concerned for him, and outside the prison
gaining without effort an interesting minority vote.

The count was:

HARDING, Republican	16,150,000
Cox, Democrat	9,140,000
DEBS, Socialist	almost 1,000,000

Once inaugurated, in March, 1921, Harding turned away, and
the people turned away with him as if they understood each
other, from all but an easy settling of public affairs. Yet 1921 was
a year when many desperate settlements were being made. It was
a year of famine in Russia, of Lenin's experiment of the NEP, and
of the founding of the Fascist Party in Italy. It was the year of a
sharp, sudden, postwar depression in the United States. In the
months of the end of that year there were probably five million
Americans unemployed. Even the great empire of Henry Ford

shut down. He laid off his factory workers, fired his office force, got rid of the top executives who bothered him by their rivalry in ideas, and sold surplus and obsolete equipment with savage concentration. His son, Edsel, and four officers of the company remembered that they employed themselves cleaning up, sweeping out, and, on one project, laying a floor.[4]

Good times began to creep back after the beginning of the new year of 1922. There was enough of a hint of the public's being able to buy for Henry Ford to begin shipping automobiles again to his dealers, whom he made go into debt to receive them. He guessed right; they sold, and at a faster and faster rate. The better times came soon enough after the inauguration to be associated with President Harding and the Republican Party. Also, the Washington Naval Conference, held between November 11, 1921, and February 1, 1922, seemed to reflect great credit upon the new administration.

Under the leadership of the Secretary of State, Charles Evans Hughes, and the Assistant Secretary of the Navy, Theodore Roosevelt, Jr.—men of the recent past, not of the present moment of 1920 or of the near future of 1920–30—the United States took the lead in proposing a naval conference, inviting the participants, and providing the scene for the working out of an agreement in Washington, D. C. It must have seemed indeed a new world to the Western European delegates who came across the ocean to this meeting.

At the opening session Secretary Hughes announced clear-cut and somewhat startling proposals: a ten-year "naval holiday," which meant the cessation of competition in large naval vessels among the great powers; a proportioned but definite limitation upon the size of the navies of each of the powers present; and a limitation upon the size of capital ships. In detail there was compromise, underneath the surface there was grumbling, but on the face of it, the conference made smooth progress. For the most part what was proposed was agreed upon, and three treaties were signed, one in December, two in February. The entire performance seemed a contradiction to the general mood of inaction.

The naval agreements, signed into treaty on February 6, 1922, allowed the United States and Britain to be first and equal as naval powers, with ships aggregating 525,000 tons; Japan was next with 315,000 tons; and France and Italy were last with 175,000 each. This was the so-called 5–5–3 ratio. What had been built or was being built above and beyond these figures was to be destroyed. The United States decommissioned more than 200 ships. A heartbreak to regular naval officers, the navy's new battleship *Washington,* not yet commissioned, was sunk, with some difficulty, off Virginia. Two old battleships, with some contempt for the sister service, were turned over to the Army to use for bombing practice.

In addition to the naval agreements, two other treaties were signed, the purpose of which was to adjust rivalries and redistribute spheres of influence in the Far East. With the principal powers present signing—the United States, Great Britain, Japan, and France—the Four-Power Treaty of December 13, 1921, took the place of the Anglo-Japanese Alliance of 1902. Its signers agreed to respect each other's island possessions and consult with each other if threatened. By this treaty, the United States moved further into involvement in global affairs, to some degree supplanting Britain's place just at the time it was insisting that this was the last thing it wanted to do. The Nine-Power Treaty of February 6, 1922 (adding to the signers of the Four-Power Treaty, Italy, Belgium, the Netherlands, Portugal, and China), guaranteed the territorial integrity of China, were each of these countries at one time or another had had ambitions, and as if exorcising the threat of one another, reaffirmed the John Hay-Theodore Roosevelt policy of the Open Door in China.

At the conclusion of the Washington conference much more seemed to have been accomplished than had been, and the apparent good allowed celebration and forgetfulness. The conference gained time in which there were no major conflicts. It also confirmed delusions that made the little wars of the thirties and the big one of the forties possible. There was bitterness underneath. Great Britain had prevented the United States from building beyond her, but had to admit equality—and did not like it. Japan chafed at its 60 per cent ratio, but gained the concession from the others not to strengthen their naval bases in the Pacific. It was not recognized how flexible, strong, and resourceful Japan was, nor what the result, twenty years later, would be. In 1941 the Philippines, Guam, and Hong Kong were what they had been during this time, "virtual hostages to the Japanese with no powerful British or American bases closer than Pearl Harbor and Singapore."[5] France and Italy had had to admit inferiority of position, but had prevented the disappearance of the submarine. The destruction of great battleships obscured the fact that there would continue to be a rivalry in the building of smaller vessels. The United States had broken up the Anglo-Japanese alliance, but had embittered Japan and continued the process of alienating Western Europe—especially Great Britain—from the spectacle of American success.

The results upon the United States were curious. There were several elements here. In addition to clever international politicking in the achievement, this was the last flaring up of Wilsonism outside the Wilson framework, a fervor against war in the way the United States destroyed ships and gave up its easy, immediate chance to be the world's greatest naval power. There was some foolhardiness too, for the conference was not a change of direction as many thought; it was merely a delay. It was to be a delay of international trouble of almost exactly the length of time of the little era of the twenties. In fact, it helped make the twenties possible. It increased the delusion of safety that the era lived in. It seemed to justify retrospectively the repudiation of the League. It seemed to prove that it was possible for the United States to operate outside the League and do so smartly and successfully, picking the time and place for particular international conferences of its own choosing.

Thus, the conference, in its swiftness and brilliance, seemed a piece of business done once and for all. At this time all troubles seemed to be easily dyked. The problems from outside did not press hard. Domestic troubles that had caused turmoil for a number of years were subsiding. The eight-hour day, irregularly complied with but generously subscribed to, eased labor agitation. This and prosperity took the fight out of the militant left. Business organizations made use of this hesitancy to push against labor membership, to see to it that antiunion laws were passed, and that attractive but powerless company unions were set up in one after another of the great corporations. All these developments apparently eased the way toward a future of peaceful, prosperous economic expansion. Two of Harding's choices for cabinet officers, Mellon of the Treasury and Hoover of Commerce, went along so smoothly and happily with this change of atmosphere that Harding's other bad choices were slurred over.

The new Republican administration repudiated the aims of both the progressive Republicans of the recent past and of the liberal Democrats associated with Wilson. After a period of government experimenting under both party labels with social and economic reform, those in governmental power denied either consciously or unconsciously that the common good was a proper aim for the Federal Government. Government became, not gradually but all at once, narrow and negative. It was a retreat to the uses of government of a time when the population was scattered, out of touch from one part to another, subsisting for the most part as groups of agricultural communities growing westward into undeveloped geography. Such conditions no longer existed, and a negative federal government no longer suited; but various attitudes, both naïve and selfish, encouraged men in power into a tacit conspiracy to behave as if this were still so.

Not everything they did furthered this retrenchment. Admiration for business methods had some part in the passage in May, 1921, of the Budget and Accounting Act, which was designed to bring "business methods" into government—government modeling itself in its restricted role upon business. The act made logical and controllable the allocation of money to various departments from year to year, allowing careful review and control. What in the long run the act did was to make the Federal Government more flexible, more answerable to direction. The Republican administrations of the twenties turned this sharpened edge of government to the service of one element of the nation: the business element. But a better-running, quicker-turning instrument was prepared by them during these years for other uses when they had gone out of power.

The purpose of such able, quiet, helpful men as Herbert Hoover, master of a newly efficient Commerce Department, was to turn the care and attention of government to the welfare of business. Such men believed that they were thus helping the whole economy. Government would be an adjunct to business, which was taken to be the proper driving force of the nation.

It is interesting that within this framework of new purpose and strengthened functioning within government and alongside much devotion, there poured into government and washed all around it a sea of calmly greeted, coolly received corruption. It was so widespread that it was at first unnoticed. It speaks well of the regard the people had for Warren Harding that it was not readily believed that he had any part in it. The instinct was partially right. Harding was never more than a naïve, frightened dupe of the grosser forms of corruption. Yet he was precisely the man to have allowed corruption to grow and spread, without inquiring into or understanding what should have been glaringly evident under his nose.

In the beginning, among Harding's personal followers, corruption was hearty and natural. Some of his friends set up office and trafficked in government jobs. Others shared in the profits of bootleggers. Some of his appointees made contracts from which they received kickbacks. With this came a coarsening of tone in the city of Washington, which under Wilson had been braced by effort and idealism. Harding, in his own loosened perceptions, probably knew nothing of tone or atmosphere. It was the world he had always lived in and had miraculously walked through good-naturedly, clean of personal dishonesty. One must picture the President just beyond the range of knowing what his greedy and eager friends were doing, playing golf in brand-new golf clothes, smoking his cigars, drinking his unhypocritical whiskey and soda, ducking out of the verbal range of a driving wife, worrying a little about foolish private indiscretions, yet capable of kindness and generosity.

Hoover and Hughes went one night to the White House early in the administration and were cordially invited to join the poker game. They rather sniffily refused and Hoover wrote that he was not asked again.[6] Colonel Edmund Starling, who served Harding, Coolidge, and Hoover in the White House as bodyguard, wrote in his memoirs that it was gross exaggeration to call Harding's poker parties orgies. The President was, he said, a one-highball man or an ale drinker. His parties were typical small-town, middle-class parties.[7]

The only remarkable trait in Harding was his extraordinary good nature. Starling tells the following story: "One day I was sitting with him on his front porch when I noticed some ants crawling along the balcony rail. I folded my newspaper and swatted them. He protested. 'Why do you kill those harmless insects,' he asked."[8] He went to the theater to see Cohan's *Mary* and enjoyed himself simply and vocally. Starling "saw him put his program to his mouth and from behind it call out to an old crony in the audience. 'Hey, John,' he said in a stage whisper, 'how do you like the girls?' "[9] Before his harassment began, Harding was already exercised by a naturally indolent man's terror of an ambitious wife and an equal terror that she or others might find out the childish adulteries he had fallen into at least twice—one enduring connection continuing into the presidential years.

With his faults, open and hidden, Harding was easy to understand, easy to like. He fitted the times and without any strenuous effort fitted the shell of the White House and the office of president to his portly frame and naïve likes and desires. At the same time, his friends were fitting other offices, honors, perquisites generously to themselves. Everywhere, new life, vital, careless, robust, was filling out and bursting old forms.

Every remote neighborhood felt the touch of new life, stimulating and sometimes disastrous. One community whose change has been recorded was that area of slum streets, alleys, blocks, houses, churches, and saloons that surrounded Hull House in Chicago. Here, Jane Addams had set up her stand twenty years before in the midst of a poor but for the most part orderly and self-respecting neighborhood of immigrants and their children. There had been crowding, huddle, dirt, hunger, and ignorance, but a slow adapting and bettering of conditions. Now the very nature of the poverty around Hull House changed. It became disorderly. The neighborhood became a disintegrating geographical area, not a community, streaked with extremes of hope and fear. Families began to break apart, children to hero-worship the small gangsters who set up cheap whiskey or beer manufacturing establishments, first in private houses and then in small factories in vacant buildings in the neighborhood. What had been an orderly, nondrunken set of blocks became gradually disorderly, openly police-defying. Jane Addams wrote, with a seasoned eye and ear for the local slang:

The "stuff" is moved sometimes in a dilapidated old grocery wagon, sometimes in a motor truck. In our neighborhood it is usually handled in two gallon cans. The inhabitants of a street near the settlement were accustomed to seeing a man sitting on a front seat beside the driver on an old Ford truck with a shotgun wrapped up in a newspaper lying across his knee; another armed man would walk casually along the pavement. This was to secure protection from hi-jackers as well as from police interference. During one half year our neighborhood was filled with bootleggers coming from various parts of the city, added to those from our own vicinity, because the local police captain had the reputation of being easy to deal with. As there have been several changes in the precinct since, it is perhaps useless to repeat the stories then afloat of the amount of money exacted for such immunities.[10]

Enforcement of prohibition was either slack or harsh. It was in the hands of too few men who were paid too little. When prohibition went into effect the first commissioner, John F. Kramer, announced:

This law will be obeyed in cities, large and small, and in villages, and where it is not obeyed it will be enforced. The law says that liquor to be used as a beverage must not be manufactured. We shall see that it is not manufactured. Nor sold, nor given away, nor hauled in anything on the surface of the earth or under the earth or in the air.[11]

The statement was soon proved nonsense, at least in big cities, where people lived close together and where there was a will to obtain, sell, give away, or transport liquor in any number of curious ways. The border between the United States and Canada, as a border between drink and nondrink, became a line of drama, subterfuge, chase, and even death. Yet, in the early years before either the trade in liquor or the prevention of that trade was well organized, the selling and the buying of the commodity was a hairbrained adventure. Heavily loaded liquor ships anchored three miles off the Atlantic coast and consumers in speedboats went out to purchase bottles. The chase of a liquor boat by a government vessel, firing guns, was a Sunday afternoon spectacle watched by thousands lolling on the beach at Coney Island.

In the early years, it was the slackness of the enforcement that was most evident. This was the era of Izzy and Moe, Isadore Einstein and Moe Smith, enforcement agents in the southern district of New York. Their exploits against the makers and trans-

porters of liquor was an illustration of the gay, half-cracked, farc-
ical side of what people were beginning to identify as "the
twenties."

Izzy and Moe never stopped, day or night, but carried on their
work with an appreciative grin over their shoulders at the newspapermen who trailed them. In his essay on the two clownish
enforcers of the early days of prohibition, Herbert Asbury wrote:

The two fat and indefatigable agents supplied human-interest material by the yard; moreover, they were extraordinarily cooperative.
They frequently scheduled their raids to suit the convenience of the
reporters and the newspaper photographers, and soon learned that
there was more room in the papers on Monday morning than on any
other day of the week. . . . One of Izzy's most brilliant ideas was
always to carry something on his raids, the nature of the burden
depending upon the character of the neighborhood and of a particular
speakeasy's clientele. When he wanted to get into a place frequented
by musicians, for example, he carried a violin or a trombone, and if,
as sometimes happened, he was asked to play the instrument, he could
do it. He usually played "How Dry I Am." On the East Side and in the
poorer sections of the Bronx, if the weather permitted, Izzy went
around in his shirt sleeves carrying a pitcher of milk, the very pattern
of an honest man on his way home from the grocery. Once in Brooklyn he was admitted to half a dozen gin-mills because he was lugging a
big pail of dill pickles. "A fat man with pickles!" said Izzy. "Who'd
ever think a fat man with pickles was an agent?"[12]

New York was not unique in its careless observance of the new
law. In the smaller cities of the South such as Nashville, deep
within the Bible belt, where liquor was preached against every
Sunday, a seeker of drink did not have to go far to secure what he
wanted. Ralph McGill was in those years a college student at
Vanderbilt University, working part-time on the Nashville *Banner*. When Edna St. Vincent Millay came to Nashville to read her
poetry, she told the impressionable young interviewer from the
Banner that she wanted some gin to make Orange Blossoms with.
He went out immediately to get the gin for the beautiful lecturer
in the "first shimmering gold-metal cloth dress" he had ever seen.
"It was simple. At Fouch's (an all-night drug store where newspapermen met in some rooms overhead to witness and discuss
politics) the prescriptionist mixed alcohol, oil of juniper and

glycerin, shook it, labeled it witch hazel, and I hurried with it to her suite in the Hermitage Hotel," full of devotion and service.[13] Not every city was as tolerant. Disapproval in smaller towns pushed the trade into corners, or prevented it. Probably prohibition, as well as prosperity, changed the eating habits of the population, who now ate more candy and ice cream and milk. But many drank more liquor than they had before, some drank who never had, and all those who drank, drank irrationally, concentratedly, with a fervent emotional concentration upon the act that dissociated it from moderating social, ritual, or esthetic circumstances.

Chicago became the characteristic city of prohibition. It had little tradition of civic responsibility to restrain destructive change. It had no character of its own and was adaptable to any kind of persuasive new thing, and the liquor trade, whose masters knew where they were going, soon controlled the municipal government. Prohibition taught people in Chicago new ways to make a living, new ways to amuse themselves, even new ways to die. The restlessness, violence, and fertility of talent already existing in the life of the city formed new patterns, which made huge profits for a few determined men.

The customs of prohibition arrived early in Chicago and were soon set ritual. "The first Federal raid on a Chicago speakeasy was on February 1, two weeks after the law became effective (at 12:00 midnight, on January 17, 1920). At one A.M. the officers burst into a basement bar named the Red Lantern at Clark and Kinzie streets and herded forty well-dressed men and women into the police station as prisoners. 'Nothing like this had happened before,' commented a newspaper."[14] But Chicago was quite willing to accept what had not happened before and go on from there. It was the purity (using the word in a special sense) of Chicago's practice of prohibition that fascinated people from the outside. The energy, vitality, talent of most of its clever young people were burned up in ten years of activity whose end, corrupt and sordid, was hardly noticed.

The official city government could not control the situation and did not wish to. This government was not trusted or respected by the people who had put it in office. It was expected, however, to amuse. During most of these years it was headed by a demagogue-buffoon, Mayor William Hale Thompson, who complied cheerfully, devising stunts to make his constituents laugh or cheer or jeer, making speeches against nonexistent enemies, earnest only in keeping Chicago "open" for the benefit of the cynical gang lords. Thompson was first elected to the office of mayor in 1915 and was reelected in 1919. William Dever, a "reform" mayor came in in 1923 and found himself unable to control the real rulers of Chicago, the gangsters who ran the liquor trade. Thompson was reelected in 1927 and stayed in office till 1931. Thus there was no effective effort to counterbalance the power of the gangs, who attracted eager recruits continually climbing out of the gutters of Hull House neighborhoods.

The liquor trade was a matter of haphazard rivalry in the early months and first years, but even in 1920 men like Johnny Torrio, who had been a respectable accountant and could have had a brilliant career in business, foresaw the necessity for rational control if the liquor business was to be profitable in the way respectable corporations were profitable. The history of the prohibition years was to be a history of increased efficiency in management by the gangs. In the end, all the agents of civic control, policemen, precinct workers, judges, legislators, the mayor of the city, the governor of the state, all held office and performed perfunctory honorary public duties on sufferance from the gangs. The real function of public officials was to organize society for the profit and convenience of the gangs. It was monstrous. But lacking a robust and contrary tradition, the corrupt arrangement was childishly and eagerly accepted in exchange for the excitement, color, and verve of the bright surface of society.

Torrio, the temporary ruler of a majority of the gangs in 1920, sent to New York for a helper in that year. The helper was Al Capone. His rise would end the spontaneity of gang life. But in 1920, when Capone first arrived, when Harding had just been nominated, the harsh efficiency soon to be exercised under the surface of this rattling life could not be imagined.

The outburst of jazz in Chicago seemed a bonus of the spontaneity of life in the city, a part of the high spirits of the time. The new word "jazz," perhaps from the French *jaser,* to prattle, to chatter, perhaps from *jass,* "a colloquialism for copulation used in the Twenty-second Street brothels,"[15] but soon vibrating with a meaning of its own, was associated with the nervous instability and the vitality of the age being born. King Joe Oliver, a Negro musician from New Orleans, had been in the city since 1918. In 1920, he formed his own band and in 1922 sent to New Orleans for Louis Armstrong to join him. So Armstrong came, at 11 P.M. on July 8, 1922, to add his raucous, vibrant sound to the unstable, generative life of the shifting musicians' community that lived as hangers-on of the ruling gangsters' world.[16]

The vitality of the music obscured the fact that the musicians themselves were inexorably bound. They were the slaves of the conditions in which the gangs made it possible for them to live, victims of dirt, dope, all sorts of prostitution. The gangsters were their patrons, the scatterers of large-denomination bills among them in the crowded, smoky, unhealthy "clubs" where they played their hot, harsh, wild music in a beat fighting for life against noise, dirt, and ugliness. This remarkable episode in the art of music, one of the few uniquely American contributions, was an amalgam of what the Negro musicians brought from the South (a mixture of the rhythm of Africa and old English hymn tunes, and an extemporaneous play in music and words upon themes of desire, faith, slave-bitterness) and what these musicians found in Chicago and other cities of the North: a harsh, driving, gritty rhythm, superficial knowingness and cynicism, the sounds of the city itself. The hungry white musicians of the city learned from the trumpet and cornet players and piano-pounders from the South and added some qualities of their own.[17] Together, in their common bondage as entertainers and buffoons for the gang lords, at the mercy of largesse or cruelty, these two elements of the North and the South made a new "popular" music. It was not "popular" long, being superseded by an easier "popular" music, but its effect upon "serious" music was pervasive, carrying an American sound all over the world.

In the lives of the gang leaders, of the government agents who pursued new varieties of criminals, in the lives of the musician-entertainers of this world of prohibition, there was spectacle and drama. Spread broadly across the pages of mass-circulation newspapers and magazines was a life of color and excitement that could be lived vicariously from day to day by passive sharers. Not all such attention, however, was benevolent. Two obscure men were to become objects of the other side of the regard of the public, a caring that was fanatical. It was characteristic of the twenties for the regard of the public to vary swiftly from the frivolous to the deadly without much middle ground of common sense.

On May 5, 1920, two men, either innocent of blood or hiding guilt, boarded a streetcar going from Bridgewater to Brockton in the outer fringes of Boston. They were Italian immigrants, spoke broken English, had not become citizens, and in spite of modest functions in the Italian-American community, were full of dreams of anarchism and fears of reprisal. They were apprehended because they had been identified as having been in the company of two other Italians, Orciani and Boda, one subject to deportation proceedings, the other under surveillance in the great campaign of the year against radicals and aliens. When Nicola Sacco and Bartolomeo Vanzetti were searched, they were found to have loaded revolvers on their persons, and they aroused suspicion by telling confused and easily contradicted stories about the weapons and their recent activities. An unsolved murder was harassing the police at the time. These men seemed all at once to fit into the suspicions. Either the state was very lucky in finding by accident the criminals it badly needed to find, or it fastened upon two innocent men who were unable to extricate themselves from a tangle of very damaging circumstantial evidence.

The *case* of Sacco and Vanzetti is not yet settled. A suffocating press of opinion during their trial claimed their guilt and demanded their punishment; a persistent mulling over and recasting of events after their execution found them innocent; a recent book has spoken again for their guilt. The *happening*, which rests beneath layers of interpretation, began in the arrest on the streetcar.

Two holdups, the second ending in murder, had taken place not long before. On Christmas Eve morning, 1919, three men tried to rob a Ford truck in which a paymaster, a guard, and a driver of the L. Q. White Shoe Factory of Bridgewater were transporting $33,113 belonging to the company. Shots were exchanged, but no one was hurt, no robbery was concluded, the

Ford truck escaped, the attackers returned to their own car, out of which they had jumped, and disappeared from the scene. One attacker had fired a shotgun; a shotgun was picked up by a passerby; presumably this was the gun used in the holdup attempt. A more serious—because successful and more deadly— holdup, similar to the one in Bridgewater, took place on the morning of April 15, 1920. The paymaster of the Slater and Morrill Shoe Factory, Frederick A. Parmenter, and the guard, Alessandro Berardelli, carrying two boxes in which the company's payroll of $15,776 was contained, were both shot down and killed in a street of South Braintree. Two men in wait had fired, grabbed up the boxes, and escaped in an automobile in which there were one or several accomplices. The car was found abandoned two days later. It was thought to be the same one used in the Bridgewater attempt.

Therefore, when on May 5 two alien Italians were arrested with loaded revolvers in their pockets, one with some shotgun shells also loose in his pocket (Vanzetti), it did not take long for a connection to be made. The police did not at first ask the two men about the holdups but asked them about the guns and their citizenship, and questioned them as to whether they were anarchists or thought the government needed changing. The fact that the police would be suspicious of any alien and that any alien would be fearful of the police at this particular time probably confused the case forever. It has never been clear whether Sacco and Vanzetti's guilty behavior, a principal point of the prosecutor, was due to their having committed the murder or to being terrified anarchists.

The day after the arrest witnesses were brought in to try to identify Sacco and Vanzetti as two of the three men in the attempted Bridgewater holdup and as the two men in the successful South Braintree holdup and murders. These witnesses identified them, saying that the men they had seen on both days had seemed foreign, that one had a cap such as Sacco owned, that one had a moustache such as Vanzetti wore. More damaging than the witnesses was the evidence of the guns. The loose shotgun shells that Vanzetti had in his pocket when arrested seemed to match the shotgun picked up at the scene of the first attempted crime. The loaded revolver Sacco was carrying held bullets, and he had extra ones in his pocket of an unusual, obsolete type that seemed to match one of the bullets in Berardelli's body. Vanzetti's gun was a Harrington and Richardson revolver, the type that Berardelli, the dead guard, was known to carry. His was never found; the implication was that Vanzetti snatched it up during the holdup and carried it away with him.

Vanzetti was tried separately and singly for the Bridgewater holdup, the evidence of the shotgun being used against him, as well as the evidence of the witnesses who said they remembered seeing him. His own defense was another set of witnesses who said he sold them eels on Christmas Eve day; they were his regular customers, knew him well. Yet their testimony had some holes in it; the prosecution made it seem at least possible that the day they remembered was December 23 and not 24. It was a matter of the preparation of the eels for Christmas day (a customary Italian delicacy). Ordinarily eels were soaked some hours ahead of cooking. The delivery on December 23 would have allowed the customary soaking in salt, which good Christmas eels required.

The testimony from both sides was not entirely conclusive. Vanzetti did not testify in his own defense, and this has been held against him as part of his alleged consciousness of guilt. (He spoke very poor English at this time. He was foreign. He was a self-confessed radical.) The trial lasted from June 22 to July 1, 1920, and attracted little public attention. Judge Webster Thayer, who presided and was to become inextricably mixed in the future fame of the prisoners, sentenced Vanzetti after his conviction by the jury to from twelve to fifteen years in the Massachusetts State Prison in Charlestown. Vanzetti did not appeal this conviction.

In May, 1921, Vanzetti was taken from the Charlestown prison to stand joint trial with Sacco for the murder-holdup of South Braintree. Again, it was a case of witnesses who were almost but not quite conclusive, of testimony about guns that was damaging but not final. The defense should have been helped more than it was by the fact that no money was ever traced to either man from the loot that was taken, that the automobile was not traced to them, that neither of them ran away or changed his style of life between the day of the first holdup and the day of arrest, and finally, that neither of them seemed like murderers or robbers.

This was too immaterial to weigh for much. The atmosphere of the time was such as to make it easy to believe that convinced anarchists would also be robbers and murderers, that foreigners were a suspicious lot, that draft-dodging aliens should not be given the benefit of the doubt. Judge Thayer apparently shared some of these prejudices and by the evidence of some incautious talk on a social occasion was heard to wish them convicted and dead; yet he presided over a technically correct trial.

The men were convicted of murder in the first degree on July 2, 1921. Judge Thayer sentenced them to death. This was not the end but the beginning of the case, for it attracted passionate attention from then until 1927, when the two miserable yet interesting men were finally executed. They were to belong to the twenties and to the color of the time in a decisive way. It was curious that two such obscure human beings should become so mercilessly known. They attracted and polarized the opposite loyalties of the time.

The amusements of the time, the scandals of the time, were new in kind. The work of the time was different too. Simplicity of motive, spontaneity of function, immediacy of achievement, were everywhere complicated by processes that took time to complete themselves. This state of being was much denied, fled from, flouted, as if it were not so—on the one hand, a wild kind of individuality, on the other, a process like movie-making or automobile-making, both requiring carefully planned sequences of work and coordinating the efforts of many people. Wobblyism would no longer do in labor. What was needed was patient, detailed, careful organizing into larger and larger unions to match the businessmen's force and resources. On the other hand, in business the daring effort of individuals was giving way to corporationwide, nationwide processes, but the change was not readily seen. It had been relatively easy for the public to grasp the brilliance of Henry Ford's accomplishment when it concerned one automobile and then one assembly line in one factory. But in the twenties, making an automobile became a linking of processes, of buying, moving, growing, and producing many things, producing power, creating transportation systems, in the end, almost incidentally, pouring out automobiles, trucks, tractors, even airplanes.

Ford sent men scouting forests for timber, mineral lands for iron and coal, jungles for sites to grow rubber; he then organized methods of bringing these needed materials to him. When Ford chose to buy some land that looked like wasteland far away from the effective resources of the city of Detroit and went out there day after day with one or another keen collaborator to assess his site, he seemed like a visionary. Yet the new Rouge plant, which was the darling of his powerful but inexpressive imagination during the twenties, was a fit symbol for the new order of elaborateness. In creating a new order that was not static but continually flowing and changing, Henry Ford was acting in a way characteristic of the national talent for meshing many acts into one smoothly flowing process. It was an American craft that survived the decay of many other old, beautiful, time-limited, place-identified crafts. The Rouge was not just a physical place where it was possible to lay out a sequence of plants and widen a river to make a harbor for the bringing in of materials.[18] The Rouge was the last segment of many time sequences, the scene of processes at last coming together in climax, an ordering that was musical and mathematical. The finishing of the product was the aim, but the enjoyment was in the movement from beginning to end.

Ford's gift for moving and organizing materials reached a pitch of achievement in the early twenties; his gift for handling people began to falter.[19] There were to be elements of tragedy in this contrast, accentuated during the decade, but only hints showed at first. In the early days of the company, there had been good close relations among Ford, his executives, and his workers. There had even been a creative give and take between all of them—ideas, methods, inventions welling upward from below as well as imposed downward. Now Ford began to be aloof from consultation and advice. Bad luck and ridicule over several projects during and just after the war seemed to harden his character. He began to get rid of gifted men in his organization if they thought differently from him. Three good men left in the spring of 1919, resigning after they were made to feel that there was no suitable place for them: C. Harold Wills, John R. Lee, and Norval Hawkins. As in the case, earlier, of the departure of James Couzens, indispensable in the formation of the company, Ford seemed to feel satisfaction at the removal of rivalry in ideas. This brilliant, limited man entered the twenties with companionship around him lessened and his own gifts no longer balanced by those of other men.[20]

Looking for a way to express his opinions about matters other than car production, Ford purchased the *Dearborn Independent*, a small, dying weekly; frugally repaired its battered press; and told his friend Edwin G. Pipp of the Detroit *News* that he intended to make this little paper, which he had redesigned in the plainest style and put on sale for a nickel a copy, "the greatest organ for national and international liberalism in the world."[21] In the early years, the paper expressed innocuous ideals for peace and the League. It contained flashes of its owner's shrewdness on scattered subjects, but it was rather dull. (It was to become lurid.) Publishing the weekly newspaper was part of Ford's attempt to express what he meant by "American."

There was much effort put into expressing the idea "American" in words, paint, buildings, roads, cities. The expressions were variously talented, mediocre, or pernicious. One expression that grew in Harding's time was the revived Ku Klux Klan. The new birth of the KKK was in part a spontaneous reaction of puzzled, bottom-of-the-ladder native white Protestant Americans over the limitedness of their opportunities and fear in the face of change. It was a fear and a puzzlement carefully fostered and guided, however. Money was made out of the KKK by the organizers, who were knowing, limited people, hypnotized by greed as well as the ideas they handled. The promoter and reinventor of the movement in 1915 was William Joseph Simmons, invariably Doc Simmons, a salesman who haunted the showings of D. W. Griffith's great, flawed movie *The Birth of a Nation* and caught from the success of the picture an idea.[22] In 1920, two sharper promoters joined and took over: Edward Y. Clarke and Elizabeth Tyler. The movement spread north and west, having as strong a hold in Indiana and Oregon as in Louisiana and Texas, losing perhaps some impetus in the states of its origin. It had 5,000 members and was local to Georgia in early 1920. After professional promotion, by 1925 it had between four and five million members and was a power in both political parties and a bullying molder of ideas in a number of communities. Clarke and Tyler milked money out of the KKK as it hit the wild, loose, hazy

prejudices of the time: "Klansmen denounced and sometimes ab-
ducted and whipped Negroes, bootleggers, adulterers, Jews, paci-
fists, radicals, Catholics, evolutionists, and other persons who did
not conform in race or ideas to what the Klansmen considered
proper standards of Americanism."[23]

A display of KKK strength in the northern Midwest took place
on July 4, 1923, at Kokomo, Indiana. A small child witnessed the
scenes and remembered the day. Robert Coughlan wrote of
that memory:

On a hot July day in central Indiana—the kind of day when the
heat shimmers off the tall green corn and even the bobwhites seek
shade in the brush—a great crowd of oddly dressed people clustered
around an open meadow. They were waiting for something; their
faces, framed in white hoods, were expectant. [A plane, wonderful in
itself in 1923, landed on the field.] A bulky man in a robe and hood
of purple silk hoisted himself up from the rear cockpit. As he climbed
to the ground, a new surge of applause filled the country air. White-
robed figures bobbed up and down; parents hoisted their children up
for a view.

The man in purple stepped forward.

"Kigy," he said.

"Itsub," they replied solemnly."[24]

By 1922 and 1923, "the twenties" existed. It was not just a
matter of chronology, for a new time had arrived in people's
habits and attitudes. The threats of the past were safely buttressed behind sufficient protections, or so it seemed. The future
went on forever. The present was full of abundance, variety, and
great patches of ignorance—as in the Klan demonstrations. There
were good and bad things to be done, material and immaterial
discoveries to be made. In different ways, strikes were made,
bonanzas were expected.

Oil was discovered in a new field, the high plains of Montana
near the Canadian border. A new scene saw the repetition of the
exhilaration of finding riches in the ground, of scrambling, developing, "succeeding." Families pulled up roots that had grown for
three hundred years and moved all the way across the country to
this lonely corner. Towns came into existence; cities grew; little
independent companies were formed; big companies swallowed
them up; narrow, straight roads were traced along the section
lines of land grants; telephone lines and buried pipes connected

new clots of population; human passions expended themselves for a temporary possessing. Children were born and grew up in a new country and made it a little less new. A certain amount of the material product, oil in this case, flowed to the south and east from this outpost and was used and misused, increasing the consequence of the changing civilization of the twenties by a little.

There were other bonanzas. Writers made discoveries too. Literature was a means of making clear the shape of the national life and the kinds of private lives possible. Sinclair Lewis, for one, made the surface contours of life more distinct; he named, satirized, caressed with rough affection all those aspects that a large number of readers immediately recognized as the things they lived among: the houses, cars, roads, streets, the outward shapes and colors of people. *Babbitt,* published in 1922, pinned upon the map of consciousness the look and habits of a numerous, shallow, widespread type of American businessman, an eager, persistent, and inescapable type. By giving a name to him and to other recognizable types, Lewis performed a boon for his countrymen, and they rewarded him.

It was the public meaning of American lives on which Lewis turned his harsh spotlight. He made the shapes of these lives cruelly visible, showed their sharp corners, their angles, their sparse limitations, the way of people in a new society, lonely and rattling about upon their large continent, huddled together in sudden new towns, how they talked, moved about, and what gigantic vacant spaces there were beyond the ends of the cluttered temporary streets: "The snow, stretching without a break from streets to devouring prairie beyond, wiped out the town's pretense of being a shelter. The houses were black specks on a white sheet."[25]

It was the private not the public meaning of new lives which T. S. Eliot contemplated. His migration from the United States to England showed the pathway that stretched now between the two worlds. Ideas moved freely and disturbingly back and forth across the Atlantic.

When readers on both sides of the Atlantic first read:

> Here is no water but only rock
> Rock and no water and the sandy road
>
> .   .   .

There is not even silence in the mountains
But dry sterile thunder without rain
There is not even solitude in the mountains . . .[26]

Or, when they read:

O O O O that Shakespeherian Rag—
It's so elegant
So intelligent
"What shall I do now? What shall I do?"[27]

it seemed a bad joke, or insanity, or the curious private
taste of an arrogant young man. But Edmund Wilson wrote in
December, 1922:

And sometimes we feel that he is speaking not only for a personal
distress, but for the starvation of a whole civilization—for people
grinding at barren office routine in the cells of gigantic cities, drying
up their souls in eternal toil whose products never bring them profit,
where their pleasures are so vulgar and so feeble that they are almost
sadder than their pains. It is our whole world of strained nerves and
shattered institutions . . . [28]

Out of a narrow, money-making background in a family in a
Midwestern city, a young man with no preparation except ambition and an unorganized talent threw up a job in the family
business of candy-making and migrated to New York. He had no
hesitation in believing that he might be "a suitable Pindar for the
dawn of the machine age."[29] In 1923, in an unknowing New
York, Hart Crane noted, "Life is possible here at greater intensity
than probably any other place in the world today."[30] He too
wished his work to express the quality "America." "It is to the
pulse of a greater dynamism that my work must revolve. Something terribly fierce and yet gentle . . ."[31]

The connection between private aspiration and public need
was not apparent. During 1923 the people of Babbitt's world read
Emily Post's *Etiquette* (in its first edition), believing that the
book would reveal to them the secret of living in the new estate
prosperity had called them to. For amusement they were still
faithful to Zane Grey, whose new book was *Wanderer of the
Wasteland*. The readers of the other "Waste Land" were not
numerous. Many coarse talents succeeded. There was a gap be-

tween high and low culture, with no comfortable cushion of middle-brow terrain between. A practitioner in the arts needed to have the same adventurousness and self-sufficiency as a bootlegger.

While the variety of American life rolled and churned below the surface, very visibly President Warren G. Harding presided over the visible scene. He seemed for a short time the crudest, most real essence of the national life. He was the representation to the people of what at the moment they thought they wanted in "a period that," as Hart Crane said, "is loose at all ends."[32] But Harding's share in the twenties ended in a shock.

In the summer of 1923, when the President was still popular and when the corruption in his administration was suspected only by a few, Harding went on a journey to Alaska and California. It was to have been a triumphal procession; the country was beginning to hum again with confident good times. But in his own person, in his faltering yet nervous manner, in his compulsive activity, in his weariness, and in the new lines in his face, the President seemed to carry a suspicion that things had gone wrong.

Herbert Hoover, Harding's Secretary of Commerce, accompanied the President and witnessed his discomfort. In his memoirs, Hoover has described the obsessive bridge game that the President launched and enforced upon his traveling companions day after day: "As soon as we were aboard ship he insisted on playing bridge, beginning every day immediately after breakfast and continuing except for mealtime often until midnight. There were only four other bridge players in the party, and we soon set up shifts so that one at a time had some relief. For some reason I developed a distaste for bridge on this journey and never played it again."[33]

In San Francisco on August 2, in the Palace Hotel, where he was stopping on his way home, Harding suffered a heart attack. He died almost at once. He was mourned unaffectedly by millions who were aware only of his kindness. Among others, Woodrow Wilson, alive but ghostlike, attended the funeral in Marion, Ohio.

VII

SURFACE
SOLUTIONS

IN THE SPRING OF 1923, the year of his death, Harding's official and unofficial administration began to crumble. On March 4, Secretary A. B. Fall resigned from the Interior Department to care for private interests in the state of New Mexico. He owned a ranch there that had had cattle added, fences repaired, a house rebuilt. On March 11, Charles F. Cramer, of the veterans' bureau, killed himself. Another suicide that spring was Jesse Smith, a good-natured hanger-on of the Attorney General, Harry M. Daugherty. President Harding died on August 2.

After the death of the President, investigations were begun of an administration that was recognized suddenly to have been corrupt. The Senate committees charged with this work had distinction because they were chaired by two remarkable men. In October, 1923, two months after Harding's death, a committee headed by Thomas J. Walsh of Montana held its first hearing into the disposal of certain oil lands owned by the Federal Government in Wyoming and California. In February, 1924, a resolution by Burton K. Wheeler (also of Montana) led to the organization of a committee to investigate the suspected wrongdoings of Attorney General Daugherty, still in office under Calvin Coolidge.

This was the premature crisis of the twenties. What was disclosed was enough to have undermined the generous public confidence that had put the Republicans in the White House and in Congress. The investigations caused headlines and stirred up an indignation that came to focus in the Progressive campaign of 1924, but the indignation was never sufficient to overthrow any but superficial and highly visible wrongdoing. It did not take very long for the uproar to subside. What came after the election of 1924 was not what might have been expected, a change of direction, but instead, a permissive cynicism. This was curious and significant.

The crisis confirmed the twenties in all its impulses and only filmed the surface with respectability. In the spring of 1924—one president dead, another not yet elected in his own right—the whole of American life seemed to be cracking open. Upon this stage, the most confident men of the moment were the two senators from Montana, Walsh and Wheeler, purging the national emotions by their conduct of the Teapot Dome and Daugherty hearings.

They differed from each other in a marked degree. Walsh was born in Wisconsin of Irish immigrant parents. Wheeler was born in Massachusetts of old New England ancestry. Walsh had earned a law degree at the University of Wisconsin in 1884, Wheeler at the University of Michigan in 1905. Both had found opportunity in Montana; in Butte and Helena in the prewar years they were as indigenous as anyone else, for everyone there had come from somewhere else. The two men made their careers out of ironclad integrity and a championing of underdogs, an activity that made them admired, feared, and quite often threatened. Montana was a genial, rough world during the early years of their maturity (Walsh preceding Wheeler by a generation) where there was an intense striving to achieve bizarre ambitions as well as to live by the everyday goodness of the Sunday school. Every man in his own person was respected for what he was and not where he came from or who his parents were. Yet these rugged individuals were to owe most of their jobs, political choices, their newspaper reading, the use of the magnificent timber, river waters, minerals, life itself, to one giant company, Anaconda. Walsh, intensely quiet, poised, sure, steady, was one kind of opponent to this tyranny. Burton Wheeler, loud, brash, challenging, improvising from year to year, was another kind; both won many wars in Montana to arrive at the center of the stage in Washington in 1923 and 1924.

The death of Harding in the fall of 1923 allowed what had been whispered to become public knowledge. The committee that Walsh chaired had been set up upon the urging of the Wisconsin Progressive Senator Robert M. La Follette even before the President's death, on April 29, 1922. It had worked quietly under Walsh until its first hearing, in October, 1923. Then its sessions began to disclose the scandal of the disposal of the government oil of Elk Hills, California, and Teapot Dome, Wyoming. The oil transaction had had many complications, but its outline was made clear by Walsh, the gentle, unflambuoyant, persistent investigator—tall, steady, quiet, with a remarkable sweeping moustache as his only colorful accent. (Wheeler, his younger colleague, was to find it easy and natural to be colorful. He had told Walsh one time that to be successful he must tell stories. "But I don't know any," Walsh answered.[1]) Walsh's investigation told a story, an ugly one with details pieced together from far places and woven into a pattern that was denied again and again, but which sank in deadly convincingness into the understanding of anyone who heard.

When he named his cabinet members in 1920, Harding imprudently asked Senator A. B. Fall, an avowed anticonservationist of New Mexico, to be Secretary of the Interior. The temptation to the Secretary's responsibility was simply the existence of public oil lands reserved from private use. As far back as 1909 President Taft had set aside certain land containing oil as a reserve for the use of the United States Navy in its need for fuel. The original reserve was later added to. Among these naval reserves when Fall became Secretary of the Interior were Naval Petroleum Reserve No. 1, of 38,000 acres at Elk Hills, Kern County, California, and Naval Petroleum Reserve No. 3, of 9,000 acres at Teapot Dome, Natrona County, Wyoming. Fall deceived the ignorant, complaisant President by a hocus-pocus of testimony from experts that there was a drainage problem in these reserves, that oil from the government lands was draining away underground into the private land surrounding them, and that the Government, perhaps by selling them, ought to use up these valuable supplies at once before they disappeared.

The President agreed. Fall next persuaded Edwin Denby, Secretary of the Navy, who did not care or know what was going on, to agree to transfer these lands from the care of the Navy Department to the Interior Department. Thereafter Fall leased Elk Hills to one wealthy oil man, Edward L. Doheny, and the Teapot Dome to another, Harry F. Sinclair. Fall's ranch began to prosper; he put money in the bank, he prepared to retire. Even as early as February, 1922, a local Albuquerque newspaper, the *Journal*, began to question Fall's sudden affluence and to nose out something questionable in the lease of Teapot Dome. (Fall, as was shown in Walsh's committee, was given in gifts and "loans" from Doheny and Sinclair through a complication of fake corporations they had formed as much as $400,000 during a short period of time.)

Fall's wrongdoing was two-sided: He enriched himself at the public cost; and in his position as official conservator of public lands, he took land from public use and gave it away into private, destructive use. The second was a greater and more lasting crime than the first, but was not minded as much. It was less easy to understand, and it was not as interesting to a public that was avid for the details of money passed to a cabinet member in a little black bag. Eventually the oil leases were invalidated and the land recovered by the Government. Various people received perfunctory punishments. Fall was convicted of bribe-taking and sentenced; Doheny was indicted and acquitted; Sinclair received a prison sentence for "tampering with a jury." Walsh accomplished his grave, steady purpose, but public attention was engrossed in the trimmings and not the essentials of the story his investigation told.

Wheeler's investigation of Harry M. Daugherty was a rocket display. His temperament was well suited to this investigation. Wheeler was a man of intense rectitude, but he also enjoyed performing in public. He sailed into a public scandal, knocked sacred cows right and left, and was happy in his work. Wheeler's nickname was Boxcar Burt, a name he earned in Montana earlier in his career when he spent the night in a boxcar on a siding guarded by one man with a rifle against a lynch mob during a touch-and-go state political campaign. Then too he said what he thought without much fear of consequences.

Wheeler was one of a group of Western progressives, Republicans and Democrats determined to work together. These new legislators, voted into office by the discontent of the depressed farming areas of the Northwest, came into Washington in the off-year elections of 1922, when the Republican majority had slumped, eager to change things, with talent and energy to spare and no reverence. When Wheeler was first introduced to the workings of the Senate, he said, full of bravado, "It reminds me of the city council of Butte."[2]

Wheeler found fit use for his talents in the Senate hearings on the career of the Attorney General, Daugherty, who would not investigate the oil scandals. Coolidge hesitated to dismiss Daugherty. Wheeler made the public see that Daugherty neglected his duties because he was implicated in some way and that his time was entirely taken up with corruptions of his own. He also forced Coolidge to the duty of ridding his administration of the Attorney General. The interesting thing is that the public scandal Wheeler created only entertained the public; it did not galvanize it into any consistent desire to affect causes. Perhaps the story was too enthralling simply as a story.

Daugherty had had a friend, Jesse Smith. Smith, a useless, foolish, devoted friend (another follower of Harding and Daugherty from Ohio), had had no job in Washington, only an unofficial office and function in the Justice Department. He was Daugherty's agent for passing out or accepting pay for favors. Smith's wife, Roxie, divorced but still near at hand, shared some of the favors freely passed out. Wheeler got hold of this witness to some of the careless graft of Daugherty and persuaded her to talk before the Senate committee. Roxie Stinson's public monologue was both amusing and probably for the most part accurate in its chatter about bribes accepted and looked for, about men in public office selling and buying advantages, about careless and easy living on the fringes of the good will of the President who knew these people and liked them but apparently till near the end had no idea of how badly they were behaving. Such vulgar business as the sale of illegal permission to withdraw liquor from storage (this involved the Attorney General of the United States and his henchman) was a regular item of extra income. Pardons were also sold. Deals of all kinds were sought as well as accepted. The Attorney General's failure to indict his colleague Fall looked like the completion of an arrangement made at the convention before the election. Daugherty had managed Harding's campaign.

The disclosures showered by the Wheeler committee upon the press and the public appalled many men and yet had a curiously stultifying effect. Knowledge of corruption simply confirmed the public in its private belief that all politicians were crooked; it did not seem to stimulate reform. Reform, which had been so alive and so passionate an interest, so dear to so many hearts in the "years before," seemed almost dead. Even the most shocking of disclosures of this period, of how Charles R. Forbes, in charge of veterans' affairs, had trafficked in the bedsheets and bandages of the sick veterans in his care, carried no result beyond disgust. The suicide of his subordinate Cramer was the sign of trouble in this department run by still another of Harding's good friends from Ohio.

The Senate investigations seemed futile in spite of the disclosures, the punishments, the recovery of public lands. The hearings and the newspaper stories seemed to cause only a kind of excitation in the public mind, a sharing of the coarse ambitions and rewards of money-making exhibited by the crude men who had come to Washington as a kind of gang surrounding the President in 1920. Cramer and Forbes, Jesse Smith and Daugherty, Doheny, Sinclair, and Fall seemed only examples; ring upon ring, circle upon circle, other men beyond the spotlight of public attention were doing likewise. A rapacious, disorderly zeal for making money seemed to have seized upon many men as a form of madness. It was a letting down of a mark held too long and too artificially through the effort of the Wilson years. Yet not mood alone caused the change, but the fact of government in new hands. The advantage given by government to the greedy seemed an endorsement of any kind of enterprise.

The public disgust at the corruption of the Harding administration seemed to promise a turning away from regular allegiances and a chance for new alignments in politics. In a planning meeting in late 1922, a council of Progressives agreed to work together as a single force in Congress. Among the group were Robert M. La Follette of Wisconsin and William Borah of Idaho, men ending great careers in the Senate; Senator George Norris of Iowa, whose days of fame lay ahead; and younger men in the House such as Fiorello La Guardia, who had as yet no national reputation. In the 1924 presidential campaign, these Congressional Progressives joined themselves in a loose alliance with other progressive elements in the political and social unrest of the times. The new force, calling itself the Conference for Progressive Political Action, included a number of unions, among them the Brotherhood of Engineers and the Order of Railroad Telegraphers; the Socialist Party, whose leaders could not understand why this was not a logical try for a third party instead of a temporary union; the Farmer-Labor Party of the upper Midwest; and what was left of the Non-Partisan League, the union of political and social reformers in the wheat agriculture of the Northwest. These dissident groups had splintered off from the optimism of the general public.

In 1924 the new union of Progressives held a two-day presidential convention in Cleveland on July 4 and 5. The Republicans had already nominated Coolidge. The Democrats were in convention in New York City from June 24 to August 10, in the act of destroying their effectiveness by displaying anti-Catholicism, pro-Ku Klux Klan-ism, and other extreme and warring elements at a time when their simple task was exposure of Republican wrongdoing. The Progressives disapproved of the immediate political scene, but their broad mood was that of undiscriminating hopefulness. They were the direct descendants of the Independent Republicans of the 1870s and of the Mugwumps of 1884. To this variegated convention came delegations of college students from Columbia, Vassar, and Union Theological Seminary. Seventy-two-year-old Edwin Markham stood up to recite his poem "Lincoln, the Man of the People." La Guardia said, "I speak for Avenue A and 116th Street, instead of Broad and Wall."[3]

In spite of being made up of diffuse elements, the convention of the Progressives was smartly handled. It was over in two days. A short clear platform was written, and La Follette of Wisconsin and Wheeler of Montana were nominated for president and vice-president. The Progressives did not expect to win office, but they

7. Herbert Clark Hoover was Secretary of Commerce under Harding and Coolidge before he assumed the presidency in a kind of natural succession in 1928. He was a fortunate man during these years. Government was to imitate business and be efficient; Hoover was thought to be the efficient manager within the Federal Government.

8. The political opposition was surprisingly lively and busy. Senator George W. Norris of Nebraska, Senator Robert M. La Follette, Jr., of Wisconsin, and Senator Pat Harrison of Mississippi, pictured here conferring on a bill to limit the president's terms to two (February 10, 1923). Norris and the La Follettes (father and son) were Progressives. This loose alliance of Republicans, Democrats, and Independents put a brake on Andrew Mellon's perfect business civilization and engendered ideas for the age to come.

did expect to exert influence. They had only the two top candidates, no local ones. They could not even get on the ballot in certain states. However, the time seemed right for them to make a showing. La Follette and Wheeler were both good platform speakers. La Follette was an old-fashioned spellbinder and had always been able to sway face-to-face audiences with his grand and thrilling manner. However, both his program—for control of the trusts and the railroads, for efficient government through the direct primary election, for tax reform—and his manner were less effective than they had been in the past. When La Follette faced a radio audience on Labor Day, he proved a poor radio orator. He was not tamable to the new device. His voice wavered on and off the range of the microphone as he moved restlessly about on the platform. His large gestures and striking appearance were of no use to him.[4]

Wheeler was an occasional success, for he was a crude but forceful speaker. He recalled years later the enjoyment he got out of a device he used against Calvin Coolidge in a number of his campaign speeches. An empty chair was placed on the platform and question after question was addressed to it.

"President Coolidge," I began, "tell us where you stand on Prohibition." After a pause, I continued: "Mr. President, why was it necessary for Congress to act before you dismissed the Secretary of Navy who had allowed the Navy's oil reserves to be turned over to the Secretary of the Interior, knowing this Secretary of Interior was frankly in favor of turning over all the nation's natural resources to private exploiters? Tell me, Mr. President, why is it you stood behind Harry Daugherty?"

I went on with rhetorical questions in this vein, pausing after each for a short period. Then I wound up: "There, my friends, is the usual silence that emanates from the White House." The crowd roared in appreciation.[5]

La Follette was speaking to the wind in appealing to those Americans who were making money and having fun in 1924. He was also somewhat ineffective in speaking to those who were discontented. His program seemed either old fashioned or visionary. He hated monopoly and made it a major theme, but it was a dead issue. A new approach to business bigness was needed. The living part of his program, the welfare role of government, a change in the weight of taxation, conservation, anti-imperialism, these themes were to rise again with the New Deal, but only after 1929. What hurt him most was that the devoted part of his audience, the farmers and ranchers, were excited by a noticeable upward tilt to the prices they were getting. "In October 1924, hog prices had moved above eleven dollars, four dollars more than in the first week of July and the highest quoted price in two years! In Minneapolis wheat reached $1.50 on the second of October, the highest price since 1921. The prices of rye and flax rose accordingly in response to a heavy export demand."[6]

The Progressive campaign in its failure was important because it was the last concerted drive of liberalism in the decade. For the rest of the time that Republican prosperity lasted, liberalism was reduced to holding actions in Congress or to individual protests that made no laws. The conventions of 1924 and the campaigns of the summer and fall indicated the cross-currents in the national scene: the ingenious yet sharply stage-managed idealism of the Progressives; the jaded hates and loves of the warring Democrats, who threw away a chance to offer an alternative; and the bland, paced, cynical sequences of the Republicans. The Republican presidential candidate, Calvin Coolidge, serving out an unfinished term in the White House, won with 15,700,000 Republican votes to the Democrats' 8,300,000 and the Progressives' 4,800,000. Yet what the Progressives accomplished with little money and amateur planning was not contemptible. They had spent $221,000 in the campaign, as against $800,000 for the Democrats and $4,000,000 for the Republicans. Yet they gained more votes in 1924 than any third party before or after. They ran ahead of John W. Davis, the Democratic candidate, in twelve Western states and carried the electoral votes of Wisconsin. They hurt the Democrats more than they did the Republicans.

The Democrats could make no good show of their own for three reasons. Their best candidate, W. G. McAdoo, could not be nominated because it was disclosed that he had been retained, honorably enough, as a lawyer by one of the chief figures of the oil scandal, Edward L. Doheny. The agricultural and Protestant Democrats of the South and West rejected the candidacy of Al Smith, the New York City Catholic liberal. And lastly, the incubus of the Ku Klux Klan fastened upon the Democrats when the party showed a reluctance to disavow the organization. Scattered, ineffective millions voted either Democratic or Progressive and thus set their mark against the placid drift of the majority, but it was useless. In the election of 1924, only 52 per cent of registered voters voted.

Calvin Coolidge was a competent, confident man in 1924. He had already made his character in the politics of Massachusetts. His neat, slight figure and tight sure face soothed anxieties, and his spare, acid wit pleased. He was completely himself and that self was trusted and admired. He fitted the moment. Ever since the Boston police strike during his governorship of Massachusetts, he had been extravagantly praised, sometimes for qualities he did not possess. He was not wise; he was shrewd. All the facts needed to debunk the man (the phrase became popular during the decade) were available. They were aired publicly, as in Wheeler's rhetorical questions to an empty chair and in magazine articles in journals of limited circulation. *The Nation* of August 15, 1923, printed an article with the title "Calvin Coolidge: Made by a Myth," which patiently explained that Coolidge's supposed courage and wisdom in the Boston strike in 1919, which had given him the vice-presidency, were spurious. "The police strike was broken by public opinion, led by a business-controlled press, while order was restored by militia in Boston called out by Andrew J. Peters, the mayor. Governor Coolidge sat discreetly on the fence until he saw on which side public opinion was gathering."[7]

Policemen in Boston in 1919 were paid less than $23 a week out of which they were expected to buy their uniforms. In those uniforms they were expected to arrest rowdy workmen making weekly salaries of from $75 to $100 a week. Coolidge's attention-getting, admired statement upon the strike was a telegram to Samuel Gompers of the AFL: "THERE IS NO RIGHT TO STRIKE AGAINST THE PUBLIC SAFETY BY ANYBODY, ANYTIME, ANYWHERE!"[8]

Coolidge was correct in demanding law and order. There was looting of stores in a policeless Boston. But as governor of a disturbed state, he had waited timidly to demand conformity to law until conditions were so bad that compromise was no longer possible. No treating with the police over real wrongs was ever contemplated. Here, he was very much the man of the decade; he would find solutions to smooth the surface and then hope the deep-seated ills would disappear. When for a time the underlying trouble seemed to subside, there was a sense of justification in thus behaving.

The coming to office of Calvin Coolidge assured the continuation of the twenties in the direction and with the momentum it had already assumed. His becoming president also set a seal of respectability upon the time that it had not had under Harding. This surface respectability suppressed some manifestations of joy that had burst forth in the careless days of Harding, but made it easier for many subsurface forms of selfishness and egotism to flourish undisturbed. Coolidge put a light hand upon the tiller, seemed to steady it, and steered a smooth way straight toward destruction.

On December 23, 1923, President Coolidge's message to Congress was broadcast on the radio. The mechanical inventions of the day were keeping up with the events. Radio not only reported the events but shaped them. Radio strengthened a tendency already working to make the people of the United States feel united and whole; for the first time, it seemed as if they could have thoughts and feelings simultaneously. For certain individuals this was comforting and strengthening. It had the effect of making people wish to have simultaneous sensations. Coolidge's period was to be a time of remarkable consistency in political thought—or in the lack of it. On February 3, 1924, an old, urgent ghost was gone when Woodrow Wilson died. Much of the immediate past seemed to die with him. During the same February, Coolidge accepted Navy Secretary Denby's resignation and after some hesitation secured Attorney General Daugherty's, too.

Coolidge, as president, was to establish the weak presidency upon an almost rational basis of satisfaction for the whole country. Which does not mean that he was a negligible quality. The country as a whole was fascinated with him and deeply satisfied with him. He seemed at the moment of his election to rebuke the faults that preceded him; in reality he preserved the essences that had flourished under Harding. He only changed the tone of the time. He allowed respectability to seem to triumph. Being the seal upon the structure, he preserved that structure. The ship of state ran a sometimes brilliant, completely off-center direction for the natural length of its course, which might have been cut off abruptly in 1924. But the rebellion of the "progressives" was not strong enough, did not have money and organization enough, did not muster enough indignation. Times got too good to support political change. Therefore, the little man from Massachusetts became very easily and safely President of the United States.

It was curious that he should end in the White House. He was a small-scale, able state politician who had climbed steadily upward in Massachusetts from small city offices in Northampton through the legislature to the lieutenant governorship and then to what might have been predicted as climax, the governorship. He was a man of stiff adherence to old ideas and small integrities, not of imagination or daring or innovation to any degree. The lucky accident of a policemen's strike while he was governor dramatized his honesty, firmness, and a certain succinct wit he used to express conservative thought. He was a popular vice-presidential nominee alongside Warren Harding in the campaign of 1920. He was quiet in his obscure office while corruption rolled around him during the Harding presidential years. When quiet, attentive, ready, he was discovered upon Harding's death, he seemed a blessed, cool, dry, unfeverish person to succeed into the hot spot Harding with his heart attack had unexpectedly vacated. The picturesque swearing in by his father, who was a notary in a remote New England village, won approval and relishment; the scene was memorable; it helped immediately to place him in the imagination.

Coolidge as president was liked first for his personal honesty and personal abstemiousness. Although Harding, as his aide Starling said, was no more a drinker than any small-town clubman, sticking generally to beer or one highball, and his orgies were only bridge or poker games, in the lurid imagination of the period immediately after the disclosure of the scandals, he was depicted as spilling whiskey on the carpets, drenching the rooms with black cigar smoke, and perhaps, it was whispered, bringing girls into the White House. This was scurrilous and untrue, beyond anything Harding himself had even dreamed of, but the damage had been accomplished. Coolidge's dry, economical management of life in the White House was a delicious change. It was true too that Harding had been common and without style, although hearty and spontaneous. Coolidge was not hearty or spontaneous, but he had a dry distinction of manner, and it caught the public fancy. He found a role. He was to stand for probity and yet not to worry anyone by fundamental honesty of the kind that upset the basic arrangements already agreed upon. Coolidge made no great point of the corruption that had preceded him; he simply behaved differently himself and he was greatly appreciated. Under Coolidge, it was easy to put the bad time behind and to move on into another atmosphere.

The new president was a Sunday School model of thrift and honesty and frugal living. With simple goodness incarnated in the White House, with Daugherty and Fall and Denby and Forbes and Sinclair and Doheny out of sight and soon out of the public mind, what more need be done but enjoy Coolidge's wise saws and get on with one's private living? Public disgust, in a great gust of feeling, was turned against Walsh and Wheeler, who had uncovered the ugliness. Wheeler was subjected to two preposterous, trumped-up indictments. Both men were used vilely by the press. As Wheeler recalled forty years later:

The New York *Herald Tribune* called Walsh and Wheeler "the Montana scandalmongers" and the Cincinnati *Times Star* said my committee was an example of "Bolshevik justice."

The principal criticism of our committee was that the testimony came largely from "ex-convicts, divorcees, discharged government employees, and men under indictment."

"Daugherty did not associate with preachers," I replied to this charge. The witnesses were not friends of the committee. They were called because they had dealings with Daugherty and his close associates. The character of the witnesses in a hearing of this kind is determined largely by the character of the central figure.[9]

Magazines like *The New Republic* protested vainly the curious turning of the tables by which Wheeler and Walsh were the ones abused.[10] They were also critical of Coolidge's slowness in asking for Daugherty's resignation. *The New Republic* on April 9, 1924 editorialized:

Although one of the most faithful purveyors of moral platitudes in these United States, he [Coolidge], like other Republicans, has silently acquiesced in the great betrayal of public confidence. He must have known the kind of man Daugherty was, the character of his cronies

and the sort of things they were doing in the Department of Justice.
. . . His behavior was a contemptible exhibition of subterfuge and
disingenuousness which Daugherty was fully justified in stimatizing as
cowardly [when the President asked Daugherty to resign].[11]

Coolidge's method of dismissing Daugherty particularly
aroused the ire of rational men. "This method of extracting an
ulcerated political tooth without admitting the existence of the
ulcer is bound to be demoralizing to American public opinion."[12]
(Daugherty was asked to resign ostensibly because he refused to
submit certain papers to the Wheeler committee.) But rational
criticism was out of tune with the public mood. Coolidge was
admired extravagantly. Even a certain prim and fussy hypocrisy
in the man chimed in with a national trait.

Criticism of Coolidge was simply not listened to at large. That
he was a part of a system of legal corruption, perhaps worse
than the kind Daugherty had taken part in, was not credited, for
everyone belonged to it and hoped to benefit by it. Coolidge
reassured each person that he was doing right, for there he sat in
the White House like one's neighbor, leading an exemplary family life, reading the *Saturday Evening Post* once a week, saying a
smart thing now and then, but chiefly minding his own business.

Besides, Coolidge was enjoyed. In his small dry way, the President from 1924 to 1928 was a decoration upon the national scene.
The people felt secure. They had time—they thought they had
forever. One sign was the relishing of personality, even eccentric-
ity, this being true in spite of a drive toward likemindedness and
being in fact a mitigation of it. Much beneficent foolishness flourished. The cult of Calvin Coolidge's personality was a sign of
the mesmerized state in which the American public lived. When
in 1924 Lenin died and Russia was embroiled in the struggle to
decide his successor, when in the same year coal miners of the
Ruhr Valley spat at the feet of the evacuating troops of France
and Belgium, in America there was only the faintest interest in
these events; what really interested and amused was the personality of the President and his sayings:

"Why don't you have artists, musicians, actors, poets around the
White House as Wilson and Roosevelt did, and sometimes Taft and
Harding?" [reporter's question].

The President pulled his solemn clown face and looked down his nose, as he drawled:

"I knew a poet once when I was in Amherst; class poet, name of Smith." A cud-chewing pause, then: "Never have heard of him since!"[13]

At the laying of a cornerstone, the President was asked for some words:

Mr. Coolidge looked over the upturned earth.
"That's a fine fishworm," said he.[14]

Elsewhere:

"What is your hobby?" a Washington social leader asked.
"Holding office," drawled Cal.[15]

Outside the range of the President's attention, forces raged—of power, desire, destruction, waste, and creation. Satisfying a public need, satisfying himself, Coolidge was the idol of an idea, the idea of function withholding itself from fulfillment. That this crippled role for government might have consequences other than good did not occur to many people during these years. It was taken for granted that holding apart was virtuous, that involvement was giving in to corruption and wickedness. A theology of isolation was taught and believed.

Coolidge personified this belief, which was passionate and total if almost unconscious. Involvement had brought scorn, complications, cost, disablements, and deaths by the thousands. It had not seemed to solve things in the final way promised: It had been foolish; one would never be so fooled again. The President was the harmless pet of society—particularly of those busy citizens who had in view private ends that could only be accomplished by being left alone, but also sincerely, devotedly, delightedly, by ordinary citizens who believed that their government must do little and be little.

Coolidge and the government in his name ignored the larger problems. The distress and discontent of the farmers was considered improper. One could do nothing for them; one should do nothing for them; when discontent eased as it did in the year of the election of 1924, it was a great relief; it seemed to justify having done nothing. As for foreign affairs, they involved only other and wicked peoples, not the people of the United States. By saying no to Wilson's League the people had set themselves against learning anything new. During the early months of Harding's administration, the Government refused to send observers to the League, and the State Department did not even answer communications from the organization.[16] It was as if a psychosis had become national and was made official; if one ignored foreign affairs they would go away. It was a curious kind of self-deception that many acts contradicted. It was an atmosphere that nourished such a brilliant piece of improvisation as the Dawes Plan of 1924.

A cheerful nation, not having suffered defeat, assumed that only some kind of European wickedness prevented the Germans from paying the Allies and the Allies from paying the Americans. A few men (not all the experts) knew better that the sequence of reparations and debts was tied together; that this settlement of foreign affairs among nations was linked to the people's lifeblood in those nations. There was no idea yet of the victor's paying the vanquished.

If a just reparations program could have been devised, I believe it might have led to far different consequences in Europe. A realistic plan would certainly have netted the Allies more than they actually received. At the same time, Germany would not have escaped so lightly from her obligations. Above all, the quarrels and animosities over the issue which poisoned the international atmosphere might well have been put to rest.[17]

So wrote Bernard Baruch many years later, with the wisdom of hindsight. He believed that the Dawes Plan (1924) and the extension of it, the Young Plan—"efforts . . . made to resolve the reparations tangle and set a figure upon which Germany's liability rested"—were only mitigations.[18]

Yet in 1924 the Dawes Plan seemed brilliant. It was no deed of vague kindness, but a vigorous piece of financial manipulation. It was the work of a clever man who had succeeded in everything he had tried. Charles G. Dawes had been a railroad rate-buster and a railroader, a campaigner for William McKinley and then President McKinley's comptroller of the currency, an organizer of banks and gas companies and the organizer of General Pershing's

European supplies. President Harding appointed Dawes as the first director of the budget bureau in 1921. Dawes shaped the first modern budget for the Federal Government. He was a more supple, sophisticated man than President Coolidge, with whom in the fall of 1924 he was to stand as vice-presidential candidate. But he had a tartness that displeased some; he was "Hell-and-Maria Dawes," who was not dainty with his words. He had none of the magical quality of the much simpler Coolidge. He functioned well in the framework provided by business and politics for the middling, hard-working, clever man of opportunity and ability. He enjoyed himself as he lived and worked, and he had no yearnings after other kinds of worlds. The United States of the twenties suited him well. He would be better remembered but that he had no disturbing margin. He fitted the times too well.

In December, 1923, Harding's budget director became the chairman of the Expert Commission on German Finances and Reparations. What Dawes did in this position was to assess Germany's immediate ability to pay and to recommend a partial stabilization of Germany's chaotic economic state. He made reparations payments dependent henceforth on continued stability. The real assets of the defeated country in its railways and industry were set in a balance against an international loan of 800 million gold marks.

Dawes was taken for a wizard. It was concluded that he had found a cure when he had only discovered a palliative. What attention existed in America for Europe's troubles was withdrawn. The contradiction of attributing so much importance to this American intervention in Europe was not admitted. Dawes' participation (and later Young's) in the international Reparations Commission was praised but not perceived as essential involvement. By the end of the decade, American observers regularly attended sessions of the League of Nations, but there was still satisfaction that the United States did not belong to the League. The face that America turned toward Europe was a dreaming face.

The look toward Europe was complacent, a refusal to see the bad, the sad, or the desperate. The look toward the Pacific was hysterical, seeing only danger, convinced that danger could be averted only by the passing of a law. The act forbidding Japanese immigration entirely was passed on April 16, 1924, over Coolidge's veto. The American law had a certain amount of influence on the success of some parties in Japan, as well as great emotional vibration there. In the twenties a frail and lively liberalism flourished for a time. The militarists awaited their chances. American total exclusion of Japanese immigrants embittered the popular Japanese view of the United States, making it easier for the militarists in Japan to come to power and to incite hatred of the United States.

Tinkering only created large problems for the future, but tinkering was the style tolerated in the government put into office in 1924.

VIII

A SUFFICIENT
FREEDOM

WAS IT A SUFFICIENT FREEDOM? Did Americans in the new
United States lead lives of interest and importance in a society
that promised plenty, mobility, stimulation, and opportunity for
all?

F. Scott Fitzgerald, a young writer from Minneapolis, could
walk the bright and beautiful streets of New York and think
himself blessed, with cash to jingle in his pockets, stories to write,
himself the topmost blossom of his time. He had come to New
York, it seemed to him, "like Dick Whittington up from the
country,"[1] and felt a confidence that in his next book he would
fully measure the time. "I have enormous power in me now,"
he wrote in a letter to a friend in April, 1924.[2]

On the other hand, by 1924 everything conspired against the
neglected architect Louis Sullivan. His original, ingenious buildings flowering with decoration stood in Chicago and a few other
cities. They had taught appropriate building to modern times, but
ordinary men had adapted and minimized Sullivan's boldness.
They signed the important contracts while Sullivan, a suffering
and increasingly bitter messiah, lived on, unused except for the
achievement of a number of small buildings in the Midwest,

banks or churches in towns like Owatanna, Minnesota, Grinnell, Iowa, and Sidney, Ohio. He poured out a stream of writings, mostly disregarded: "The Tall Office Building Artistically Considered" (1922), praise for Frank Lloyd Wright's Imperial Hotel (1923), praise for Eliel Saarinen's design for the new Chicago Tribune Building (1923) and scorn for the timidity that failed to give Saarinen first prize and, instead, awarded prize and contract to a mediocre design. In 1924 Sullivan completed his *Autobiography of an Idea,* still expressing a fatalistic belief in democracy:

The orbit, the inertia, the momentum, the creative power lies in the imagination and will of the people. It has always been so; it is so now. Hence, special virtues are exalted when the multitudes so feel and will; and when the exaltation of vice is particularly in evidence, it is a sure sign that these are dominant within the thought of the people . . .[3]

Louis Sullivan died in poverty in Chicago in April, 1924. His example and his person passed away without much notice taken. The lives of Fitzgerald and Sullivan only illustrate the partiality of the time. It was very good for some talents, bad for others. Opportunities opened up and were seized upon joyously or were lost forever. There was indeed sufficient freedom for a distinct kind of life and energy to flourish; yet many talents suffered.

What was noticed first by visitors—and for the first time many visitors from Europe came to the United States—was prosperity, movement, power. J. A. Spender was a journalist who visited the United States from Great Britain as the first Senior Walter Hines Page Memorial Fellow. Under the auspices of the English Speaking Union and newspapers on both sides of the Atlantic, he tried to ferret out the truth about the United States for transatlantic readers. He wrote: "In the world's history can there have been such a display of wealth, power and energy as is spread out across the whole continent; never such feverish activity in breaking and making." However, all was not blind energy; as he looked, he found moments of delicacy and precision within the apparent confusion. "The assembling of the magneto struck me as an especially delicate and beautiful operation."[4] The visitor was troubled, however. In spite of the amazing energy of new processes, which he described with some exaggeration in order to shame Europe—and particularly England—into making larger efforts toward more efficient methods, he took comfort in assuming that Europe preserved human qualities and America destroyed them. "At Detroit," he wrote, "you begin to understand the new sort of American business as Henry Ford shows it to you. And also you understand the cost of it for those who can't keep pace, the ruthlessness, the concentraticn, the unsleeping demand for efficiency, and intolerance of inefficients which are the price of its success."[5]

Spender's view was the conventional European attitude. A more original insight, through literary criticism, came in D. H. Lawrence's book *Studies in Classic American Literature*, published in 1923. During the long spiritual winter of the war, which he sat out in Cornwall and London, Lawrence reread the masterpieces of the short American past—Franklin's maxims, Poe's stories, *The Scarlet Letter, Moby Dick, Leatherstocking Tales*. He read them for clues as to the new American soul, which he took for granted was struggling to be born and which, unlike most Europeans, he was interested in—half repelled, half fascinated. What he found in Poe—a disintegrating and sloughing of the old consciousness; the forming of a new consciousness underneath[6]—he applied quite consciously to the contemporary American soul of the twenties.

Spender's conventional view and Lawrence's unconventional view might be kept in mind. Underneath, there were questions to which no answers were proffered, and, also, underneath there were people and institutions hurt or neglected—to the harm of the general good of society. On the surface there was a great bustle of bland, boisterous, and generally optimistic nature. The tension between the obvious and the hidden produced much of the quality of the twenties. The leaders of the IWW were live men, yet the fact that they continued to exist, incarcerated for sentences stretching beyond the lengths of their expected years could almost be forgotten. The issues they had once argued noisily still hummed below the surface. The fears and hates existed, as the men existed, but buried below the surface of society.

Another sign in 1924 of the quieting down of the surface was the passing in May of the Adjusted Compensation Act, increasing the benefits of the Government's veterans' insurance, granted to the former members of the American Expeditionary Force to France. This bill placated the veterans. Occasional later gatherings during the prosperous twenties glowed with a threat of vigilante action, and when organized veterans turned their attention to a subject, the gaze was that of reaction or censorship; but the veterans in uniform or on parade became, for the most part, only a childish symptom of the twenties' own censorishness and prudishness.

What made for a general peacefulness of atmosphere was the sense of opportunity. Much the same attraction of vitality and power that foreigners saw in the great American centers of population was felt by those from the fringes of the country, the dull towns, the poor farms, the underpopulated coasts and mountain coves; they saw and felt and smelled opportunity and poured into the cities to obtain their share. Even when they themselves did not share in the prosperity, they could think of Henry Ford as a man of their own kind, the man they might have been.

The brilliant spectacle of material achievement seemed offered as if there could be nothing finer or better to share in. For the majority it all seemed good, to be admired and to be desired. A kind of official cheerfulness spread over the scene—a tyranny of attitude aided cleverly by advertising, an art not new, but now consolidated and pervasive.

In an American world more closely knit and stitched together than it had been when families and settlements had trekked into wilderness beyond knowledge or help of one another, everyone shared a community of ideas and things. This was probably the first time that on a giant scale a society developed a set of manners, a provision of wants and needs, and a faith from the selling and buying of goods. Wearing a particular style of suit or driving a Ford or a LaSalle indicated a scale on the upward or downward path. It would be an overstatement to say that this changeable, flexible, malleable people, moving about from place to place on a wide continent and yet finding the same goods available everywhere, were completely gullible to the appeal of advertising. They were a people readily aware of the underhanded cleverness of the appeal. They made the fact of advertising and the power of it, and scorn for it, a sort of joke; but it was humor living within a faith. Any people so saturated with a new thing would necessarily be different from those who had not been. This was the first decade of the widespread use of brand names in selling. There was some freshness, some looseness and experimentation, some joy in the business of advertising; inventive Burma Shave verses decorated brave new roads. The audience for the advertisements was unjaded, naïve, uncritical.

What was lost or overlaid was the old modest traditional culture of the crossroads preacher, lawyer, teacher, newspaper man, editor. This folk culture had existed securely below the intellectual or literary culture that, in any case, had never traveled very far from urban centers. Now the whole country was receiving powerful blasts from the new wind. It was a new faith that was destroying the old one.

The new faith spread by advertising was business, a very limited answer to the range of human possibilities, desires, ambitions, imaginings. However, human nature could hardly know how limited a choice it was being offered, for this was all it knew: business was everything, the proper occupation for individuals and for the country; business sharpness was the only kind admired and considered useful; business gave one rewards—houses, clothes, cars, things that one's neighbor valued; business success made one important and happy.

By the mid-twenties it was the appurtenances, the luxuries that one enjoyed as the result of the proper life of devotion to business that the ads pictured prominently: a sybaritic persuasion. Among its articles and stories, the pages of the *Post*, the bible of the period, flowered in alluring advertisements of cars and motor oils and gasolines and asphalt; of California as the end of the continent and the end of the rainbow; of silk stockings on shiny, slim legs; of congoleum floors to walk on; of white kitchen stoves with easy controls; of the movies, easy entertainment around the corner.

The world that a whole population was being asked to find desirable was narrowed down so that the kinds of emotions to be experienced were limited, in keeping with linoleum floors and shiny white stoves and straight, smooth roads leading on and on from one similar town to another. Like the new federal highways, long anticipated before being built, the new life of the twenties promised particular kinds of joys to a whole population. The enthusiasm with which many responded to the promise obscured the fact that not all so responded, not all so enjoyed. There was in fact a very partial agreement to the propositions put forth by advertising, the agent of business. Rewards did not shower down impartially and democratically upon everyone. The structure of this society was powerfully manipulated. Only certain people, certain areas, benefited. There were various segments, many scattered individuals, whole geographical regions seemingly cast into outer darkness by the ordering of benefits. And, more significantly, there were people who conducted their lives by preference so as to have little or no part in the gaudy goods scattered about by a certain kind of living; there were others who were bored and simply stepped aside; there were some so rapt by authentic work of one kind or another that they never considered what so concerned the days and hours of their neighbors. The gigantic success of the dominant interest of the time was never complete. It was so emphatic that it aroused strident rebellion. It was so unfair that it excluded many who might indeed have been willing to share in it. In addition, the country itself did not behave in a way to live up to what its own citizens believed of it; it was large and varied and in part undeveloped and there was room for vacant and backward and curious pockets where all sorts of individuality existed.

From 1924 till near the end of the twenties was a period of prosperity, but it was a thin prosperity. Men of wealth like Andrew Mellon lived in grave elegance without display. Men of wealth like Al Capone handled unestimated millions and lived garishly. There was money to be had by some. Although by 1924 the average individual income had risen since the dip of 1921 and 1922, for many the gain was not great. The average minister of the gospel earned a salary of $1,428 in 1920, $1,556 in 1922, and $1,622 in 1924—$200 a year better off than his worst year. The average federal employee had climbed painfully from $1,375 in 1920 to $1,515 in 1924. The average construction worker had had a more spectacular fall and rise; in 1920 he had made $1,924; by 1922 his income had fallen to $1,459; in 1923 it had risen to $1,815; and in 1924 it continued to gain, to $1,822. At the bottom, and staying there, the average agricultural worker had slumped from $830 per year in 1920 to $551 per year in 1922 and had climbed only to $614 a year in 1924; never in all the prosperity of the twenties did he again gain the $800 he had had in 1920. The professions were never to do as well in the twenties as they were to do in the next period of great prosperity. Medical men at the peak of the boom (in 1929) did not average more than $5,224, a solid, respectable income for those days, but not dazzling. In the same swollen year, 1929, other averages were: college teachers, $3,056; lawyers, $5,534; and dentists, $4,267.[7]

There were geographical exclusions and exclusions by occupation. The areas where textile-making was a strong local industry were in trouble. Coal mining continued to lag, and whole countrysides suffered as a result. Wage-earning in general was poorer than in boom times during and after the war. Certain easy crops, like wheat, continued to do well as long as the weather allowed. Dairy production near the cities prospered. For the most part the rural regions of the West and the South were excluded from the general prosperity as if they had been other countries.

In one whole geographical area, a great natural disaster compounded poverty already present and in static possession. For the South, the decade of the twenties was the boll-weevil decade. By 1922 the little snout-nosed beetle covered the entire southeastern cotton-producing region to its northern limits. It had been on its way since the fall of 1894, when the first occurrence in the United States was noticed just over the line from Mexico in Brownsville, Texas. It had reached Louisiana in 1903, Mississippi in 1907, and Georgia in 1916. Its effect was as all-encompassing as an Egyptian plague. Losses were "from one-third to one-half of the yield. . . . Farmers, merchants, and bankers were bankrupted; farms and homes in whole communities were deserted; labor and tenants were demoralized and moved to other sections; and a general feeling of panic and fear followed the boll weevil as it moved into locality after locality."[8] Songs were sung about this disaster; babies of tenant farmers were named Weevil.

Those enjoying the glow were in limited economic categories in certain geographical areas or were temporarily fit for the time. This was not all blind chance. The prosperity was also further limited by manipulation. With a very good conscience, the principal manipulator, Secretary of the Treasury Andrew Mellon, planned a tax program and after two major rebuffs saw it become a system of law. He put his aims quietly and modestly and seemingly for the good of everyone; it was as if he averted his face from the fact that such a man as himself with his hundred million benefited greatly, too. He wrote:

The existing system of taxation was framed to meet war-time conditions. . . . The burden is now being borne chiefly by the man of initiative attempting to make money under the usual conditions of business competition. These rates bear most heavily on the producer, the salaried man and those engaged in trying to make a competence for their later, unproductive years. They penalize principally the middle incomes, while permitting wealth to escape by investment in tax-exempt securities and by other available methods. . . . The United States is no mere happy accident. What we have has been achieved by courage and hard work. The spirit of business adventure has built up in this country a civilization which offers unprecedented rewards to any man who is willing to work. But where the Government takes away an unreasonable share of his earnings, the incentive to work is no longer there and a slackening of effort is the result.[9]

The man who put the religion of business so reasonably was much admired by his age. His views were exemplary; he possessed a personable, discreet, unshadowed demeanor. Harding, Coolidge, and Hoover, in an unbroken succession of Republican power, trusted and admired him. He was the pivot from which the curiously negative, shallow, but determinative policy of the three administrations was exercised. To the public as well as to the three presidents, he was a magician who made the prosperity of the twenties work. That he was blind, also, along with the three presidents, and the millions, and helped bring on crash and depression, was not seen except by embittered hindsight—much, much later.

The policy was called laissez-faire, but it was not that; it was a careful buttressing of wealth and wealth-making by the Federal Government. It was a period of the abasement of politics as an independent or balancing force in which government was not unimportant, but acted as the agent of business. Mellon's policy did not become an almost perfect instrument until 1926, when his tax laws were enacted in the form he wished. In his early efforts he failed because there was still a great deal of loose

opposition. Some of the opposition was that of people who had
been active in Wilson's reform years, when government played
the role of the regulator of business, not the abettor of it. Some of
the opposition came out of the depression of 1921–22. A great
deal arose from the disgust felt at the corruption of the Harding
years. Mellon had to wait quietly and try again, but he was a man
capable of waiting. He bided his time until the election of Calvin
Coolidge in 1924 smashed all kinds of opposition. Then he caused
to be enacted into law exactly what he wished.

Mellon's principles were two: that wealth should be encouraged to pursue its own ends; and that government, except for
its usefulness in helping to promote these ends, should retire into
as small a compass of activity as possible. His program, which did
not become law until 1926 but which the election year of 1924
made possible, altered the weight of federal taxes upon different
sections of the public. The Progressive alliance in Congress
opened Mellon's eyes to the need to include the sop of lower
taxes for the middle and lower levels of income; his initial tax
proposal in 1921 had not included benefits for anyone but the
wealthy; his later proposals included what looked like exciting
benefits for everyone. However, the important changes were at
the upper levels. In 1921 he proposed that the maximum surtax
be cut from 65 per cent to 50 per cent; he got by no means what
he asked for. In 1923, he asked quietly that the surtax be cut from
50 per cent to 25 per cent. That effort failed in part, but the surtax
had been worked downward by this time to 40 per cent.

When the new Congress elected with Coolidge came into
power, Mellon offered his program again. He received everything
he asked for and more. The protests of such men as La Follette
had no effect after the election. The maximum surtax came down
to 20 per cent, the basic income tax was scaled down, the inheritance tax was lowered—soon to be repealed—the gift tax was
repealed.[10] The pattern was set: The United States was to be a
society built upon a slender framework of government, narrow in
its application, inexpensive to run, while society's motive power
was to be an expansive, minimally regulated business enterprise.

Because some parts of the business enterprise expanded greatly
in the twenties and the Government instituted few positive pro-

grams, Mellon retired part of the national debt each year until by 1928–29 he had cut it by eight billion dollars. It seemed a vindication of his policy, and a thousand Rotary Clubs and Chambers of Commerce hailed it, but it was accomplished by the Government's abdication of many positive functions. Mellon's budget for the fiscal year 1927 was below three and a half billions, three billion less than in Wilson's last year as president.[11]

In its aid to business, the Mellon management policed or regulated other elements of the national life. New labor laws and decisions within the federal court system, especially the use of the injunction against labor agitation and strikes, prevented organized labor from becoming a force to rival or threaten organized business. Inside several agencies of government, particularly within Secretary Hoover's Commerce Department, bureaus and agencies worked efficiently as arms of business within government. Hoover, like Mellon, was an element of intelligent continuity in the three successive Republican administrations.

While American foreign policy answered the blind need of a whole people shuddering away from involvement in the affairs of other peoples, the same foreign policy—and the business interest was hardheadedly aware of the fact—seemed also to help American business. Foreign policy was in two parts: higher tariffs, to protect the expansion of domestic business; and a businesslike and purposefully coldblooded collection or attempt at collection of the war debts of the allies of the United States in the 1917–18 war. Neither policy was successful, but did not show obvious failure because other forms of prosperity hid the truth. Hindsight would show that high tariffs hurt rather than helped American trade. In the matter of war debts, Mellon's view was no sharper than the average man's and as narrow as that of President Coolidge, whose remark about the debts Europe owed to the United States was "They hired the money, didn't they?" echoed to leg-slapping approval during the years Europe crawled along the edge of disaster, a disaster that the amused, comfortable witnesses across the Atlantic did not know that they were going to share.

To see the twenties whole, it is necessary to acknowledge the quite conscious manipulation of the economy for the benefit of one element. However, it was a time that permitted the luxury of contradiction. Everything went so easily and smoothly along the road that business wished that all those outside the mesmerism of the dominant interest could be allowed, like harmless children, to play their games.

Andrew Mellon himself was pleasantly contradictory in his personal behavior. He made for himself a hobby of completing Pierre L'Enfant's plan for the city of Washington, seeing to it that one grandiose, heavy, but generally impressive building after another was erected—to give the city the look at least of federal power. In his personal life, Mellon did not believe that business was all; he appreciated fine wines and food; he collected paintings. In his function as enforcer of Prohibition, he was an anomaly; Overholt whiskey was among his investments.

Mellon's policy never won unanimous approval. Hard times in the country regions remained constant. A cure for rural poverty in the shape of a bill in Congress, the McNary-Haugan Bill, was offered for vote again and again; and although it was never passed, it dramatized the continuing agricultural distress. It kept before the eye of the nation the fact that everyone was not happy. The bill itself was much like what was to become accepted policy in the days of the New Deal, the proposition that the Federal Government should subsidize the purchase and disposal of farm surpluses. Another continuing Congressional battle dramatized a deep split in opinion. This was Senator Norris' successful series of stands against disposing of the government-owned public power facility at Muscle Shoals. His belief that waterpower should be public power was also premonitory to the New Deal. His stubborn struggle led directly after 1932 to TVA.

Exploitation of natural resources was the norm, as the careless misuse of oil showed, but at the very time that Daugherty was conniving with Sinclair, Gifford Pinchot's men still remaining in the government service initiated the most quixotic and extreme of conservation ideas, the preservation of the national wilderness. In 1924, the head of the Forest Service set aside a certain part of the Gila National Forest in New Mexico as a wilderness preserve; in 1926 an area of woods and lakes and streams bordering Canada in the Superior National Forest was set aside to be forever roadless; in 1929 the Secretary of Agriculture established procedures by which other areas in the future could be reserved.[12]

Thus, even within the Government, there was an option to differ—even if faint, disregarded, or unheard. The differences did not completely die in the gush of enthusiasm for unanimity of purpose.

Even in law, which was for the most part subservient to the dominant enthusiasm, there was a critical presence. It did not prevail, but it existed and was to be a point of departure for the future. In the Supreme Court, Associate Justice Brandeis was the focus of this by no means timid criticism. He had allies—often Justice Holmes, sometimes Justice Stone, less often Justice Butler —yet in his own person he was the most balanced, studious, assiduous assorter of justices and injustices in a great unbalanced, energetic, thoughtless civilization.

Wilson had appointed this remarkable man to the Supreme Court in 1916 against a remarkable rally of inflamed respectable opinion that feared Brandeis as a radical, although some of them knew the man as personally unobjectionable in Boston "best society." Louis Brandeis was a Jew, the son of Polish revolutionary parents who had left the bitter deprivations of their country in 1848. He was also a Western and Southern individualist who had spent his years of growing up in the open, rural life of uncrowded and unsophisticated Kentucky. He was in addition a keen, hard-working lawyer who had worked in the complex world of growing capitalist organization—corporations, unions, trusts, banks, railroad companies, insurance companies—learning their functioning from the inside out in intimate detail. He was a formidable man to be where he was, nobly optimistic, with a naïve, fresh belief in democracy as it ought to be, sophisticated about the economic structure of the democracy he found himself in, believing without cynicism that economic democracy ought to be made to work as well as political democracy. He had made his way through varied experiences of democracy and remained unscathed in his hopes and determination. He was formidably equipped with detailed, hardheaded knowledge.

In the Court he gave his ingenious attention to every intricacy of fact—being the master of fact himself—in cases of the most resounding significance and of the homeliest detail. This was a new kind of concern, infinitely upsetting to the traditional way of thinking, infinitely fructifying for the future development of the country. In one typical case, *Gilbert v. State of Minnesota,* in 1920, without even Holmes agreeing with him, he dissented from a majority decision that seemed to him to damage free speech. A Minnesota law of April, 1917, forbade public speeches "against enlistment and the teaching of abstinence from war." Majority opinion held that the state's doing this was a "simple exertion of Minnesota's police power." Brandeis said no and said it quietly, delicately, precisely.[13]

The Minnesota statute was enacted during the world War, but it is not a war measure . . . Unlike the Federal Espionage Act of June 15, 1917, it applies equally whether the United States is at peace or war. It abridges freedom of speech and of the press, not in a particular emergency, in order to avert a clear and present danger, but under all circumstances. . . .

[Therefore] the right of a citizen of the United States to take part, for his own or the country's benefit, in the making of Federal laws or in the conduct of the Government, necessarily includes the right to speak or write about them . . .

Full and free exercise of this right by the citizen is ordinarily also his duty; for its exercise is more important to the Nation than it is to himself. Like the course of the heavenly bodies, harmony in national life is a resultant of the struggle between contending forces. In frank expression of conflicting opinion lies the greatest promise of wisdom in governmental action; and in suppression lies ordinarily the greatest peril.

I cannot believe that the liberty guaranteed by the Fourteenth Amendment includes only liberty to acquire and to enjoy property.[14]

In less exalted cases, Brandeis put admirably the way society really worked in small but complicated matters. Nothing was too ordinary to evade his probing. In 1922 a typical case was a matter of underwear. Brandeis wrote the majority decision upholding the FTC, reversing the United States Circuit Court of Appeals, saying that a manufacturer of underwear must not say his product was wool when it was partly cotton:

The labels in question are literally false, and, except those which bear the word "Merino," are palpably so. All are, as the Commission found, calculated to deceive and do so in fact deceive a substantial portion of the purchasing public. . . . The fact that misrepresentation and misdescription have become so common in the knit underwear trade that most dealers no longer accept labels at their face value does not prevent their use being an unfair method of competition.[15]

In another case, *Jay Burns Baking Company v. Bryan,* 1924, he spoke with lofty dignity about the way one found out cheats:

Knowledge is essential to understanding, and understanding should precede judging. Sometimes, if we would guide by the light of reason, we must let our minds be bold. But, in this case, we have merely to acquaint ourselves with the art of bread-making and the usages of the trade, with the devices by which buyers of bread are imposed upon and honest bakers or dealers are subjected to their dishonest fellows . . .[16]

With a smile perhaps, the keen, patient judge acquainted himself with wickedness and exposed wickedness to light and air. Whether assenting or dissenting, he set down irrefutable facts. His mild and deadly opinions and his steadfast life became examples to the decade and to the time beyond. In the decisions of Brandeis, business received almost the only intelligent criticism during the decade.

While business was praised as the only occupation, the activities of practical science gained some approbation from the general public. Applied science seemed an immediate, touchable, profitable kind of knowledge. Much of what men like Edison, Firestone, and Ford did was also entertaining and exciting to the national imagination, somewhat starved in its everyday life. The magical ways in which George Washington Carver converted the wastes of farming to useful products was fantastic and delighted the popular mind. The twenties were the years of Carver's greatest triumphs in research through the founding at Tuskegee in 1920 of the Department of Agricultural Research. The work by this man of genius in diversification of agriculture for the South was a practical reaction to the blow of the boll-weevil infestation. Turn away from cotton; raise peanuts and other crops, he said in effect, and see how they multiply into products.[17]

Abstruse, selfless science suffered in comparison with business except in spectacular practical results. The applications of science to flight were particularly enjoyed by the public, as if the dangerous testings of the limits of this new knowledge were a kind of national sport engaged in by few but followed by nearly everyone in the daily papers. Between April and September, 1924, the United States Army Air Service achieved the first round-the-world flight. It was a small affair and, therefore, more noteworthy to the imagination. Four planes carrying eight men set out from Lake Washington, in Seattle. Two planes and six men of the original group succeeded in returning—two of the men in a substitute plane. None of the men had been seriously hurt, although one of the fliers came home suffering from heart strain, and there had been damage and danger along the way in a crash in the Aleutians.[18]

While the decade seemed a completely new world to many men absorbedly employed in activities unlike any their parents had known, the twenties had many subterranean connections with the time before. There was even a scattered, uncoordinated seeking of that past. The unkind present repudiated the established New England literary heroes or found new qualities in them and lost interest altogether in the second and third rank of popular writers of the recent past. Thus, Longfellow, Bryant, and Whittier faded away into neglect. Hawthorne, Emerson, and Thoreau were understood in a new way. Rediscovered were Whitman at his most disreputable; Melville at his maddest; Twain at his blackest; Emily Dickinson, new in her witty cross-purposes; new also were the stylish and sardonic Henry Adams and the not so respectable Henry James. Not all this happened at once, but a new national self-knowledge was unfolding during this decade and the next. In 1924 a sign of this overturn of taste was the publication of Melville's deeply questioning story *Billy Budd*, never before published. Another sign in 1924 was the appearance of Martha Bianchi's *Life and Letters of Emily Dickinson*.

All sorts of scattered cultural events were taking place. An adulteration of jazz possessing great charm in its hungering and thrilling cadences, George Gershwin's *Rhapsody in Blue* was played in public for the first time in 1924. Eugene O'Neill's monotone of lust and greed, *Desire Under the Elms*, fascinated audiences who felt these live roots in themselves and yet were able to be comfortable because the writer portrayed them as inhabiting recognizable rural types. *What Price Glory?* by Laurence Stallings and Maxwell Anderson, dramatized the ordinary soldier's war. In the guise of hack writing, a former baseball reporter,

Ring Lardner, presented the essence of the vulgar and vapid and well-meaning existence of many citizens in *How to Write Short Stories*.

In 1923 Isadora Duncan married the Russian poet Essenin and carried her individualistic dance to Russia. Eric von Stroheim directed the movie *Greed* in 1923, a sharp, hard masterpiece, and lost more ground in his battle to keep a place in the movie industry. Maurice Prendergast, a painter, died in 1924 and might never have lived; it would take a generation and more to recover his quality.

A writer like Robert Frost protected himself by wanting very little that his time had to offer, by stripping himself of superfluous desires and relationships, and concentrating in total loneliness upon aspects of life and nature suitable to his gifts. He taught in short-term appointments at colleges and universities; he farmed not very efficiently but with some satisfaction; he lectured. He made his independent way and developed a bitten, pungent style of being, suffering from living in a time whose interests were not his own, but became interesting and a little frightening through being himself. His *New Hampshire* in 1924 won the Pulitzer Prize; his popularity grew, based in part on a public misconception of who he was and what he was—a belief that he was giving his readers easy answers instead of hard questions.

There was an American sky, as D. H. Lawrence said, that united satisfactions and dissatisfactions in one atmosphere. The rich bent on keeping, the broad middle "class" bent on getting, the Bohemian, the eccentric, the angularly individual bent on holding off the claims of the others—all had a decidedly original, new, and strictly American flavor in their commitments and non-commitments. People suffered and went without both materially and immaterially to shape this new time, but there was margin enough—under the American sky—for a life of some passing interest to be lived.

IX

THE EVOLUTION
OF THE FLAPPER

THE OPPORTUNITIES and the pressures of a new age created new kinds of people. Whether or not there was freedom and a new chance for all—and there was not—there existed an erroneous but cheering belief that there was change ahead. The openness of the future and the accessibility, as it seemed, of success produced a froth upon the times, and many short-lived, heedless, sometimes graceful, careers danced upon this foam of confidence. A later, more solid time that would have more real opportunity would lack this effervescence, which was a unique attribute of the twenties. An English observer characterized a conspicuous part of the population: "Dancing as aimlessly as gnats in winter sunshine it brings to bear on the jolly business of being *ephemeridae* the same hard and cheerful efficiency that it uses in its money making."[1] Observers from overseas were keen, but never got in quite right. They assumed in Americans a hard, deliberate choice in the universal career of money-making with other choices discarded, whereas, for Americans, there was nothing else they knew, and they put into money-making the traits reserved in Europe for other careers: sports, gambling, politics, status-creation, even remotely, a kind of esthetics.

The most effervescent symbol of the twenties was the flapper. She was a new American girl, a new woman, a new arrangement of the elements of sex and love. She no longer exists; she existed for only a few years in the mid- and late twenties, but during that short epoch she was a completely defined and recognizable type. In the twenties she was suddenly there, it seemed, and welcome.

Yet the flapper evolved.[2] She was born perhaps in the experiences some few women had in the war of 1917–18, when all sorts of freedoms and equalities with men occurred during the exigencies of Red Cross and other welfare work among the soldiers or particularly in the excitements of entertaining them. Travel, informality, closeness of contact between the two sexes in situations of danger changed the relations between men and women, at least for short periods in certain places; and some of this carried over into the period after the war, buried at first, but asserting itself at last with impudence and self-assurance.

Mary Pickford was not a flapper, and the Mary Pickford type of sweet, confiding, shy, and yet gay innocent female dominated the early after-the-war covers and illustrations in the *Saturday Evening Post*, which may be taken as a place to watch for the flapper's arrival. A change appears first in the familiarity of the boy and girl on the innocuous covers. In a Norman Rockwell painting for the issue of March 12, 1921, the girl is more kittenish than hoydenish; her hair, her dress, her attitude are soft and tentative, but she is unafraid and a little bold, whereas the boy whose hand she is holding—to tell his fortune—is awkward. She looks into his eyes with confidence and no assumption of consequences to her boldness. A year later, in a cover by Thomas H. Webb for the issue of May 13, 1922, the closeness of the boy and the girl, while still playful, is more self-conscious; he is standing close in an attitude of embrace, ostensibly showing her how to hold a bow and arrow; her dress is beginning to be tomboyish: a skirt and sweater, the sweater belted in leather, an Indian beaded band across her forehead. Her glance backward at the young man—awkward boy no longer—is more conscious of possible consequences of this exciting intimacy.

During 1922 and 1923 the girls in the stories still wear soft, full dresses, rather awkwardly long. Sometimes the heroine in sweater and skirt wears her hair in a long, thick braid down her back. Older women wear ample clothes, which denote maturity. In 1924 there is a change in an occasional cover or illustration. Out of the cover of January 5, 1924, a gambling girl looks straight at you. Her dress is the slightest, flimsiest silk, cut low and square-necked, thin straps over her shoulders. Her bobbed hair is almost hidden by a soft, wide, shirred bandeau of the same silken material as the slight, slim gown. She handles gambling counters as she sits at a table; the look she gives says that she handles her life as a gamble, too.

Dresses in many of the stories remain rather indefinitely long, but the nice young girl's position in society is infinitely free and easy; one story shows the heroine sitting at her ease at a drug counter, exchanging pleasantries good-naturedly and unselfconsciously with the sleek young man behind the counter. A boy and a girl in an Alice Duer Miller story sit at ease upon a beach. They wear the new bathing suits; his is one-piece, armless, but high-necked; hers is one-piece, reaching a few inches down the thigh, the skirt of the suit gaily and boldly striped. She has on some kind of stocking below the knees and slippers. As late as January, 1925, a cover shows a fond and fatuous portrait of a Mary Pickford girl who has long corkscrew curls trailing down to a soft and modest neckline. But inside the same issue, on the first page after the cover, there is a bold girl in a hosiery ad who seems to herald a new age. She is perched carelessly but gracefully upon a glossy mahogany table, dangling one silken leg off the edge. Her hair is softly waved and bobbed and her dress is sleeveless and short, held up by straps that look like flowers. Her slippers are slight things with pointed toes. At this moment the flapper is here, and all girls, the good ones and the bad ones, try to be flappers; the time is the end of the year 1925 and the early part of 1926. So long did it take her to come. Girls with skirts short to the knees or just below the knees become frequent if not universal.

In a story in the issue of April 3, 1926, there is a girl who is the very type: a girl seen in a careless pose, her back to us, on tiptoes, her dress hem hitting the back of her knees, her waist low and bloused. On her head is a cloche hat with a soft brim. Another story shows the same kind of girl dancing the Charleston, the caption comments, "with imagination and abandon." Girls, by this time, are shown putting on lipstick in public, confident of their own importance, and displaying a breezy independence of opinion. Many girls try to be flappers. The generic flapper is the nice girl who is a little fast, who takes the breath of staid observers with her flip spontaneity, her short-lived likes and dislikes, her way of skating gaily over thin ice. Would-be flappers are often heartless little ignoramuses, gum-chewing, vulgar, wearing ridiculous clothes, imitating a mode in second-rate style; others are overdecorated, costly, gangsters' girl friends. Many girls of the mid-twenties, however, grew up, finished school, fell in love, married, all without any whiff of the style of the type—yet bobbing their hair, doing up their hems, learning to Charleston.

By 1925 the phenomenon of the flapper was so conspicuous that many words were put on paper analyzing her. In 1920, before the full-blown type existed, Scott Fitzgerald gave a book of short stories the title *Flappers and Philosophers.* A magazine like *The New Republic,* given to the serious study of politics and economics, had space on September 9, 1925, for a piece by Bruce Bliven, an attempt to describe the new girl. Bliven thought he knew how she made up her face and what she wore and told it in a piece called "Flapper Jane":

She is frankly, heavily made up, not to imitate nature, but for an altogether artificial effect—pallor mortis, poisonously scarlet lips, richly ringed eyes—the latter looking not so much debauched (which is the intention) as diabetic. . . .

[Her clothes] . . . were estimated the other day by some statistician to weigh two pounds. Probably a libel; I doubt if they come within half a pound of such bulk. Jane isn't wearing much this summer. If you'd like to know exactly, it is: one dress, one step-in, two stockings, two shoes. [No petticoat, no brassiere, of course, no corset.][3]

The flapper seemed the most notable new character upon the scene. She attracted the most attention. When she smoked a cigarette conspicuously on a public street, reporters made a front-page story of the incident. She rallied a whole new circle of male types around her. Her beaus, boys in Joe College clothes, or sharp young gentlemen in belted jackets and new Van Heusen soft collars, and trousers with wide flapping legs, shared her good times, learning to drink in a dry age, dancing the fox-trot in roadhouses, riding about in rattletrap flivvers or expensive Marmons, going to the movies and the speakeasies, traveling across the Atlantic to a gay, superficial Europe that seemed to belong to Americans. Oddly, the particular, identifiable flapper faded away very quickly, to be replaced, so that the fact was hardly noticed, by another. She and her boy friend, after a short season of gaiety, a year or two or more, vanished and became part of a solid, respectable, and inconspicuous mass of settled, older, married folks, upholding the standards of the good life as sketched so preposterously and winningly in Sinclair Lewis' *Babbitt*. Flappers and Babbitts had to be rather well off. Unprosperous folks did not have the time or cash to belong to either type, so the double layer of gay young people and stuffily proper middle-aged ones was after all very thin, the two-tiered icing upon the cake of the age.

N. W. Ayer & Sons took a full-page advertisement in the *Saturday Evening Post* on January 10, 1925, to state the facts of life that fed business. A drawing showed three young people striding forward clothed in confidence and pride as well as of the costumes of youthful success: two girls wearing dresses belted low and carelessly across the hips, the boy in a pinched-in jacket and loose fitting trousers and wide-brimmed fashionable hat. The copy read:

You may regard the new generation as amusing or pathetic; as a bit tragic, or rather splendid. You may consider their manners crude, their ideals vague, their clothes absurd. Their cynical, humorous discussions of social conditions may stir you to admiration or fill you with helpless rage.

But it is useless to deny that these youngsters have a definite bearing on the thought, literature and customs of our day. And particularly do they exert a powerful influence on buying habits and the movement of merchandise.

The tremendous increase in the sales of cosmetics and silk stockings in the last ten years is a revelation of power. . . . Practically all men's clothes are young men's clothes. Most frocks are designed for young women.

Today they are careless of tradition, heedless of responsibility. But tomorrow these young women will be home executives. These young men will conduct our businesses. They will buy enormous quantities of every conceivable kind of staple merchandise.

9. Political opposition might be fettered; intellectual opposition was free and easy, frightening to some, invigorating to others. In law, Clarence Darrow was a force in himself, utilizing magnificent showman's gifts to defend lonely and sometimes pitiful and repulsive individuals against the might of legal and moral condemnation. The Scopes trial of 1925 was only one climax of his career.

10. Dwight Morrow at the White House on December 2, 1925, after presenting to President Coolidge the judgment of the special aircraft board of which he was chairman that the nation did not need an air force and had nothing to fear from air attack. Morrow functioned beautifully within the horizons of the decade, helping to make it seem to work. As ambassador to Mexico, he initiated the "good neighbor" policy before that policy had a name.

The flapper fascinated because she flaunted respectability. But respectability usually caught up with her. There was another type of the time who fascinated because he really broke through the crust of respectability and showed the hellishness down below. This was the garish gangster. He exerted a strong pull of half-denied interest upon the solid middle group, for he showed in his awful, destructive, yet sometimes stylish and purposeful activity traits in human nature that everyone felt the tug of, but usually denied.

The age was held spellbound by the gangster, but in most of the territory of the twenties, the gangster was an exotic, seldom seen, only talked about. He was rampant in restricted areas. In Chicago he was most blatant. Solid citizens in comfortable beds had no reason, or so it seemed, to fear him. (Poor folks feared him, those out of the swing of the general prosperity.) He attracted as well as terrified. The point has been made that the gangster, in his perfected and organized form, was the business-man as the businessman wished to be but dared not be, without restrictions or aims but those of power alone. He was therefore a caricature in burning-bright and ruthless shape of what all the good, small men praised and desired in success. But this is to make Babbitt into a bigger, freer creature than he was. Babbitt was the middling mover and servicer of society, not the maker and organizer and producer. The real makers and producers were larger, more unhampered men whom the Babbitts did not really know at all, although they flattered themselves that they modeled themselves upon such men. What the gangster meant to the good, tight, well-behaved middling Babbitt was an extension of personality. Superficially, Babbitt deplored the fact that such people existed, but he never exerted himself to control the gangster till the end of the period; then his own world and the gangster's both ended.

A dying gangster, shot by rivals in Chicago, kicked at the hospital attendant who was helping to carry him on a stretcher, aiming at the face of the man who represented society to him, saying, "Take that, you dirty son of a bitch." This was his "valediction"; and, once pronounced, "he fell back and died."[4]

Gangster dominance in certain areas showed in an uncontrolled violence. Gang-killings in Chicago accelerated:

> 1924—16 men shot to death
> 1925—46 men shot to death
> 1926—76 men shot to death

In these particular killings only six men were brought to trial. All were acquitted except one, who certainly went out of his way to be offensive: "Sam Vinci, who pushed public settlement of quarrels a little too far. He drew a .45 automatic during an inquest on his brother Mike and shot John Minatti dead, his explanation being that it had begun to look as if the jury were going to set Minatti free, and he did not wish this to happen. Vinci went to Joliet Penitentiary for twenty-five years."[5]

The epitome of gangsterism was Al Capone, in his flashy clothes and freehanded spending of a fat bankroll for friends and for the poor, his killings, his organization of liquor into a gigantic business at the top of a great terror-ridden pyramid. His operations by the end of the twenties had given him a fortune of probably forty million dollars and his organization an income of a hundred million a year.[6] Capone showed a chilling public display of power in taking over and remaking one innocuous suburban town, Cicero, Illinois. Capone's men supported the Republican ticket of Cicero and then took over the city completely. Capone moved into Cicero to line its streets with gambling places, which gave him one certain supply of money. He made the Hawthorne Inn his personal headquarters, covered its doors and windows with steel shutters, and turned its second floor into a sort of castle from which he looked down upon the activities of his personal domain.

Mayor Klenha and his circle dispiritedly endured what they had brought upon themselves. Now it was Capone's voice that was listened to; his orders transcended law. Police, city officials and local businessmen took instructions direct from the Hawthorne Inn.

Once when Klenha had failed to carry out a command, Capone paid him a personal call, knocked him down the steps of the City Hall and kicked him repeatedly as he scrambled up. A policeman stood watching the assault, twirled his night stick and strolled off.[7]

The twenties created the flapper and the gangster, who were exceptional and notable. It created also the middle businessman, who enjoyed being part of a great, undifferentiated average. The normal view was from the middle. However, the colorful off-shoots of the age, the types with bright or angular distinctions enlivened Babbitt's satisfactions.

The work of the professional entertainers pierced through the blandness of the time. So excellent were the entertainers of the twenties that a later time remembered them and forgot the middle people. Yet in entertainment, perhaps most in entertainment, there were contradictions. There were two popular kinds of entertainment in the twenties: one that soothed and edified and put to sleep; another that inflamed, sharpened, and intensified emotions and wills.

An advertisement of Universal Pictures in the *Saturday Evening Post* of January 19, 1924, signed by the president of the company, Carl Laemmle, states exactly what producers of entertainment thought the broad audience wanted, and what for the most part that audience thought it wanted:

I don't want to go to the theatre to weep. No, and I don't like death scenes. I don't like to see the hero shot or hanged, or the heroine die in the arms of her lover when they can just as well live and send you home with pleasant impressions and memories.

While the techniques of movie-making improved during the late years of the silent pictures and a few producers made movies of enduring intellectual brilliance to go with the better technical means, a blandness in agreement with Carl Laemmle's prescription crept over much that was offered, a placidity of entertainment suited apparently for the happy people of Middletown.

But strangely enough, it was entertainers of a kind of demoniac possession who were the ones best loved. Lon Chaney in his career was an example. In a series of horror movies, his special and intense gift burned out the dross of preposterous surroundings and left an impression of purity and genius. Edmund Wilson found Chaney's American motion picture *The Unholy Three* not far below the acknowledged German masterpiece of the type, *Dr. Caligari,* and "admirably acted. . . . [In] its parrots that cannot talk, its misanthropic midget, its infernal scene around the Christmas tree where the tranquil benevolence of a family circle serves as a mask for the murderers, it is quite comparable in imagination to the German nightmare."[8]

Wilson, beginning to exercise an individual gift for criticism, assessed motion pictures or nightclub entertainers as seriously as a new poem by T. S. Eliot or a novel by F. Scott Fitzgerald. In the enthusiastic proliferation of living, doing, being, without forethough or afterthought, there did not lack some minds such as Wilson's who saw that this life was all of a piece and all interesting. The American environment itself was as rewarding a study as American books or paintings or buildings. Wilson found the contemplation of the nightclub hostess Texas Guinan well worthwhile: "This prodigious woman, with her pearls, her glittering bosom, her abundant beautifully bleached yellow coiffure, her formidable trap of shining white teeth, her broad bare back behind its grating of green velvet, the full-blown peony as big as a cabbage exploding on her broad green thigh."[9] Wilson saw in her raucous salute "Hello sucker" an honesty and a spirit that many in the busy age lacked and that was refreshing and good in itself.

Gilbert Seldes, another new critic of the anonymous or popular or vulgar arts, praised Al Jolson. "Mr. Jolson sublimely lives. His daemon attends. He is ageless and radiant and terrible."[10] Seldes was writing for a highbrow audience in a highbrow magazine, *The Dial*. An anonymous critic in the same magazine attested devotion to "Krazy Kat." "Here is a veritable creation."[11] A comic-strip artist, a popular singer, a motion-picture actor, a gifted director—such individuals drew vitality from the general life of the time and gave that life form and style. Such people were an irritation as well as a stimulation to the general viewer. Main Street life flattened out angularities. Its environment encouraged sameness rather than difference. Yet Main Street kept always a sneaking admiration for those others, the outrageous, the different, the entertaining. Entertainers and entertainments flourished just beyond the borders of the well-regulated areas where the numerous, sincerely imitative Main Streeters or Middletowners lived.

So a director like von Stroheim or an actor like Chaney lighted up the mediocre scene of the movies, or a Texas Guinan the tawdriness of the places where bad liquor was sold. In other fields, other gifted individuals were not lacking. The unknown and almost interchangeable jazz musicians of Chicago and New York played in reeking, sweating, ugly surroundings, but achieved a kind of lighthearted innocence of aspiration and single-minded ambition. The scene of the speakeasy itself, the nightclub hostess' and jazz player's world, a stronghold owned by gangsters, serving rotgut liquor, charging outrageous prices, provided a stage for creativity. With the exception of O'Neill, it was the lighter, more popular side of Broadway that attained first-rate quality. Edmund Wilson wrote about "The Follies" in August, 1923, in *The Dial:*

... Ann Pennington has been added, so that, with Cantor and Gilda Gray, you have perhaps the three highest pressure performers in the city all under the same canvas. The tempo of the show is now uniform and it is the same as that of life outside. It is New York in terms of entertainment—the expression of extreme nervous intensity to the tune of complicated harmonies. When you take the subway after the theatre, it speeds you straight with a crash to your goal, like a song by Eddie Cantor; and in the roar of the nocturnal city, driven rhythmically for all its confusion, you catch hoarse echoes of Gilda Gray singing her incomparable Come Along!

In September, 1923, Seldes wrote in *The Dial:* "One man on the American stage, and one woman, are possessed—Al Jolson and Fanny Brice. Their demons are not of the same order, but together they represent all we have of the Great God Pan, and we ought to be grateful for it."

Appreciation for the gifted and "possessed" entertainers came most literally from the highbrow press, not at all from the *Saturday Evening Post,* which existed to smooth away the sharp perceptions of its middle people, who yet, almost ashamedly, enjoyed Jolson and Brice and Chaney and Krazy Kat. The best entertainment of the twenties was brilliant and extreme because it played itself out against its audience, not for it.

One must put off any solid analysis of the world of Middletown and the possible reactions against it that were valid and not merely hectic. But here, in glancing at the types twisted into shape by a divided world, at the flappers, the businessmen of middling range but extreme monotony of type, at lurid gangsters, and at brilliant entertainers often wasting talents upon poor material, one can study the binding world of knowing and feeling in which they all lived.

It was a new civilization trying with young energy to be one. After having been thin, poor, scattered, it found itself rich and influential, its spiritual means not quite grown up to the occasion. Some of the ways people bound themselves together were commendable and even noble, others were pathetic or improper or harmful. The popular culture that wrapped around this people was made up only in part of older elements of tradition from smaller regional cultures or of the successive traditions of immigrant waves. These elements spread thin and lacked depth and force for the children of the old settlers and the children of the new settlers living in new conditions. The new popular culture built itself up out of the pristine elements of life that this young generation found itself immersed in. The going quickly from place to place, the hearing of news almost as soon as an event occurred, the sense that all the parts of a large continental country were tied together—these new facts changed people. Making the change radical was the way goods were bought and sold.

The world of persuasion, in a society whose business, as President Coolidge said, was business, *was* the new tradition—lacking any other—in which people lived and felt close to one another and knew themselves one people. The very means by which this unity and closeness were accomplished—transportation, communication, persuasion—were part of the culture.

It has become a commonplace notion that an uncritical, ambitious, rising culture becomes itself through imitating the life of advertisements. In the twenties in such a typical magazine as the *Saturday Evening Post* one can see it begin to happen. What people ate, what soap they used, what clothes they wore, what they did for amusement, what thrilled them with a sense of adventure—in advertisements all these things were invented, named, joined together, in a continuous pageant of life to be emulated. The young industry made life exciting for a people eager to improve themselves and their families. That the being better and the doing better was worked for the benefit of corporations selling goods was slurred over willingly both by the sellers and the buyers. It was a conspiracy happily self-imposed. A sampling illustrates the way the new world of goods and ideas hit the eye and the mind of the casual reader.

A Cream of Wheat ad in the *Saturday Evening Post* of March

12, 1921, made gentle fun of the hick farmer who held up a box of cereal and exclaimed, "Empty, by Heck," as he stood by his pot-bellied stove, his kindling in an empty Cream of Wheat case. This was a way of including all the people in the knowingness of the brand name—even those isolated like the farmer. This approach was quickly abandoned. Increasingly, the advertisements painted the consumer as sharp, sophisticated, more sophisticated than the advertiser believed him to be, but therefore sophisticated as the consumer wished himself to be. Taught like a lesson, plainly and pointedly emphasized again and again, as if for a bright but lagging child, was the new importance of the brand name. In the issue of May 13, 1922, the Victrola ad asks the reader to look for the label: "Important: look for these trademarks. Under the lid. On the label." The Campbell's Soup ad says firmly, "Look for the Red and White label." In the issue of January 5, 1924, the Del Monte foods ad reads:

You can be just as sure of quality in canned fruits as you want to be.
It's the easiest thing in the world. There's only one condition—you must *know* what you want. Then make sure you get it. Quality is bought only through knowledge—and *not* by chance.
That's why it is so important to insist on a brand like *Del Monte*.

Simple insistence gave way to enticement, the association of all sorts of allied advantages to the basic good ensured by the product. An Ivory Soap ad of January 5, 1924, showed a young woman playing the piano surrounded by five attentive men. She had bare arms, her dress had a square low neckline, its fabric fell straight and soft, in simple lines. She wore a bandeau across her forehead to catch and hold her short hair. Another smaller picture showed her among her beauty aids in her bathroom; cleanliness was of course understood, but attractiveness was stressed. The ad states: "In Sally Jollyco's own gleaming white bathroom lies one of the chief secrets of her charm."

Magazine advertisements sold ideas as well as products. A full-page display on January 5, 1924, sold "California—Where Success Means More." It pictured an idyllic valley farmhouse surrounded by orchards; in the foreground of the picture were a youthful father and mother and a little girl with an armload of flowers.

Many people plan to succeed, and then come to California. California invites you to succeed here. People who can make good somewhere else can make good in California and in many cases do it more quickly. California is developing faster than any other section of the country. . . . There is, on the average, an automobile for every family and every farm. Modern kitchen conveniences are common in the country. Rural homes are on smooth highways. Even the humblest abodes are flower-clad, and can nestle against great foothills beneath mild skies. . . .

California spends money to be better. Better roads, better schools, better parks. A $12,000,000 bond issue was recently voted by San Francisco for a greater public school program. California spends money to be happy and comfortable. . . .

Success means more in California because children are given advantages here. Success means more because the average Californian sees his youngsters grow heavier and taller than the nation's average. . . .

There is comfortable room in California for 26,000,000 more people.

The very means of communication and transportation that bound together the parts of the country, a comparatively old East and a comparatively new West, were romanticized in advertising.

A General Electric advertisement of Mazda Lamps in the issue of January 10, 1925, conveyed a relationship between the homely electric lamp of household use and the lamps used to light airplanes to dangerous landings at night. A dramatic picture showed a biplane, as if seen from above, square-winged, single-engined, its two searchlights on: "When the mail plane swoops down from the sky at night, it sails into a flood of light that makes landings safe as at noon. For the air mail landings, the Laboratories have developed Mazda Lamps of ten thousand watts."

Radio in thousands of homes linked people in simultaneous enjoyment and excitement. Advertising was from the first the skeleton upon which the enjoyment and excitement were fleshed. An ad for radio batteries, in the *Saturday Evening Post* of January 5, 1924, showed two boys with earphones on, grinning with excitement at each other, one saying, "There's another station we never had!" The advertiser's comment, patronizing, encouraging, was: "Fishing for the new ones—that's half the fun, isn't it?"

Another radio-batteries ad, for Willard Batteries, on January 10, 1925, conveyed the communion of people listening to new programs carried regularly by large and powerful stations, a standardization in listening and enjoying that was a pleasure:

When "The King of the Ivories" is tickling the keys at WOS—
When WOR comes rolling in from the East and KFI, in its turn brings greetings from the Pacific coast—
When your Saturday evening dance from WTAM is making just the biggest kind of hit—remember that Willard Radio Batteries are contributing to your enjoyment—

Advertising was false in promising more than the seller delivered to the buyer, but it was false also in seeming to be a world to which real life must bring itself into relation. It was false to particular American life and it was false to particular human nature in its blandness, narrowness, its smoothing away of individual corners and all inconvenient or tragic exultations or despairs. It was so pervasive a surface, so willingly adjusted to by many people that it was like a lowered, limited horizon. Strong emotions and fierce beliefs were stoppered down so that when they burst forth they rushed out with violence and exaggeration.

The true twenties, the real twenties, was a society of contrast, of an amazing sameness and acceptance, and also of violent emphasis, revolt, and jagged and exceptional development. The violence and waywardness of achievement were ways of reacting against an impervious blanket of satisfaction. Yet the rejecters and the accepters shared a similarity of confidence encouraged by the widespread sense of national and personal security. It was a security that seemed to roll around and lap all the contingencies of life; it included patronage (pity or scorn) for other peoples and was so basic as not to know itself: Hopes and ambitions were thought not to have limitations.

X

THE YEAR
NOTHING HAPPENED

IN 1925 AN AMERICAN PRESIDENT was inaugurated and departed almost immediately upon a vacation that lasted through the tranquil mid-part of the year. The year 1925 was the subject of a report from the vantage point of 1926, "The year 1925, from the standpoint of national politics and government, was uneventful." And: "The relations of the United States with foreign countries was almost universally friendly during the year. Practically the only friction was with Mexico."[1] [Oil, of course.] The year 1925 was the emotional as well as chronological dead center of the decade. Everything of the twenties had arrived, and a new equilibrium of habit, taste, and manner seemed to float securely upon a *now* that was going to go on into forever.

Calvin Coolidge, having won the office in his own name, was fully accepted in his position as President. His importance was anecdotal, as the office was. Important things happened beyond the quiet center of nominal power in Washington. Coolidge was happy as the people were happy in this fact. However, as president he was important in his personality, which emphasized the easily understood small integrity of this still center of the great brawling turmoil.

Starling, the personal bodyguard of presidents, caught in his memoirs the Coolidge note. The President had time to walk and liked to walk, particularly along F Street, and to window-shop. One day he noticed the wretched condition of the broken sidewalk bordering the Treasury Building. Starling and the President noticed "a young lady whose stockings were wet half way to her knees with water splashed from these puddles." About the pavement, the President spoke drolly that day. "Yes," he said, "the Treasury Department ought to fix it. If they don't, some day my Secretary, ol' Andy Mellon, will come walking along here counting his coupons and stub his toe."

Starling comments:

Everybody was "ol'" to him. I was "ol' Colonel Starling," Frank Stearns was "ol' man Stearns," Rudolph Forster was "ol' man Forster," and his Cabinet members were "ol' man Mellon," "ol' man Denby," etc. In the same way they were all "my": "my Secretary of the Treasury," "my Secretary of the Navy," "my Secret Service man." All the material trappings of the Presidency were likewise "my": "my car," "my house," "my lawn," "my garden," etc. . . . It was as if he were a small boy whose daydream of being king had suddenly been made real by the stroke of a magic wand. He would almost tiptoe around, touching things and half smiling to himself.[2]

A fact underpinning the presidential vacation of 1925 and the presidential unconcern even of his work year was the state of the budget. More impressive to hindsight than to the contemporary view (there was a considerable amount of *Saturday Evening Post* editorial grumbling about the proliferation of bureaus—to help women, to help babies, even—in the new efficient government of Andrew Mellon and Herbert Hoover) were the amounts taken in and the amounts expended by the Federal Government during 1925:

Receipts	$3,780,149,000
Expenditures	$3,063,105,000

Unimaginable were the figures to come within twenty years: expenditures in 1945, $98 billion; receipts, $44 billion. Easy and pleasing to the understanding, however, was the contrast to the figures of just five years before:

Receipts for 1920: $6,694,565,000
Expenditures for 1920: $6,403,344,000[3]

Government expenses had been cut in half; that was the fact that Coolidge and Babbitt could grasp. Coolidge and Babbitt were better off. It seemed a good world.

What there was was time. There was leisure to look at the sky and the stars and the sun. A total eclipse of the sun in January was one of the great events of the year. Some solemn talk was made about the happening, and a good bit of nonsense was written. The point to be made is that people looked at the eclipse and listened to the talk. "Millions awed as total eclipse shadows earth from cloudless sky" was a headline on the front page of the New York *World* of January 25, 1925. Two days later, Heywood Broun made personal matter of the eclipse in his column in the same newspaper:

"The solar Follies of 1925" was a great show, but certain reservations must be made by this reviewer. It should have been orchestrated. I feel the need of music. Best of all would have been a great chorus of male voices singing some negro spirituals while the shadow held.

And I was by no means wholly satisfied with the stars. This feature of the pageant seemed to me a bit mechanical. Out they came, perfect in step and alignment, and then, almost as if Mr. Belasco had blown a whistle from the wings, they trooped away. Somewhat more casualness and a slower pace would have heightened the effect. . . .

Having read that the eclipse would attain totality at 110th Street and parts north, I went to 104th Street, as I believe in moderation in all things.[4]

There was a tendency upon the part of a whole population to become amused spectators at events. The new hobby of radio listening encouraged the tendency, but the set of mind was a new thing, a feeling that one's country and oneself were exempt from unpleasant consequences. What happened happened to other peoples and other individuals, mostly other kinds of countries and individuals. One lived, one lived indeed well, and had a predictable kind of success, and the tragedies and comedies of life were performed as in a show.

The public refused to get excited about many of the old reform movements. The concern of Margaret Sanger for birth control made headlines from time to time, but general interest deteriorated. By 1925, birth control for the well-to-do was simply a private matter. Contraceptives could be procured from one's own doctor. It was not seriously considered important to extend the benefits to the poor for their own good or to the population at large. Margaret Sanger and her followers had been agitating for years. She had been arrested. Churchmen continued to become publicly upset at her persistence, but her public passion was deprived of support by the fact that the birth rate seemed now to decline. There were 2,909,000 live births in 1925; the previous high rate had been 3,055,000 in 1921.[5] Urgency evaporated from this cause as from others. Miss Sanger's antics seemed, like the doings of many other people in the headlines, designed to entertain rather than to move to action. In 1925 upon the occasion of the Sixth International Birth Control Conference in New York City, Miss Sanger wrote earnestly and probably with some conscious sense of impudence and irrelevance to President Coolidge, calling upon him to aid her cause: "It is imperative, Mr. President, that as a nation the United States meet the problem of an uncontrollable birth rate. I respectfully suggest that you, as Chief Executive of the United States of America, take steps toward the formulation of a Federal Birth Rate Commission."[6] The answer was a pregnant silence.

Other matters that had moved people to frenzy seemed to cure themselves. Inner threats and outer threats to security seemed to disappear and the various cures advocated seemed no longer urgent. The KKK, which was one virulent cure for domestic troubles, had reached its peak membership in 1924. In 1925 it suddenly collapsed. The malodorous doings of one Klan-made public official, sufficiently aired in all the newspapers of the country, helped kill the Klan as a public force. A headline in the October 31, 1925, issue of the New York *World* read:

DEAD WILL ACCUSE
D. C. STEPHENSON

· · ·

The dying declaration of Madge Oberholtzer, after certain deletions, will be admitted in evidence tomorrow in the trial of D. C. Stephenson. [*from Noblesville, Ind.*]

Stephenson was a governor of Indiana elected in part by the Klan. For a time he had gone roughshod on his way as the Klan had, but in 1925 the publicity in the case of Madge Oberholtzer ruined his career. The story of his abduction and rape of the girl (a story that she told while dying slowly of self-inflicted mercury tablets) was too much. It was read with gusto across the country and the governor was finished. The fear of the Klan suddenly evaporated; its membership dropped. The expectation that the Klan might take over the city government of Detroit was seen to be an illusion. Returns on November 3 showed an anti-Klan mayor and city council elected. The major bogey of the early twenties seemed after 1925 not very frightening.

Urgencies in foreign matters were rejected, too. Wilsonian appeal even in the mouth of Calvin Coolidge did not carry far when he asked for participation in a World Court. No Congress went so far as to act upon the suggestion. Complacency ruled the American viewpoint of Europe. Either Europe was hopeless and American help was a waste, or Europe was doing pretty well on its own and did not need American help. In October a number of European nations signed a series of pacts in the Swiss town Locarno that allowed Americans to feel happily relieved of responsibility. The agreement, signed by France, England, Italy, Germany, Poland, and Czechoslovakia, guaranteed the peace of the Rhine and called for arbitration of any conceivable conflict between the nations involved. The Foreign Policy Association (of the United States) was filled with triumph. As reported in the International Yearbook of the following year, the association found that in these meetings the "'victor and vanquished policy' went into the discard . . ."[7] In this hasty congratulation of Europe, there was self-congratulation, also. The United States could now lull its conscience to rest. If it had done wrong in not following Wilson's lead, it was all right now. Europe was going to be safe, and without American help.

The news from Germany brought back by two successive American ambassadors strengthened the prevailing view that troubles were smoothing themselves out almost spontaneously in that country. Germany seemed to be transforming itself. Americans heard what they wanted to hear. Before Alanson B. Houghton "left his post in 1925, he pronounced German militarism dead and declared that the Reich's ambitions were limited to economic rehabilitation." At this very time, the American millionaire Otto Kahn visited his birthplace, Mannheim, and with sufficient publicity reported "that the Germans were recovering because they had given up flag-waving for hard work and sacrifice." The American ambassador who succeeded Houghton in 1925, Jacob Gould Schurman, previously an energetic president of Cornell University, continued in the same tone of American encouragement and delight. American capital began to flow toward Germany, and the ordinary American shared in a diffuse pride in his former enemy, a warmer feeling than he could muster for any of his former allies.[8]

Curiously, even in areas where there was keen although sporadic interest, there was little sustained support. The conquest of the air accomplished itself by the efforts of small numbers of men during the twenties. Isolated adventures and disasters attracted attention. On September 3 a dirigible (the U.S. airship *Shenandoah*) was caught haplessly in wind currents over Caldwell, Ohio, and broke up. Thirteen crewmen were killed, dramatizing to all newspaper readers the hazards of man's hoisting himself precariously into the air. On August 31 the Navy sent two planes across the Pacific toward Hawaii from San Francisco. One, the PN9 No. 3, went down 300 miles from that city and was towed back. The PN9 No. 1, under Commander John Rodgers, almost completed the journey, but came down at sea 200 miles short of Honolulu. Rodgers and his men made sails and navigated the plane as a ship to within fifteen miles of Kauai island, and were then found and towed in by a submarine. They were nine days at sea.[9] This epic adventure caused a brief stir, then vanished into the maw of the public's insatiable appetite for news.

The year 1925 was also the year of crisis for air power and its position in the armed services. It was the year when the Government formally rejected air power as having an important future. The report of the President's appointed air board, which pronounced the decision, was not swayed by the deliberate scandal and outrage that a flying army officer, General William D. Mitchell had provoked. Mitchell had seen air power develop into a powerful, well-organized arm of war. He conceived the threat air power could be in later years—toward the United

States, or by the United States. He became persistent, impolite, one-track-minded in preaching his message. The *Saturday Evening Post* carried articles by him illustrating for the public what he had already proved to no one's great interest: Air power could destroy sea power.

In an article in the January 10, 1925, issue Mitchell showed, with photographs and narrative, how he had trained fliers to hit battleship targets, some laid out on the ground, some old ships at sea. In the March 14 issue he continued his appeal to the people above the heads of his military superiors in an article, "How Should We Organize Our National Air Power?" He was not kind to blindness: " 'Where there is no vision, the people perish.' This old Biblical quotation is more applicable to the development of aviation and air power than to any other undertaking. We are at the turning of the ways in the development of our air power . . ." The pictures showed ships hit, sinking, and sunk by airplanes.

Although these articles created a stir—mostly through the force of character of the author—Mitchell found blindness as strongly entrenched in the public as among his superiors. There was an unquenchable optimism in the air that would not admit that danger existed. There was a vague new morality held by this gaiety-loving people that to think of war was to be predisposed toward it and that the unforgivable sin was the earnestness of the past that had led to the misfortune of going to war.

Mitchell fulfilled his prophetic Biblical mission when he succeeded in forcing the army to bring him and his views to court-martial. He criticized not only general policy, but the preparations for the Hawaii flight and the uses of the *Shenandoah*. The trial began on October 28. It ended on December 17. He was inevitably found guilty.

Parallel to the Mitchell disturbance, showing the equanimity of official and public confidence, was the report, already referred to, of the special air board appointed by the President to investigate and pronounce upon the precise importance of air power to the United States. The board, which included among its members Congressman Carl Vinson of Georgia, in the early stages of his career of concerning himself with the military requirements of the nation, duly considered air needs and issued its findings: "We do not consider that air power as an arm of national defense has yet demonstrated its value—certainly not in a country situated as ours—for independent operations of such a character as to justify the organization of a separate department."[10]

Thus, the age drew in upon itself.

In drawing in, it did not become less lively. It discovered itself as a center for activity and as a spectacle. The year 1925 can aptly demonstrate the range of self-consideration. At one extreme was the discovery of the existence of an audience for a new magazine, *The New Yorker*, which began publication in 1925. At the other extreme was the ready availability of a great national audience for the Scopes trial in Dayton, Tennessee, a happening long drawn out and heatedly reported during the summer of 1925. The two events have this in common: They illustrate the fact that by 1925 the national life itself had become a spectacle, for sophisticated or naïve comment. There was a great revulsion away from commitment but an eagerness to watch others commit themselves, as if at comic or tragic bear-baiting or cock-fighting.

The New Yorker was begun modestly by a group of acute young people who happened to come together in the city and who directed the magazine, as they thought, at others like themselves in the city. Very quickly they found that they had struck a vein responsive to their critical and impudent mood. They found sufficient material in the life and entertainment of the city to succeed with that thin but intense group of reactors. The city of New York, in its entertainments and its movements of life, continued ostensibly to tie the magazine to a locality. The theme of the city gave a center and a gravity to what was shortly a stylized display of American life. The editors of *The New Yorker* viewed, for the most part, life in its lighter aspects, yet found in lightness many sharp and subtle things to say. For forty years *The New Yorker* has preserved certain aspects of its original inspiration buried increasingly amidst the fat plenty of its advertising, but the qualities of the original year were sharper and reflected the time.

It was local and it was brief. A "Profile" of Harold Lloyd by Robert E. Sherwood was only two pages long, a typical length. The advertisements were at first so unimportant as to be compressed sometimes to a "shopping service" on a page. The local reference was continuous. "Why I Like New York" was a continuing head. E. B. White, on August 22, 1925, tried to state why:

> Because it is the only city in the United States that takes itself with a grain of salt.
> Because the noise of Elk, Owl, Lion, and Moose is drowned in the general roar.

It carried much light verse, not all signed. An early effervescence characterized the 1925 flapper:

> A coonskin coat
> To warm her throat;
> A tea-date at the Ritz;
> Most any maid
> Thus well arrayed
> Need not depend on wits.[11]

Its covers were artificial, cartoonlike, and striking in their weekly succession—presenting a version of privileged life. Its criticisms were to the point. An early review of the play adapted from Michael Arlen's novel, *The Green Hat* said, "The renowned hat placed on Katherine Cornell, who wears it very well."[12] It was irreverent. A profile was not determined by the subject's absolute importance, but by his importance relative to the little world that read the magazine. Thus, Joe Leblang, the theater-ticket agent, received such a biography. What resulted was an attitude, as in a section from "Talk of the Town" toward the end of the first year's publication:

> The artificializing effect of Metropolitan life is very great, but we flatter ourselves that we retain sufficient freshness to thrill at the homelier and more lovely things when we see them. Riding on a bus, our eye fell on a load of hay. Misty-eyed, we made an entry in our notebook:
> "Load of hay crosses Fifth Avenue at Forty-second Street at 4:12 P.M., Wednesday, August, 11, 1926."
> "Did you see that?" we ejaculated, turning to a fellow passenger. "Yes," he said sourly, "but forty nude chorus girls will probably jump out from under it when it gets to Broadway." Heaven preserve us from such cynicism as this.[13]

The magazine succeeded in two illusions (that were probably not entirely illusions for the group that worked together in a small office to get the magazine out): that it was a little world one looked at and that by witty words, one could communicate humor or nostalgia about any number of happenings; and that what one experienced was a gay tolerance or a limited sadness, both comfortably wrapped around by satire, a jeering at those others who failed to share with one the inwardness of it all.

The New Yorker did not create the lighter temperament of the time, but it helped give it edge, and in its success it attracted imitation. The frivolous surface of society approximated more and more the attitude of the new magazine. This was no mean achievement, for it was a frivolity with style and definition.

On the surface, in the hot summer season, when there was not much news from anywhere else, the Scopes trial from Dayton, Tennessee, seemed to tell of a confrontation between two bitterly opposed views of life between which there could be no accommodation. Yet in the strangest way in the world, the mood of the twenties blurred the sharp edge of difference between the religious fundamentalist and the rationalist. The fundamentalist believed that teaching Darwin's theory of evolution in the public schools destroyed belief; the rationalist, that Biblical fundamentalism held back progress. However, the sharpest observer of the trials (not Mencken, who got the most amusement out of the experience), Joseph Wood Krutch, saw the incident as something different from confrontation.

Krutch was the best equipped of all the reporters who swarmed into the small town, most of them determined to give it a merciless drubbing in words to be sent all across the country. He was a certified, sophisticated New Yorker, the recently appointed drama critic of *The Nation,* sent southward to report the live drama of the courtroom in Dayton; but he was also a native East Tennessean who understood these people from having grown up among them. He had objectivity and sympathy, as well as an artist's gentle, unblaming relish of the quandaries in which people so readily trap themselves. He was a "modern" man, at this time almost morbidly enthralled by rational thought. This side of his intellectual explorations would find expression a few years later in *The Modern Temper* (1929). But he did not, like many of his colleagues, find the people of Dayton objects of ridicule. What interested him was not the bigotry in Dayton, but the gentleness, the mildness, the politeness of the people who, after all, had never heard anything like Clarence Darrow before. "Dayton heard for the first time the voice of an enlightened man who was not afraid to speak his mind . . ."[14] Bryan's defense of fundamentalism was disappointing to a people reared in its tradition: "His chief plea—a plea for ignorance as uncorrupted as possible by any knowledge" seemed flat. Darrow, in the short time he had been among them, had shown them that other things counted. "It seemed almost true that, as Mr. Mencken, seated behind me, excitedly exclaimed, 'Tennessee needs only fifteen minutes of free speech to become civilized.' "[15] At the end, when the court decided against the defendant, the schoolteacher Scopes, it did so in a perfunctory manner, almost apologetically. The fine was merely nominal. Tennessee and the nation would not ever be the same again. Tennessee had joined the great American public. From the highly critical reader of *The New Yorker* to the intent auditor at the Scopes trial, the American had become a spectator rather than a partisan. He disregarded serious troubles abroad; he disregarded serious troubles in the depths of the American society—that is, he did so if he were sufficiently cushioned by prosperity or buffered by hope.

Below the level of this self-satisfaction was the American farmer. On July 29, 1925, *The Nation* published an article called "The Defeated Farmer." The author noted that "farming in the Northwest, and in parts of the South is virtually, and to a considerable extent actually, in receivership. . . . Georgia showed a 1,000 per cent increase of farmers' bankruptcy cases in ten years . . . Montana, 900 per cent."[16] There could be no mildly humorous savoring of life for those badly fed, overworked members of the population.

It was their physical condition that worked on the nerves of Rexford Guy Tugwell: ". . . the unpaid labor of men and women and children in fields and barns and stables in extremes of cold and heat, underfed, ill clothed and badly equipped with the tools of their craft."

The condition of the farmers was a fatality of the twenties. The situation was aggravated by two natural disasters. The boll weevil continued to eat through the wealth of all the large and small farmers of the South. Superfluously, drought afflicted not only much of the South in the summer of 1925, but large regions of the West. The news that farming was somewhat more prosperous this year than it had been since 1920 (the improvement accomplished by better methods in favored regions) would not have been believed by many gaunt farmers and their wives, whose view was all of dusty fields and unpainted houses and unimproved roads. Tugwell wrote in vain, "Agriculture needs protection now; and it ill becomes that section of industry which has had protection for nearly a century to deny it."[17] Ruefully, he admitted that that section would in fact deny it.

The cooperative movement among farm producers had grown in ten years, between 1915 and 1926 from a business of 651 million dollars a year to 2.5 billion dollars. Farmers had persistent friends in the United States Senate. In 1922 and 1926 Congress gave palliative relief. The law of 1922, the Capper-Volstead Act, acted simply to recognize that farmers might "act together in associations in collectively processing and marketing their products." The law of 1926 created the Division of Cooperative Marketing in the Department of Agriculture, "the work of which shall be to acquire, analyze, and disseminate economic and statistical information regarding the organization and business methods of cooperative associations."[18]

The help accorded farmers was done in the spirit of not spoiling their individual initiative. No humor was seen in the contrast of the administration's general concern and day-to-day help given the business interest. No infringement upon the businessman's initiative was feared. Appointments and the shifting of offices and bureaus from one department to another completed the system by which three Republican administrations put themselves at the service of American industry and commerce.

On July 1, 1925 by executive order the Bureau of Mines, the Patent Office, and the Mineral Resources Division of the Geological Survey were transferred from the Department of Interior to the Department of Commerce. President Coolidge appointed a new member to the Federal Trade Commission in 1925, William E. Humphrey, and thus reversed the balance of voting on the commission from the progressive to the conservative side.

Sweeping investigations of industrial malpractice were curtailed. Procedures became more informal, with greater emphasis on voluntary reform if grievances were indeed discovered. This meant a reduction of unfavorable publicity. All in all, Humphrey's new approach was "friendlier, more trusting, and more co-operative toward business." In the main, when regulation was needed, business could regulate itself, and government would smile benignly, using its authority only against incorrigibles.[19]

In 1925, the twenties also completed its system in foreign affairs. One Secretary of State took the place of another, the change being downward toward mediocrity. Charles Evans Hughes had shown brilliance in his conduct of the office. Frank B. Kellogg diminished the American role abroad. In his own person, he fulfilled the idea of the twenties that government officials should be inconspicuous and unenterprising.

The Kellogg years were destined to mark the nadir of Republican postwar statesmanship. . . .

In fairness to Coolidge and Kellogg, it is necessary to concede that the spirit of the day had made constructive world leadership most difficult. Harding might possibly have re-ignited the fag-ends of war-time idealism. But by 1923, internationalist zeal had waned, while the isolationist front had broadened and deepened. The isolationist coalition now represented more than a pooling of groups who hated Wilson for diverse reasons. It had become a genuine groundswell of public opinion, formidable enough to give pause to even intrepid and far-sighted makers of foreign policy.[20]

It was not merely the Federal Government that retreated into mediocrity. Local government was notably timid in the face of pressure or corruption. Chicago was notorious, and New York in 1925 entered upon its gaudiest episode, the mayoralty of James J. Walker. He had voted for a number of progressive measures when he served in the state legislature. His campaign for mayor, however, was vague and sentimental. An almost full-page campaign advertisement in the New York *World* of October 29, 1925, said:

I am, always have been and always will be, for the five-cent fare . . . [and for] liberal and humane measures . . .

I was born in this city and still live in the street where I was born. I love every inch of my town.

I was reared in a God-fearing home. I declare to you out of a heart filled with precious memories of my home and parents that, if I am elected Mayor, New York City will be the best, cleanest, most wholesome and most orderly place in America.

Jimmy Walker was to become the brilliant image of the time and the city, but orderliness and wholesomeness were to fall far behind wit, insouciance, and even a quite irresistible joy in life— all of which at that moment meant far more to the people who had voted for him than ordinary honesty. The voters literally got what they wanted, although they could not have named at the time they voted what that quality was. Walker's kind of government, superficial and rapacious, did not shock, and did not seem very important. But even in 1925, the year when nothing happened, public and private things occurred that began to create a new future.

A great unfolding into the future was hidden in 1925 in the completion of a hydroelectric power dam at Muscle Shoals on the Tennessee River, to be called the Wilson Dam. It was to be the foundation structure of the whole TVA system, its existence the peg upon which the history-making government corporation was to depend in the next decade. In 1925, not much might have been given for any future for which the dam stood. It was an orphan, almost an accidental product of a conception of the war years that seemed in 1925 outmoded, out of step with the contemporary emphasis upon private industry and business accomplishing the work of the nation. It was part of a project of Wilson's war years, by which the rapids and shoals of the Tennessee River near Florence, Alabama, a serious obstruction to navigation, were to be used for the manufacture of nitrates for government munitions. Foreign sources had been cut off by war blockade. After the war, the product was to be fertilizers for farm use or the site a station for government experiment in fertilizers. In either case, a series of dams, the Number 2 dam (later Wilson Dam,) being the most important, was to furnish the electric power derived from the fall of the river for this specific manufacture. After delays, arguments, stoppages, the dam stood complete, and in 1925 it generated its first quantity of electric power. Beginning in that year, the War Department operated the power plant and for a number of years sold this cheap power to one customer only, the

Alabama Power Company—the only beneficiary at this point of the whole development. But the future history of American public power inhered in the fact of the existence and operation of the dam. Without it, the whole subsequent development of public power, control of rivers, development of regions, improvement of agriculture, preservation of natural resources—the entire conservation movement itself—would have been slower and certainly different. In 1925, Senator George Norris had enough influence to prevent sale of the assets at Muscle Shoals to Henry Ford, or to delay acceptance of his offer (an offer ostensibly public-spirited and popular with the farmers of the South, since it promised cheap production of commercial fertilizers, but which was in fact a low bid for a great deal of potential power) until Ford withdrew his offer. Norris educated himself and a number of his colleagues to see the importance of public power, and he gave them the cohesiveness to hold firm against delays and two presidential vetoes and to wait.[21]

Nongovernmental energies started other projects in 1925. The John Simon Guggenheim Memorial Foundation was established in that year by a gift of three million dollars from former U.S. Senator Simon Guggenheim and his wife. The first fellows were to be named the succeeding year. They were to receive, it was reported, $2,500, for a year's freedom to do their own work. This foundation set up to assist private individual study was the forerunner of others, a pouring out of private industrial money for ends not foreseen by the original money-makers.

A surplus of individual energy and investment poured itself in an almost spontaneous way toward Florida in 1924 and 1925. The movement was helped by any amount of false or near-false advertising. A Seaboard Airline Railway advertisement proposed to move people to Florida in luxury. "Baths" were included in the refinements of rail travel between the Northeast and Florida.[22] The excursion from north to south, whether by Orange Blossom Special or by Model T Ford, attained a high gear of momentum in 1925. The Florida boom was the final, the most delightful icing upon the cake of prosperity.

The excitements of the year were for the most part benign. Air mail was authorized on February 2, 1925, by the Kelly Act in Congress. By July 1, night air mail, which had a rugged excitement attached to a new routine, became a fact in a route maintained between New York and Chicago as a government service. The modest purpose of the service was accompanied by pride in its being accomplished at all: "The object of this service was to provide that letters leaving either city in the evening should be delivered in the first mail of the following morning." Danger was thwarted by individual valor, as the planes winged across mountains and vacant land and cities, the mail pilots doing a lonely, tough job, fitting it into the American context of passionate regularity. The mail plane of the first established route left Hadley Field, New Jersey, upon the stroke of 10:30 P.M. each night. Cleveland was an intermediate stop where all sorts of busy, concerned activities took place to meet the mail and send it on its way again. Like a modern pony express, pilots were changed at this point. The second man carried his fragile craft onward through the night to Chicago. There, the letters were pulled out of the innards of the plane in organized haste and were forwarded in various directions.[23]

The migration to Florida, the leap into air mail service, many important new things seemed to accomplish themselves dumbly. The great happenings of the year were large-scaled movements, not isolated events. Yet a great contradiction existed during this year when nothing happened. It was dazzlingly the year of the twenties when the time interpreted itself. The twenties did not really exist until this began to happen. That it occurred crystallized the twenties. The wonder of 1925, and the years immediately following, was a spontaneous boiling up of patterns that fixed the era. The patterns were mostly those of words; in music only in jazz; in painting and sculpture, patterns were those of Edward Hopper, Charles Sheeler, Charles Burchfield, Arthur Dove, Charles Demuth, Stuart Davis, William Zorach, Alexander Calder, Arthur B. Davies, Robert Henri, John Marin, John Sloan, and Walt Kuhn, who were all at work.

It was not seen at first. It seemed that American quality fulfilled itself in car-making or road-building or in the reorganization of business, but American quality at this moment in time fulfilled itself supremely in words.

In the year nothing happened, three works of fiction struck powerfully through the false assumptions of the age in order to locate real hungers and thirsts. They interpreted the time while picturing it. The three remarkable books were *An American Tragedy*, by Theodore Dreiser; *In Our Time*, by Ernest Hemingway; and *The Great Gatsby*, by F. Scott Fitzgerald. One displayed the yearning of a poor boy for the kind of money and position his rich relatives had, a panoramic and solidly built study of the kind of life every reader recognized as true. The second, in stories, concerned itself with loneliness and boredom in a world where everything was void except certain emotional and physical honesties. The third was a contemporary legend about the dream and deception of American success, a bootlegger's dream of money and love, a story that hung like a soap bubble about to burst above the facts out of which it was made: the displays of ignorant wealth, the threat and actuality of violence. In an age that had shuffled death out of sight, the three books treated death as a principal subject. They were remarkable in appearing in one calendar year. They demonstrated the flawed American civilization's spewing out in profusion in the midst of trash much vital artistic material, and certain gifted individuals' seizing upon this inchoate matter and making use of it.

Aside from the three novels, so pertinent to 1925, aside from best sellers, the kinds and qualities of American books published in 1925 made a record to put alongside the accomplishments in automobile manufacture or corporation organization. In verse there were published: Marianne Moore's *Observations*, E. E. Cummings' *XLI Poems*, Ezra Pound's *Cantos I–XVI*, and Robinson Jeffers' *Roan Stallion*. In fiction there appeared: Sinclair Lewis' *Arrowsmith*, DuBose Heyward's *Porgy*, Ellen Glasgow's *Barren Ground*, Willa Cather's *The Professor's House*, and for high and low comedy—both characteristic of a vein of feeling of the time—Elinor Wylie's *The Venetian Glass Nephew* and Anita Loos' *Gentlemen Prefer Blondes*. It was the year of John Dewey's *Experience and Nature* and William Carlos Williams' *In the American Grain*.

Here was an assimilation of European influences (Pound, from Idaho, was also an influence in Europe) and a new appreciation of regional experience (Virginia in *Barren Ground*, the Southwest in *The Professor's House*, Charleston back-street culture in *Porgy*, early American history and earlier American writing in *In the*

American Grain, California coastal physical and human geography in *Roan Stallion*). Here was also play with words (Moore, Cummings, Hemingway) in the interest of expressing contemporary meanings. Here was philosophic self-examination (Dewey), esthetic self-examination (W. C. Williams), sociology in fiction (Lewis), elegant escapism (Wylie), humor (Loos), many, many different ways—all valid—of taking life. Having turned aside from commercial aims, these writers found in a rampant commercial age resources of life, energy, and ambition for the appropriate shaping of their books. In this spout of creativity, instigations toward excellence operated with great power. These writers seemed to owe something to the historical moment, and to repay much to that moment, in spite of the fact that in order to function, workers in words had to separate themselves in some manner from the life of ordinary men.

This separation damaged the creators and it damaged society. The whole artistic motive seemed set apart from and to one side of the life of the average American citizen. Art was suspect. The separation caused ordinary citizens to have contradictory feelings toward practicing artists. Writers (and painters and musicians) were scorned, yet if successful—that is, if they made news or made money—they were admired extravagantly as people who had somehow gotten away with something. Writing seemed a superfluous kind of activity when there was so much else to do, yet the ability to write winningly was an attractive one. Dangers came to popular writers. The popularity of such a writer as Sinclair Lewis was to be as dangerous to him as popularity was to be for Charles A. Lindbergh.

What was not understood was that the art of the time was not a frill upon its edges but a basic interpretation, a finding of meaning in all the lives joined together in joy and pain, delight, sorrow, anger, compulsion, and spontaneity. The three remarkable books of the year received for the most part respectful reviews, but certain critics expressed public doubts. Of *In Our Time,* one said, "One may not like this prose. . . ," adding, "but it would be impossible to deny it a vigor and actuality that is unusual."[24] Of *An American Tragedy,* one wrote, "The commonplaceness of the story is not alleviated in the slightest degree by any glimmer of imaginative insight on the part of the novelist."[25] Of *The Great Gatsby,* one wrote, "[It] is not a good book,"[26] and another, "What has never been alive cannot very well go on living."[27]

Yet advocates were not lacking. Champions they had to be, for they knew that Dreiser's, Hemingway's, or Fitzgerald's candid gaze at the United States of 1925 was not welcome. Paul Rosenfeld said of *In Our Time,* "He looks upon the world without prejudice or preconception and records with precision and economy, and an almost terrifying immediacy exactly what he sees."[28] Joseph Wood Krutch said flatly of the Dreiser novel, "It is the greatest American novel of our generation."[29] Gilbert Seldes wrote of the Fitzgerald story, the most easily misunderstood of the three, "The plot works out not like a puzzle with odd bits falling into place, but like a tragedy, with every part functioning in the completed organism."[30]

The reception of works of art by critics is not altogether a literary matter; it is a hinge where two parts of society are joined. The two parts in 1925 were not hitched smoothly together. The confusion of the critics was only a sophisticated version of the general public's unease in the face of the honest candor of the well-made and significant *thing* of art. The public, ravished by the splendors of pervasive advertising and publicity, "arts" that were after something in them, did not know what to make of books or paintings that did not ask anything of them but to look, to listen, to understand, to feel.

And yet, despite a gap between the producers and consumers of these works, there was vigor on both sides. It was a queer kind of society: the unconscious members living lives of color, complication, urgency, for which they had no words for describing, no tones for singing; the conscious interpreters, in some manner stimulated by the same circumstances, living also at high speed and creating remarkable works, and not able to touch fundamentally the lives of Everyman. It was a society that did not understand itself and did not want to understand itself. American culture could not come of age until it could tolerate a thicker layer of knowledge and artistry and self-criticism than the twenties could endure. Although in that heedless decade there was a happy and spontaneous flowering of individual artists, the total number of scattered talents more brilliant perhaps than in any decade to succeed it; the soil underneath was thin. "Culture" was an outlaw in the twenties, and so was "art." Therefore, the twenties remained adolescent.

XI

HOW SOME
PEOPLE LIVED

THE TWENTIES WERE YEARS RICH ENOUGH to reward social investigation in midstream. It was possible for two sensitive
observers and their helpers to go into an approximately typical
Midwestern city in January, 1924, stay unobtrusively and sympathetically with their scientific wits about them among these
natives of their own land until June, 1925, and come away with
material to be sorted, analyzed, and made into a narrative to be
published in 1929 with the title *Middletown*.[1] To this point already did the twenties reward self-study. By describing the
everyday life of a typical small city of the northern Midwest, the
Lynds' work helped the twenties see the twenties and later decades see the twenties; it characterized with infinite compassion
and sharp sociological skills real people caught haplessly within
the lines and limits of category. It discovered among these people
two classes, the business and the working, and six areas of activity, getting a living, making a home, training the young, using
leisure, engaging in religious practices, engaging in community
activities. Forty years later, the study was to be even more
poignant than it was to the twenties—to see 1890 disappearing in
1924, to perceive the push toward conformities and the wistful

pull toward individuality, to notice certain concerns hardening into habits for the first time, to catch sight of ourselves in these intentions, ambitions, lacks. For this study seemed to be reporting to succeeding generations: This is where you began. In the book's honestly tentative conclusion the Lynds wrote, "In case after case the preceding pages have revealed Middletown as learning new ways of behaving towards material things more rapidly than new habits addressed to persons and non-material institutions."[2] Thus, the Lynds' study, a product of the twenties as well as an investigation into it, allied particular Americans of the decade with humanity elsewhere. Its hardheaded particular findings—the dominance of business, the uncritical worship of education coupled with a callous disregard for teachers, a suspicion of culture and a fear of intelligence, the worship of success, and a generous and even humble love for goodwill and kindness—were a remarkable exercise in self-criticism, in a time's studying itself.

Veal cutlets for breakfast, listed on butcher's order books as a popular Middletown breakfast, might seem a lingering tradition from a former time, but traits big and little that were being established in 1924 were part of a new tradition that would hold sway undiminished for unknown decades into the future:

a. Gadgets and mechanical things—radios, Ford cars, toasters, electric irons, Hoover cleaners were becoming a central part of everyday living.

b. Women, supposedly free, were showing stresses in their new, unprecedented American lives.

c. Business, and everything related to it, took precedence over everything else. Politics, religion, art were not rivals to this one dominant interest.

d. Intellectuals and artists lived lonely or different lives, necessarily in some sort of quiet or noisy conflict with their neighbors.

In spite of the sensitivity of the researching effort of the Lynds, the result of the statistical composite in their book was dull and monotonous. There was in the reality of the life of such a place a certain insipidity.

The individual accomplishments of the twenties must be set

over against the dominance of the middle range of human endeavor. The time is remembered as lively, individual, daring,
reckless. Is it a trick of memory, or if the collective national
memory is true, how account for the contradiction? Certainly
statistical averages melt away in particular perspectives, and
country is not like city, nor South like North, nor rich like poor.
Yet the average, ascertained by a certified social science, was not
at all like memory's picture.

Contradicting the statistics in a tentative way, the observer
might claim that general conditions in the twenties supported
the strong individual (not the average or the weak, who approximated willingly to an approved standard). A relatively high
standard of consumption, food to eat, a sound roof above the
head, good wages, opportunity to be heard and approved or at
least argued with, space to move about in, variety in the levels to
be climbed to, above all a general hopefulness and a widespread
sense of personal and national security: these factors of life in the
twenties encouraged stout-minded individuals to exert themselves
to the utmost. In addition, the blandness of the middle range of
life aggravated strong personalities into differences in behavior or
stimulated talents of various kinds to embellish the scene, to disregard it, or to overcome it. Thus, to appreciate the varieties of
individual experience in the twenties, it is necessary to remember
the good-hearted but poor-headed sameness out of which the
spectacular individual sprang. Individuals did flower out of the
dull background. Illustrations come readily, and the only necessary connection among them will be the way in which each one
stood in relation to his time.

Some among them did not question fundamental assumptions,
but only made the twenties a more interesting, more complex
time to live in. Such a one was Dwight Morrow, an excellently
functioning, essential cog of the age. He was also an individual of
decided charm who made headlines in one valuable role after
another during the span of the decade. His biographer, Harold
Nicolson, has described him:

A little man of gentle gaiety, of sweet unworldliness, of brilliant
intellect. True it was that Morrow's unflagging zest, even in small
things, titivated and amused; that his intelligence was as various, as
volatile, but as intent, as a pack of hounds. . . . Essentially Morrow was

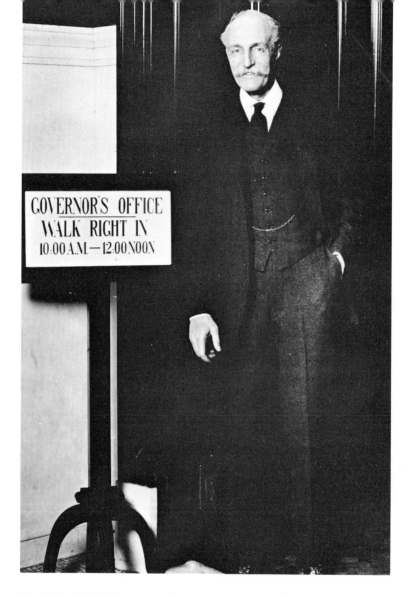

11. Gifford Pinchot was the progressive Republican governor of Pennsylvania who arbitrated a coal strike in 1923 so that the workers benefited in the settlement. He had been, before the World War, the first chief forester of the United States and had created the Forest Service. He preached the conservation of natural resources, including man.

12. Dr. Robert H. Goddard at a blackboard at Clark University in 1924 explaining a method by which a rocket might reach the moon. Goddard carried on his explorations in the theory and application of rocket propulsion and space flight at a time when nothing could have appeared more futile or ridiculous.

a man of action. He was ambitious, determined, precise, cautious, unremitting, and shrewd.[3]

He was the child of strenuously conscientious and striving Presbyterian parents, his father an unprosperous schoolteacher all his life in West Virginia and the Pittsburgh area; he was to have himself a nightmarish fear of becoming "enormously" rich. He became so, and handled the condition modestly, indulging only in large telephone bills and a costly library, but keeping an old car.

Morrow became a partner in the J. P. Morgan & Company just as that firm undertook the handling of British and French loans in the United States before the United States entered the war. He also served his own government in various capacities. He instituted penal reforms in New Jersey; and in Englewood, where he lived, he found the local garageman as interesting as Aristide Briand. Criticism of party hacks and tired techniques did not interrupt an intense personal loyalty to the Republican Party. He excused Calvin Coolidge for not putting him in the Cabinet. Morrow had known Coolidge since college days and had managed the abortive 1920 Coolidge-for-president campaign. He continued to support the President loyally. Morrow handled two notable controversies of the decade to the satisfaction of his contemporaries.

He was the dominant member of the Board of Trustees of Amherst College in 1923 when that body decided to let President Alexander Meiklejohn go. The disturbing president had been brought to the college before the war to upgrade the faculty and had done so, causing an uproar in that intensely conservative group by bringing in men more interested in research than in the local New England scene. A local observer wrote, "One of my neighbors looks upon the controversy as centering upon the failure of four of the men to keep the lawns mowed."[4]

At the time of the Meiklejohn controversy, Morrow was hurt by an open letter in *The New Republic* questioning his liberalism. Morrow's character determined the action taken. He lived intelligently within the context of his own time, but was altogether immune to prophecy. He defended Meiklejohn longer than most of the other board members. He saw the littleness and unimportance of one of the charges brought against him: that he had mishandled his personal finances. But the charge that finished Meiklejohn, that he failed to "get on" with the faculty, was one he might have disregarded. Meiklejohn was hired to transform the faculty; the function at least for a period of years precluded his getting on with them. The president was adored by the students, admired by educators elsewhere. He had made Amherst famous for its willingness to experiment. Morrow disliked something overly emotional in Meiklejohn's public pronouncements.[5] The two men in their personal styles were incompatible. When Morrow took action, he dexterously took the onus off the board by asking the faculty to vote. The faculty voted by a majority of over two-thirds to let Meiklejohn go. Morrow, as chairman of the investigating committee, had then the appearance of only concurring.

The Billy Mitchell affair of late 1925 displayed the general as a tactless prophet of disaster. It exhibited Dwight Morrow as a skillful conciliator. He was one who helped keep the twenties on its temporary course by moderating one difficulty after another. The air board enquiry was one of the occasions of his calling attention away from danger and making inattention seem intelligent.

From among the citizens appointed by President Coolidge to the air board, Dwight Morrow seemed perfectly suitable as the promptly self-chosen head. Many witnesses were called to testify, Mitchell among the most important. His importance was carefully deflated by the manner in which he was questioned and listened to. Morrow's skill muted Mitchell's strictures. The board, embodied in Morrow, listened politely to the general and remained incredulous, skeptical, and derisive, in a gentlemanly way. Through Morrow's quiet management, the general was made to seem exaggerated and hysterical in his claims of the possibility of air attack upon the United States. The hearings came to a close; Mitchell (who went on to his court-martial) and the other witnesses were dismissed; and the board recommended a limited number of sensible, small changes in the organization of air power. They did not find necessary the establishment of a separate air arm. From the air board enquiry Morrow went on to further quiet triumphs in the service of his country.[6]

The gaps in Morrow, not faults, for he functioned flawlessly, illustrate how completely he belonged inside the twenties and never glanced outside the prison of his times. He made the period more interesting and helped make it work. He had no hypocrisy. Unlike most public men of the time, he was refreshingly honest about the failure of the Prohibition Amendment and recommended its repeal. Morrow was at his best in his diplomatic dealings with Mexico in his term as ambassador between 1927 and 1929. The problem in Mexico was oil. Morrow solved the problem neatly by finding a Mexican way of doing so, convincing the Mexicans that the most onerous part of the new laws passed by their revolutionary regimes against foreign investment was unconstitutional within the framework of their own tradition. But this that he had been sent to do was the least he did. He created the beginning of at least temporary better feelings between Mexico and the United States and the climate for better general relations between all the Latin American countries and the United States. His work, while first benefiting the American businessman who had put money in the ground of Mexico, was a compromise of interests and was also the forerunner of the broader "good neighbor" policy of the thirties.

He exercised his personal gifts in accomplishing these ends and surpassed the easily stated purpose of his coming to Mexico. Harold Nicolson has described Morrow in Mexico:

From the first moment of his arrival it became obvious even to the most nationalistic Mexican that Morrow had come to placate, to appreciate, and to please. His insatiable friendliness, his utter simplicity, the very exuberance of his good will, held them enthralled. He applauded their food, their climate, their agriculture, their hats, their ancient monuments, the bamboo cages in which they kept their tame parrots, their peasant industries, their patriotism, their volcanoes, even their finances. Here at last was a North American who neither patronized nor sneered. His boyish enjoyment of his task was infectious. In the sunshine of his zest, under the warm breeze of that creative credulity, even the most morose suspicions melted. . . . His small size, his untidy clothes, the utter collapse of his hat and trousers, the curious contrast between the slow deliberation of his walking stick and the upturned scuffle of his little shoes, the general zest and bustle which he created around him, the gentle wistfulness of those deep blue eyes, his utter absence of selfconsciousness, aroused delighted feelings such as are evoked by the spectacle of a happy and bright-mannered child.

Upon the fascinated receptiveness thus induced the effect of his high qualities of intelligence and character were overpowering.[7]

Dwight Morrow was the best-equipped and most intelligent Babbitt of the time, a man functioning beautifully for the benefit of a limited kind of society.

Some kinds of ability were unwanted and unclaimed by the twenties. The owners of such talent reacted in different ways: William Mitchell with obstinate public insistence, a man like the scientist Robert Hutchings Goddard with silence and silent work. Goddard mined below the surface of the time, preparing for the future. He was a physicist at Clark University in Worcester, Massachusetts. In the mid-twenties he was fully engaged in his life's work, exploring the mathematics and physical realities of a kind of flight that had as yet no vocabulary: space flight and rocket flight. He had had some help from the Smithsonian Institution and he had worked in a modest and disregarded way for the army during the 1917–18 war. For the army he designed a weapon that was tested and put aside. It was not used during the American participation in the war against the Kaiser. It was not used till the next war, but was to be used then with some notorious success. This was the bazooka. Goddard attracted the attention of Colonel Lindbergh, living in the heat and light of publicity after his flight to Paris. Lindbergh visited Goddard in New England and directed the attention of the Daniel Guggenheim Fund for the promotion of aeronautics to Goddard. The fund gave Goddard modest support after this date.

In snowy fields outside the New England town where he lived, to the derision and alarm of the townspeople who called him "moon-man," Goddard set up fragile tripods with tiny rockets mounted on top and shot them up into the frosty air. With a little money from the foundation that had befriended him, he escaped from the close surroundings of jibing curiosity to the spaces of the Mescalero Ranch near Roswell, New Mexico. Here, through the later years of the twenties and into the thirties and forties, he played with what seemed his mad toys. They were not toys at all, but in the climate of the twenties, perfectly inert discoveries. A changed historical situation was to make them formidable tools and weapons. During these indifferent years he discovered, and in some cases patented, a projectile rocket (1918), a liquid-fuel rocket (1926), a rocket faster than sound (1935), a gyroscopic steering device, the conception of a multiple-stage rocket, a mathematical theory of rocket propulsion and flight, mathematical proof "that a rocket not only works but works better . . . in a vacuum, and so can operate in space."[8]

Some men worked with the current of the times, some underneath; others were flung off to one side. The good health of certain American lives seemed to require in this decade the long perspective that Europe gave, and many went abroad: the frivolous, the earnest, the gregarious, the solitary, the rich, the stinting. Europe, viewed from at home by the families of Main Street, was suspect, but also infinitely attractive. Bohemian exile proved a peculiar benefit for a few. Ernest Hemingway was one of those: typical yet unique.

He was in the early twenties a young unknown American living in various unheated apartments in the Rue Notre Dame des Champs or the Rue Cardinal Lemoine in the sixth *arrondissement* of Paris, eating when he could afford it in students' or artists' cafes, sitting often for hours, disregarded by a selfish, self-absorbed yet creative and tolerant life swirling around him, his back to the wall, literally and figuratively, putting down painfully and slowly on the ruled pages of little blue exercise books the memories of his boyhood's Michigan. A short walk from the Dome, the Select, the Rotonde, was the liberating salon of Gertrude Stein, who in grand egotism, surrounded by her huddle of pictures and albums and nineteenth-century shaded lamps, encouraged many young talents. We were like brothers, Hemingway said of her once, and recalled walks, talks, arguments, misunderstandings, and understandings, all in a context far removed from his own childhood background of Michigan and Illinois. Paris was a world where the difficult, slowly developing gift for words had a chance to grow. "Paris was always worth it," Hemingway wrote near the end of his life.[9]

Another different world from that of normal business occupations and middle-range ambitions was Greenwich Village. It was a Village not so militant in its bohemianism or in its fervor for revolution as it had been. In 1927 Edmund Wilson reported a night expedition into a Village street in search of a friend and of the dilapidation he encountered on the way. The very houses were sad: "Those high halls, with their dismal lights, with their expanses of stale yellow plaster, with their flat odor of unventilated bathrooms and their monotonous trickle of defective toilets, closed me round with a void of abandonment even more formidable than that of the streets." Even his friend Jane Gooch, the solitary editor of a magazine that had not had an issue published in eighteen months, admitted the difference between this day and an earlier one. People were getting married; they were taking respectable jobs. Jane spoke to him of a Village man redoing a house for a bride: " 'It's just like what you read about in the old novels,' said Jane, 'making a nest for the bride! First nest I ever saw down here! All I ever knew them to do at most was to have the bed made the night they were married. And they used to be ashamed of getting married.' " The old enthusiasm flared in his friend, however, when he asked her about the next issue of her magazine, *The Vortex:*

"Well, we're planning a big hydraulic number," she said. . . . "Hydraulics?" "Yes: pipes and oil pumps and plumbing fixtures—and all those things. We've got some photographs by Leo Kleist of bath-rooms that are the most marvelous things you ever saw. There's a series—of wash-basins at different angles that looks just like that tomb of the Medicis of Michelangelo's. And then there are some paintings by Jacques Ducran of oil stations—bright red and orange and bright blue and gold—he took them out on the Coast—that look like something Chinese. Look at this!" She showed me a still life in rich brown and yellow water-color, with a background of dazzling white. "Isn't that luscious? That's a rubber bath sponge and a piece of soap. Of course people will laugh at us—but we're used to that, and if anything is going to be done to bring the American public to a real appreciation of art—to a realization of the beauty, of the possibilities for beauty, of these things that they use every day—it will have to be done in the teeth of the sneers and ridicule of all the kept art critics of the bourgeois magazines."[10]

More remarkable even than those who fled to Paris or to Greenwich Village were those who lived a kind of double life, both in and out of the common, broad, ordinary, everyday America. Robert Frost, farming and teaching and lecturing, a man whose private occupation was writing poetry, was one. Wallace Stevens, executive of an insurance company and poet, was another. William Carlos Williams, obstetrician and pediatrician in a small New Jersey city, was another.

Interested in the motives and behavior of his patients, gentle with faults, curious about virtues and vices, Williams wrote verse and stories and essays in the interstices of his busy daily life in Rutherford, contributed to little magazines, and went on occasional literary expeditions to New York or to Europe. Yet his farthest expeditions only brought him back to circle around the humanity he admired in everyday life, a life that seemed rich to him even in its routine and waste.

Williams was a rebel against the scholarly domination of the literary scene by T. S. Eliot, and particularly his busy followers. He wanted to find a local inspiration for poetry. He wanted to exercise his senses to keep them alive. He detested a crust of learnedness growing over the fresh taste of life. He found his own ground of inspiration in Paterson. His making a long poem about the town belonged to a later time. In the twenties he wrote short, scattered, sharp impressions of life. He was full of enjoyment and indignation. His recollections written in the forties catch the mood of young artists in the twenties. "Damn it, the freshness, the newness of a springtime which I had sensed among the others, a reawakening of letters . . . [and] the stupidity, the calculated viciousness of a money-grubbing society such as I knew and violently wrote against."[11] Publication was a battle: "Our poems constantly, continuously, and stupidly were rejected by all the pay magazines except *Poetry* and *The Dial. The Little Review* didn't pay. We had no recourse but to establish publications of our own."[12] He was, like Sam Dodsworth, wary of Europe. Yet he wrote, "The Paris of the expatriate artist was our only world—day and night—and if bread is the staff of life, whisky, as Bob [McAlmon, founder of the Contact Press] was fond of saying, is the staff of night life, both products of the same grain."[13]

Williams had one curious passage across the Atlantic on the SS *Pennland* in January, 1927. He found himself coming home with a boatload of celebrating American Legionnaires. Drunken rowdiness threatened to take over the boat. The writer looked on with impartial curiosity and even sympathy. The riot subsided, he wrote his wife, "Perhaps the change in wind yesterday, with the subsequent clearing of the weather, was due to the passing of one of the Carolina boys on board, who died of pneumonia. The ship was quiet all day because of this. We now have three dead men in the hold. Legionnaires who died in Europe."[14]

In his verse in the twenties, Williams made sharp intellectual observations:

> The pure products of America
> go crazy—

or translated into focus what he saw with the clear hard eyes of a child:

> so much depends
> upon
>
> a red wheel
> barrow
>
> glazed with rain
> water
>
> beside the white
> chickens

but he seldom invoked moral warmth at this time. It was only in the next decade that he wrote the contrasting:

> To A Poor Old Woman
>
> munching a plum on
> the street a paper bag
> of them in her hand
>
> They taste good to her . . .[15]

Williams in 1925, *In the American Grain,* cast a strange and original look at American pasts, translated into a new relationship to the American present. Holding back and letting go, puritanism and rich self-indulgence, twin traits of the national character, seemed to him to have deep roots.

He wrote about the Pilgrims:

The Pilgrims were seed of Tudor England's lusty blossoming. The flamboyant force of that zenith, spent, became in them hard and little. Among such as they its precarious wealth of petals sank safely within bounds to lie dreaming or floating off while the Restoration throve, a sweltering seclusion of the hothouse, surrounded by winter's cold.[16]

He wrote about Daniel Boone:

There was, thank God, a great voluptuary born to the American settlements against the niggardliness of the damning puritanical tradition; one who by the single logic of his passion, which he rested on the savage life about him, destroyed at its spring that spiritually withering plague. For this he has remained since buried in a miscolored legend and left for rotten. Far from dead, however, but full of a rich regenerative violence he remains, when his history will be carefully reported, for us who come after to call upon him. . . . So Boone lived to enjoy ecstasy through his single devotion to the wilderness with which he was surrounded. The beauty of a lavish, primitive embrace in savage, wild beast and forest rising above the cramped life about him possessed him wholly.[17]

While a scientist like Goddard and a writer like Williams failed to find public support for their work, Goddard ridiculed and Williams ignored, the latter known only as a hard-working physician to his neighbors, the former as a gifted man only to a few scientists, other dexterous citizens skated across the surface of public attention and thrived in limelight. It was a period of wanton, fickle, united public gaze directed here, there, everywhere, but not anywhere for long, by daily papers, daily radio, widespread magazines, billboards. The public might be divided by analysis into the higher and lower browed, but was really one in being willing to be entertained if not called on to act. For there was nothing to be done about any public matters, and only money-making was serious and private.

Some people lived in the public eye almost as a full-time career, or at least to achieve certain aims. The personal existence of H. L. Mencken of Baltimore (student of language, music lover, lover of Baltimore street life) was not much known, but Mencken's public personality became notorious during the decade. He wore this public personality like a uniform for combat, and he behaved with such gusto and bounce that his courage and persistence were discounted by lazier citizens who let him fight for them. In his various joustings against stodginess (Babbittry in general), censorship, fundamentalism, and other bindings upon individual freedom, he carried on a public career at the top of his journalistic voice.

A notable adventure of April, 1926, was his arrest on a street corner in Boston. The sequence of action began in his Baltimore office. A *Sun* reporter telephoned him that the April issue of the magazine he edited, the *American Mercury*, was being banned in Boston. This was expected, for he had been prodding Boston sensibilities deliberately with a series of articles. However, the April offense was not deliberately anti-Boston; it was a chapter of reminiscence by Herbert Asbury, a compassionate essay about a small-town prostitute known as Hatrack. The essay was essentially noncensorable even for 1926 and Mencken knew it. Boston seemed ripe for buffeting and Mencken ached to do it. The city had allowed itself for eighteen years to be censored in its reading by one man, the Reverend T. Frank Chase, secretary of a private organization, the Watch and Ward Society. Mr. Chase pored over books and magazines as they were published and issued monthly lists to retail booksellers of titles they must not sell. The booksellers were helpless, because under local law they might be liable, if police prosecution were brought upon them by the Watch and Ward Society, for stiff fines or two-year jail sentences. Mencken knew that he might bring on himself the same punishment, but he resolved to act.

He went up to Boston, secured from a police station a license as a peddler, and set himself to wait upon a street corner for Mr. Chase, who had agreed in perfect seriousness to the public scene and the test of strength. The place was Brimstone Corner outside the Park Street Church, and a crowd of three thousand gathered around the slightly nervous Mencken, his lawyer, and a number of Harvard students cheering him on and yelling for the arrival of Chase, who was a little late. Chase appeared, accompanied by the captain of the police vice squad and a plain-clothes detective. He handed over fifty cents for the magazine, and when Mencken gave it into his hand, he said, "I order this man's arrest." The two police officers closed in on Mencken, and marched him off to the police station to be booked. Trial was set for the next day, and Mencken was let out for twenty-four hours on bail.

Next day at the trial, though his nerves were frayed by a slight delay in the appearance of his lawyers, Mencken spoke strongly for the dignity and decency of his magazine and its right to a wide range of subject matter:

> I came to Boston to find out whether so-called reformers were or were not to dictate to the citizens of this country what they should read and what they should not read. These reformers can smell out what they term "immorality" in any publication from the Bible down, if they are so minded. Now I should not want the prosperity of my magazine to depend on its being obscene. It appeals to intelligent and decent people and assumes that such matters are open to debate and discussion.

Although he spoke well, the crowd and the community seemed against him, and Mencken realized what a force he had set himself against. He thought, and his friends standing by him thought, that the judge would rule against him. He came prepared the second day to face a stiff sentence and was shaky and depressed. But Judge James P. Parmenter, who had kept a poker face through the proceedings, ruled handsomely in Mencken's favor:

> I do not find anything in any other article that touches upon sex except "Hatrack," but there the subject is not made attractive—in fact, the contrary is the case. It is a rather frank expression, but at the same time an intellectual description of prostitution in a small town, and I found nothing in it that would arouse sexual impulses or lascivious thoughts as prohibited by the statute. The magazine is rather high priced and this makes it unlikely that it would get into the hands of youth, but if it did, the quality of its articles is such that they would not understand them and, accordingly, would suffer no harm.

The charges were dismissed.[18]

Such fights as Mencken undertook were not frivolous in the climate of the twenties.[19] His temper and aggressiveness were needed if there was to be any chance to defeat a very persistent tendency toward censorship. Incuriosity, fear, and hate blanketed a broad portion of the population against new or foreign or upsetting ideas. Many people could not be aroused even to want mental freedom. Many people thought that such a cause was not "nice." The mediocrity of the half-educated also continued to weigh as a tyranny on fresh and inquiring minds.

Mencken was not interested in democracy, in fact he disapproved of it, for he understood democracy to be the lumpish, conforming, and undiscriminating mass opinion that was always in some way threatening liberty. He was interested in preserving personal liberties. The entire age took democracy for granted and did not worry about its lack for certain parts of the population, as the progressives of the Wilson period had, and as the liberals of the Roosevelt period would. For fortunate people, the twenties was often a period of privilege. Considering themselves licensed to be themselves, above the timid likemindedness of Babbittry, a variety of individuals prospered.

Although the twenties was the confident age of big business, many little businesses flourished, some of them thriving upon daring and individual effort. This was particularly so of intellectual and artistic effort. Many holders of Guggenheim awards in the twenties were writers or artists, unaffiliated with a university, venturing independently to write a book, paint pictures, or compose music. There were many small producers of plays in the Broadway section of New York City, and a vigorous little-theater movement prospered. It was possible also to begin book publishing upon a shoestring and to prosper artistically and financially. Donald Friede retold a typical twenties kind of success story in his own career in his memoir, *The Mechanical Angel.* In 1925 Friede, a brash twenty-four-year-old, joined the firm of Horace Liveright. He went into book publishing independently in 1929. He was in many ways the typical bright young man of his time.

Friede was accustomed to patronizing new music. He did not see why he should not produce a concert if he wished. He and his crowd, he explained, were in love only with the new. If Stravinsky's *Sacre du Printemps* were to be played at Carnegie Hall, he would call the box office beforehand to ascertain the exact minute of the beginning of the Stravinsky number in order to skip the rest:

We would stand out in the lobby smoking until the orchestra had finished playing that old fuddy-duddy Haydn. Then we would troop in, swoon orgiastically over the atonal music we had come to hear, and troop out again, careful to be safely in the lobby before our ears were assailed by the horribly melodic music of Johannes Brahms. The chances were excellent that we were not sufficiently intelligent to truly appreciate his art.[20]

So without an ounce of forethought but with presumption and gusto, he invited the American composer George Antheil, at that time living in Paris, to come home to perform his "Ballet Mecanique" at Carnegie Hall; Donald Friede would manage the occasion. The result was a disaster that was gigantic, comic, and endearing, in retrospect perhaps more enjoyable than a success would have been.

Upon the evening of the performance, after difficulties in programming and rehearsing, audience and performers were got together. An innocuous string quartet preceded the main event. Then a drop-curtain was raised to disclose the composer's special orchestra assembled before "the billowing buttocksy backdrop of the colossal Charleston," which Friede had had painted for the occasion, and "the audience roared with laughter. I had not realized how utterly incongruous it would seem to use such a backdrop in hallowed Carnegie Hall." The orchestra included ten pianos, to be played by ten pianists scraped together with difficulty, a mechanical piano to be played by the composer, six xylophones, two bass drums, electric bells, a wind machine, and a fire siren. The audience never recovered from its visual shock when aural shock was added; the crowd disintegrated into helpless laughter. The musical evening concluded in a wild scene of disrepair onstage and off. However, anything undertaken so playfully could be laughed off. "As I came out of my box I ran into a friend of mine, a wit in high standing at the Round Table in the Algonquin. 'Too bad, Donald,' he said. 'You tried to make a mountain out of an Antheil.' I managed a mechanical smile."[21]

The easygoing, loosefitting freedom of the time helped some people become themselves. Compulsions and deprivations helped others. Prison life for seven long years, and the living under sentence of death, sharpened and stylized the individuality of the two most famous prisoners of the time: Sacco and Vanzetti. The last year of their lives, 1927, was a year of widening interest in their case, of protests and appeals.

At this late date, in response to opinion, Governor Alvan T. Fuller appointed a committee to reconsider the trials, testimony, and judgments of the past seven years and to give him advice upon the repeated requests for clemency. The three-man committee, President A. Lawrence Lowell of Harvard, President Samuel W. Stratton of the Massachusetts Institute of Technology, and a former probate judge, Robert Grant, could not have been more distinguished. They decided against Sacco and Vanzetti as two panels of juries had done earlier. Innocence could not be established. Felix Frankfurter, however, thirty-three years later, gave short shrift to the balanced fairness that may have tortured the three men in their decision: "Lawrence Lowell was incapable of seeing that two wops could be right and the Yankee judiciary could be wrong."[22] Men were to go on arguing decade after decade whether Sacco and Vanzetti were innocent or guilty.[23] And during 1927, physical death came closer and closer.

Sacco continued almost inarticulate and did not seem to change. He spoke out on a rare occasion to condemn the Charlestown State Prison: "That horrible death-house, that should be destroyed with the hammers of real progress—that horrible house that will shame forever the future of the citizens of Massachusetts. They should destroy that house and put up a factory or school, to teach many of the hundreds of the poor orphan boys of the world."[24] Vanzetti, a more flexible man, changed greatly. He learned to read and write English and corresponded with a wide circle of those concerned about his and Sacco's doom, some friendly, some merely curious. Vanzetti was intensely aware of himself, of others, of the world outside. He went through only a short period of the insanity of despair. He developed a style of utterance to match the movements of his emotions. He wrote of himself, "I did not spittel a drop of blood, or steal a cent in all my life." He wrote of Sacco, "Sacco is a heart, a faith, a character, a man." He said in a speech to the court on April 9, 1927, "I would not wish to a dog or to a snake, to the most low and misfortunate creature of the earth—I would not wish to any of them what I have had to suffer for things that I am not guilty of."[25]

Men suffered and yet it was a callous time. Being amused and being amusing were the characteristic stance of the individual who had freed himself from belonging to the world of Babbitt. Indignation hung around Mencken, yet his partner in the *American Mercury*, George Jean Nathan, was not in the least bit indignant and had no intention of ever being so. He wrote characteristically in his twenties mood, "If all the Armenians were to be killed tomorrow and if half of Russia were to starve to death the day after, it would not matter to me in the least. What concerns me alone is myself, and the interests of a few close friends. For all I care, the rest of the world may go to hell at today's sunset."[26]

XII

HIGH TWENTIES

THE YEARS 1926, 1927, 1928, AND 1929 until October might be labeled the high twenties or the golden twenties. It was a time of benign self-satisfaction. Things happened in foreign countries, far away, to threaten the equanimity of this state of mind, but such pricks were only flea bites upon the skin of a dog-happy, ignorant, generous, self-regarding society that could not imagine that it was dreaming in the sun of only temporary good times.

In these years Józef Pilsudski in Poland grasped power. Pilsudski was only a name and Poland was far away. In Italy, Mussolini finished off his opposition, sometimes by the most curious and brutal murders. To Americans Mussolini was only an unusual kind of Italian who made trains run on time and whom the *Saturday Evening Post* bade one admire.[1] In England, national despair and pride united in deadlock in the crisis of the general strike. In Russia, Trotsky lost control of the changing, growing Soviet Government, and a new, unknown man, Stalin, grasped power. Such happenings brushed with only the lightest strokes the preoccupied, dreaming American consciousness.

The public attitude was careless and generous. It thought it had solved political problems and that they did not in any real sense exist. Therefore, it had time to turn away to private affairs. All sorts of personal selfishness could flourish undisturbed. Individuals defined themselves; the national type (if there was such a thing) defined itself. In any case, recognizable American traits crystalized.

A rapt public attention fastened upon the beauty of process in Henry Ford's changeover from Model T to Model A. Nothing ever dramatized the system of factory organization so well as the break in Ford automobile production stretching across a good part of the year 1927. Ford was the epitome of everything in the world of everyday work that the citizens of the twenties admired. His faults were overlooked or accepted as virtues, and his success in this great mechanical and business venture seemed a test of the health of the nation itself. The public found itself absorbed, entertained and delighted by such toys as Model Ts and Model As. If Ford should fail, they all in some measure failed. But anticipation was joyous. Even the suspense was delicious, and it would be a misunderstanding to think that it was all a matter of sober self-interest, that this man would again bring out the car that suited at the price that was right. As a matter of fact, Ford had fallen behind, or at least was beginning to slip, as his competition among the other automobile makers became sharper. People had begun to buy slightly more expensive Chevrolets in increasing quantities and small cars to fit a softer style of living with which the better times of the high twenties allowed some people, often for the first time, to indulge in. Ford could no longer count on keeping his first place. Against the advice of men brave enough to give it, Ford had hung on too long to his beloved utilitarian, well-proven Model T.

In a little ceremony on May 26, 1927, Henry and Edsel Ford walked along the line as the 15,000,000th Model T was assembled. They drove it away from the line, and fourteen miles through the rain to a reunion in front of the Dearborn Engineering Laboratory where Henry also drove briefly a surviving example of this first horseless carriage of 1896. The ceremony of the ending of one phase of his industrial life was a pause before a second supreme effort. His men knew the possible consequences of the gamble. No firm plans yet existed for a new model, yet the company could not afford to be out of production for over a year. Ford's dealers had suffered in 1926. Many had gone into bankruptcy. They would now have to wait many months for the new car. Everyone waited.

While there was not a detailed understanding among the public of the problems Ford and his men faced in tearing out all their equipment, in making new tools and creating new routines as well as a new car, there was a general appreciation of the dilemma and the challenge. It was a drama in which the public participated. Allan Nevins has written:

The magnitude of the reorganization which had to be completed within the calendar year (a longer delay would be fatal) was something new in American industry. It was almost as if the Panama Canal had been closed by earthquake in a time of international tension, demanding the swift completion of a Nicaraguan waterway in its stead . . . Rumors and reports about the new model constantly pushed into the headlines.[2]

While the fierce, unrelenting work went on in the Rouge and Highland plants, where engineers worked themselves without mercy or stop, only Henry Ford himself seemed unhurried but, on the contrary, keen, absorbed, slow-moving. Dealers pleaded for details and were refused; newspaper stories speculated; the public waited, adding to the slump in purchases for the year. The first Model A was produced in the factory on October 20, 1927. Rapid production did not come all at once; many difficulties had to be corrected that slowed the assembly line, yet when the car appeared, it caused both sensation and satisfaction; it was clean-lined and convenient—lower and more attractive than the old car, faster, safer, in tune with the time, an excellent product, worth the sweat and talent poured into the process. Crowds poured into the showrooms where it was displayed. Police were needed to control them—as if at some great public event, and so it was.

Work that was often not individually interesting but that might be a part of a long-linked, important process, took most of the foreground of man's life (not woman's, and for that reason she was more detached, more dangerous, less predictable). It was a hard-working civilization that believed in work and had little time in which to give serious attention to anything else. Yet with the regulation of the businessman or the working man in his days and hours (the man regulated alongside his product), he had a larger and larger fringe of time to devote to amusement. It was all right to play in this fringe of life; it was dubious in the extreme to play or to think or to contemplate all the time; the word "playboy" was the derogatory category of those drones who did not march hitched to the daily work schedule. Still, the permitted margin for relaxing must be filled. The American man found more and more time to spend, and made many efforts at amusements that were pointless and trivial. Yet the expenditure of energy in leisure was important. Perhaps the most significant expenditure of energy away from the daily job was in admirations. The American integer (who did not feel himself an integer, and was not one except in his forced meshing with his fellows) needed to admire.

The qualities he admired were often elemental ones that were not allowed to function in his own well-regulated working life. He hardly knew that he was missing them, but when someone outside the kind of life he knew possessed these traits, he poured out to him extravagantly a tribute of limitless adoration. The objects of the average man's adoration were often those who lived to entertain him, less often those who lived beyond the boundaries of everyday life, pushing into unknown territories of technical or scientific or physical exploration.

Athletes often possessed some of these vital qualities. An example was the baseball hero Babe Ruth, who possessed to an extraordinary extent not just a genius for the game, but the quality of gusto. It showed in every gesture as he lived and moved and breathed, always in the merciless glare of public attention. The year 1927 was his greatest year, when he hit sixty home runs, a record number in one season. Ruth played ball with an ease that seemed a sort of magic. His playing, to which the crowd leaned and cheered and moaned in unconscious sympathy, seemed to belong to them too, "as though by having been there when it happened, some of his magic stuck to them."[3]

Although the player's private life was untidy and unregulated, it shared the quality of wholeheartedness that was in his game and added to his attractiveness.

Ruth did not look like a hero: "the big burly man with the ugly face, blob nose, curly black hair, cigar stuck out of the side of his mouth." He did not talk like a hero: "his speech is coarse, salty . . . with 'son of a bitch' used so frequently, genially, and pleasantly that it loses all of its anti-social qualities and becomes merely another word that does not particularly disturb." He did not behave like a hero (particularly in his innocent younger days):

He drank, he smoked, he cursed, he wenched, he indulged himself, he brawled and sulked, and got the swelled head and got over it. . . . All the food he could eat, beer and whiskey, girls with red or black or yellow hair and soft lips, baseball every day, nice warm places to sleep, silk underwear, fine warm clothing, plenty of pals, money in the pants pocket, more where that came from, name and picture in the papers, a big shiny automobile to ride around in—wow![4]

Yet Babe Ruth belonged at the very center of American glory.

Another person who was to be regarded with an even more extravagant worship by the American people was until 1927 an unknown and unregarded citizen. His fame was waiting securely at a point ahead of him. Meanwhile, he was flying straight toward it.

A young air mail pilot of the St. Louis–Chicago route of the new commercial system for the delivery of air mail by contract, he was the chief pilot of the section run by the Robertson Aircraft Corporation of St. Louis. There were only two other pilots. The three shared all the flights, keeping the mail going through bad weather even though often only a few letters were sent. The pilots landed if need be on small emergency fields for which at night they could not afford electric lights. If their home field could get in touch with someone to help, the emergency field might on a bad night be lighted by a row of six kerosene or gasoline lanterns set up on a line of fence posts. In windy weather after such a landing the pilot tied his plane to a fencepost and telephoned the local gas and oil company (from the lonely telephone box set up in the deserted field), which sent out a truck with fuel supplies. The pilot then asked the obliging and usually interested truck driver for a ride to town, carried the mail to the nearest railroad station, and saw it safely on its way. "Slim," as he was called, was a young man neither unaware of his abilities nor particularly forward about them, but all through 1925 and 1926, he used them tightly and rationally to accomplish one purpose: to buy a plane and prepare himself and the plane to fly and win the New York-to-Paris nonstop Orteig flight contest, in which a number of heavily financed and highly publicized aviators were announcing entry from week to week.

He went straight to his destination. No small detail on his way was neglected. He must buy a new coat and hat and suit and gloves to wear for an important visit to an aircraft company. He must make a list of businessmen in St. Louis who might be interested, and he must visit each in turn. He must find out what kind of navigation could be used by one man in a plane and then learn how to use it. He must determine who had the plane or would build and sell one within the possible $10,000 to $15,000 it seemed possible to raise, for by this time his unselfconscious but formidable straightness and purity of purpose had interested some St. Louis bankers and businessmen and they assured him that, with his own savings of $2,000, the sum would be raised.

Several likely opportunities fell through. Then he persuaded the Ryan Company of San Diego to build his plane, having secured the cooperation of the company for which he flew mail— the owner becoming a small but enthusiastic backer, the pilots taking over his flying duties in his absence. In a low-keyed, terribly practical application of energy, he and the designer of the Ryan Company decided that they could sacrifice high stability (one did not need a highly stable plane to fly a long distance, said the experienced pilot) for other qualities: lifting ability, fuel space, strength for takeoffs and landings. He found the kind of charts he needed and assured himself that a simple navigation by dead reckoning and carefully marked charts would be sufficient. He found that a radio weighed too much and so took none. He carried army rations for food for the possible forty hours, the taste of which he tried and did not particularly like. He included a small rubber raft as a minimal defense against drowning; he calculated needs at takeoff, needs at landing, and needs for himself if he should survive a crash in the ocean, and he balanced the three needs against each other. He tested his plane, lightly loaded at first, upon a deserted army base near San Diego, a field covered with loose rocks dangerous to his tires; then he built up fuel load till he was convinced that he could carry enough fuel to fly a few more hours than it seemed likely he would be in the air. He argued and won the argument to put the pilot's cockpit blind behind the extra fuel tank, which blocked out what might have been a front cockpit. He had a preference for that place as a pilot of mail routes, being used to taking his bearings at an angle rather than straight ahead (some of the mail pilots customarily blacked out their windshields to cut down on dangerous light glare on night flights). The back seat would save him from being, as he said, a sandwich between the engine and the gas tank. A crash for a pilot seated that far back from the nose was not so likely to be fatal. He was not heroic. He did not strike poses, he went straight on with his preparations, a modest, thoughtful young businessman planning all the angles of a complicated venture, involving other people whom he used as he used himself. He spared only a few hours—flying at night—to savor what he was trying to do, rating himself as one who might help aviation advance the great general flying business of which he felt himself thoroughly a part as a mail pilot. He was aware that his feat would help aviation but apparently saw not much beyond that, except that he would do something important and then himself be able to go on to other important operations.[5]

The flight that took place on May 20–21, 1926, changed the whole face of aviation, and for the young pilot changed his circumstances beyond anything he could have imagined. The response to his feat and to himself was extravagant and unrestrained.

For the period between May 21, 1926, and the end of 1928, the *Reader's Guide to Periodical Literature* lists the following outpouring of words about the new hero: 7 pieces by Charles A. Lindbergh; 24 poems to him or about him; 91 articles with him as subject. Among the poems were the following titles: "Ave, Lindbergh"; "Ballad of Lucky Lindbergh"; "Flying Fool"; "Lyric Deed"; "Our Boy"; "Skoal! Charles Lindbergh, Skoal!"; "Slim"; "White Bird." Among the articles were those entitled: "American Viking of the Air"; "Columbus of the Air"; "Galahad"; "Lindbergh the Exemplar"; "O Pioneer."

The possible collision between imagination and reality (tragic for Lindbergh, tragic for the American people) was suggested as early as February 1, 1928, by Heywood Broun. In *The Nation* of that date he wrote about the dubious effect upon American diplomacy of sending Lindbergh, the hero, on a circuit tour of

Central America after his triumphant stay in Mexico. Broun wrote:

From Managua he [Lindbergh] wrote for the *Times* and said that he was impressed by the great friendliness which all Nicaraguans expressed for the United States. This was a few days after a bloody skirmish between the marines and Sandino, and only a week or so before Díaz grew irritated at American interference. The largest entertainment given for Lindbergh was a party prepared in his honor by the leader of the reactionary group. Does this mean that Lindbergh is conservative in his politics and that he bestows approval upon everything his country has done in Nicaragua? No, but some people will be certain to impale with significance his lightest word or deed. . . . Lindbergh will have to fight hard to keep from being forced at last into politics.

Too much supermaning can hardly help one.[6]

Gusto, purity of purpose, these floated one hero or another into the special merciless glory of the twenties, a time turned in adoringly and destructively upon itself. The private pursuit of a talent might also seem a glory or a consolation. Such a one was Hart Crane, a writer unequipped for the daily struggle, but knowing himself equipped to make music and sense out of that struggle, and so he launched upon a flight of words. Crane's overweening ambition was to twist and braid together elements in the American life never put together before: history, technical achievement (bridges, skyscrapers, electric welding), and the human longing for meaning, and to fuse all this in one great poem. Drunk, apart, poor, Crane partly achieved his wish. Between 1925 and 1929— all his glory private and concealed from the American moment in which he lived—Hart Crane worked on and completed his partial masterpiece, *The Bridge*. It would be seen then that an American moment had found words:

> Down wall, from girder into street noon leaks,
> A rip-tooth of the sky's acetylene . . .

His symbol of aspiration uniting all the extremes of life was the great Brooklyn Bridge, which in the decade of the twenties withstood much concentrated gazing by painters and writers.

O harp and altar, of the fury fused,
(How could mere toil align thy choiring strings!)
Terrific threshold of the prophet's pledge,
Prayer of pariah, and the lover's cry . . .[7]

So, in character, act, creation, the twenties fulfilled themselves, contradictory in public and private achievements.

Those who did not perform to achieve some sort of glory hungered for news of those who did. Admiration and interest became a lust for sensation. Nothing could have exceeded the concentration upon a kind of village news now accessible through the newspapers and radio to the whole nation. During the Hall-Mills murder trial, eight daily papers rented houses in the town of Somerville, New Jersey. The New York *Daily News* sent sixteen men to cover the story, the *Daily Mirror*, thirteen.[8] The public supped on horrors in other notable murder cases of the decade, the Gray-Snyder case and the Loeb-Leopold case. A lingering accidental death, Floyd Collins', in a cave in Kentucky, carried ordinary interest into morbidity.

Even in the last days before his flight to Paris, the straightforward purpose of the candidate for the Orteig Prize, Charles A. Lindbergh, was disturbed by public attention. Flying out across the Atlantic, away from the heavily breathing crowd that had dogged his heels in New York, he felt free. Years later he looked back to that moment, of leaving behind the mob: "But I've left all that behind, with the mud and the telephone wires. Now the air, the clouds, the sky—these elements are mine." And he recalled his independent-minded father, who had repeated to him a saying of the settlers of the old northwest:

"One boy's a boy. Two boys are half a boy. Three boys are no boy at all." That had to do with hunting, trapping, and scouting in days when Indians were hostile. But how well it applies to modern life, and to this flight I'm making. . . . I haven't had to keep a crew member acquainted with my plans. My movements weren't restricted by someone else's temperament, health, or knowledge. My decisions aren't weighted by responsibility for another's life. . . . I've not been enmeshed in petty quarreling and heavy organizational problems. Now, I can go on or turn back according to the unhampered dictates of my mind and senses. According to the saying of my father's, I'm a full boy—independent—alone.[9]

Two constants in American life were in conflict here. The first might be called the Daniel Boone attitude in Charles Lindbergh and Hart Crane, the desire to step out alone beyond the noise of neighbors, the dogs barking at the next house, the cocks crowing in the near barnyard, to go on ahead. This would be one way. The other and opposite habit might be called the husking-bee habit, the barn-raising or house-raising instinct, when people of a community worked hard together to do quickly a complex thing that had to be done, enjoying the meshing of effort and the accomplishment of many hands and purposes all directed to one end, as in the assembly line, the charity drive, the making of a movie. These opposites would exert conflicting pulls upon many citizens; the conflict was a necessary stretching of a society to fulfillment over a wide range of endeavor.

It was the cooperative instinct, the husking-bee instinct, which worked in the great natural disasters of the period: the Florida hurricane of September, 1926, and the Mississippi flood of the spring of 1927. At a distance, these two natural happenings were spectacles described in the newspapers and on the radio, and so to be enjoyed. People in the devastated areas held a different view. For them, after the water receded, there was a real choice to be made. Could they depend in the future on the brilliant volunteer effort that had been improvised, or should they delegate to the Federal Government the planning of means to counter future emergencies, or to prevent them?

The Florida hurricane that hit the Miami, Fort Lauderdale, Hollywood, and Lake Okeechobee areas in September, 1926, seemed a redundant blow, the last unfair hammering home of bad luck, for 1926 had seen the boom busted that had filled so many with a wild Florida fever. The year before had been the year of frenzy, when speculators in real estate sold $1,000 lots in sand pits or under water to gullible purchasers who had come in their Ford jalopies and trucks to Florida to buy land, resell it, and get rich. "The smell of money in Florida, which attracts men as the smell of blood attracts a wild animal, became ripe and strong last spring [*i.e.*, spring, 1925]."[10] Before the natural storm broke, the human storm of hope had been pricked into flat disappointment and despair. The sand pits remained, the swampy subdivisions, the almost finished giant hotels along deserted waterfronts. "The larger cities," wrote one reporter in July, 1926, "like Tampa and Miami, where but lately the streets were teeming with traffic, forcing the installation of new traffic and parking systems, are now nearly as lifeless as the street on a theater curtain."[11] "Dead subdivisions line the highway, their pompous names half obliterated on crumbling stucco gates. Lonely, white-way lights stand guard over miles of cement sidewalks, where grass and palmetto take the place of homes that were to be."[12] Into this discouraged area, where the boom had been most extravagant, the hurricane hurled itself—unexpected and unexplained. There were no hurricane-hunter planes then, no long-range forecasts of storms, no preparations, no general understanding even that, when the storm came, the dead quiet after the first blow was the eye of the hurricane. The second blow that came at the city from the other side came as if out of pure malice.

Into the muck and debris, valiant amateur relief poured: the Boy Scouts, the Knights of Columbus, and then, more professionally, the Red Cross, in the biggest job it had undertaken since the San Francisco earthquake. The Red Cross counted heads, and in one week, October 2 through 9, gave

Medical aid to	113,200
Food to	6,500
Clothing to	4,650
Materials to repair homes to	3,000
Tents for	1,900

Where a house remained, the family characteristically remained at home, built a cook fire in the front yard, and lived in the open for weeks. Statistics were assembled: 472 killed; 6,381 injured; 21,500 families affected.[13]

The next spring, the spring of 1927, the valley of the Mississippi suffered an even greater and more long-drawn-out disaster. The great rolling spring flood destroyed land, crops, animals, human beings, and all the delicate connections of transportation and communication. During the height of the flood, a reporter, visiting the scene of frantic preparation for breaks in the levee, saw:

Flame on the earth and flame in their faces. Two thousand men at work on the levee. Orders, shouts, curses. Shadows running, torches burning. Activity. Bags being filled with mud, mattresses made of

willows being sunk, stones piled on the mattresses. Powerful black
men, backs bending with rhythmic ease, bearing bags of earth. Piling
the bags and singing as they work.

> Come on sand bag
> Git your place
>   erumphh
> Gotta stop dis ribber
> Flood be comin' soon
>   erumphh[14]

A crevasse, 2,100 feet wide, broke in the levee near Tallulah,
Louisiana. A woman safe in the second floor of a flooded house
looked out to see others less lucky:

. . . not a hundred yards from the break several hundred Negroes and
a few white people, with their accompanying train of dogs, horses,
cattle, and pigs, are camping on the levee, calmly pursuing their daily
lives. They spread their mattresses and scanty covers on the sod,
regardless of sun and rain, place their battered remnants of furniture
about them, build their fires, prepare their meals, feed their stock,
comfort their crying babies, and go their ways with a patient sto-
icism.[15]

The relief of the Mississippi Valley was a notable effort, a
combination of volunteer labor and loosely strung together organizations coordinated by Herbert Hoover, the Secretary of Commerce, whose work in this pressing season of emergency made
him once again the humanitarian hero of the nation, as he had
been in the relief work during and after the war. To the Cajuns of
the backwaters he became a legendary figure: "Hoover had arrived and told them they must leave their homes. Within a few
weeks 'Hoovair' had become a great man to them, a man of fable
and legend, and so they left."[16]

The Governors of the six endangered states asked for Federal cooperation, and suggested that I should be placed in charge of the emergency. President Coolidge complied. I went at once to Memphis and
took hold. . . .
    As at this time we all believed in self-help, I financed the operation
by three actions. We put on a Red Cross drive by radio from the flood
area, and raised $15,000,000. I secured $1,000,000 from the Rockefeller Foundation to finance the after-flood campaign of sanitation to be

matched by equal contributions from the counties. We organized a nonprofit organization through the United States Chamber of Commerce to provide $10,000,000 of loans at low rates, for rehabilitation, every cent of which was paid back. But those were days when citizens expected to take care of one another in time of disaster and it had not occurred to them that the Federal Government should do it.[17]

The relief organizations saved people first, then animals, but could do little for land or crops. The Red Cross fed, sheltered, clothed, and warded off typhoid and smallpox epidemics. The spirit of the effort was remarkable. It was also deceptive for the future. It seemed to prove that this way was the only way to combat large national emergencies. Coolidge forced himself, scandalized, to sign the Flood Control Act of 1928, which put the Mississippi River under broad and federal public control. He had intended that the states "directly benefiting [be] liable for a portion of the cost." Southerners, who had endured the worst of the flood, and progressives saw to it that the Mississippi River Flood Commission was empowered "to acquire for the Government by purchase or condemnation in Federal courts all land needed for floodways, spillways, and levees."[18] The new law overturned the limited policy of "levees only" administered with single-hearted devotion by the Corps of Engineers, but proved ineffective. It opened the door to many dangerous and alluring possibilities, depending upon the attitude of the viewer. The prospect was a delight to such an old progressive as Gifford Pinchot, the Republican Governor of Pennsylvania. He reiterated in 1927 the good doctrine of 1907, recalling a report of the Inland Waterways Commission of that year linking past and future together to enunciate a doctrine that in the 1930s would justify such a development as TVA:

Every river is a unit from its source to its mouth; . . . it must be handled with due regard to every use of the water and benefit to be derived from its control; . . . every good or bad influence on stream flow from the source to the mouth . . . Forests, swamp drainage, soil drainage, levees, and everything . . . must be combatted or made use of in the unending struggle of men to utilize the earth without upsetting the natural balance which alone makes it habitable to man.[19]

On the crest of this modest progressive wave passing over and disappearing under the calm surface of the decade was the enactment at the very end of the year December 21, 1928, after being delayed by a Senate filibuster of the bill to empower the building of a dam on the Colorado River, the Boulder Project Act.

The Flood Control Act and the Boulder Project Act were exceptions. Legislation to empower the Federal Government to conserve human or natural resources seemed to have little chance of passage. Yet the history of the latest defeat of two perennial bills, one to promote public power at Muscle Shoals, one to level up the income of farmers to the national average, was exciting. President Coolidge defeated both bills in 1928 by vetoes.

The latest bill that Senator Norris of Nebraska sponsored' to make national use of the installations already in existence at Muscle Shoals envisioned a government-owned corporation to operate the power plant, surplus power to be sold by the Government, and additional dams to be built. The Senate passed his bill over a filibuster by McKellar and Tyson of Tennessee by a vote of 43 to 34 on May 25, 1928. By the peculiarly frustrating expedient of failing to sign the bill within a requisite ten-day period, President Coolidge vetoed it.

The latest version of the McNary-Haugen Bill had strong Congressional support. The Senate passed it by 53 to 23, the House by 204 to 121. President Coolidge vetoed it after waiting a week and spoke in unusually strong language of his detestation of this effort at government support of farm prices. Under the terms of this legislation, the Federal Government would have purchased agricultural surpluses at home and marketed them abroad, protecting and raising farm incomes at home. Coolidge labeled the measure "bureaucracy gone mad."[20] The Senate voted to override the President's veto. The roll call was 50 to 31, failing to attain the necessary two-thirds majority.

Controlled and supported farm prices and cheap electrical power remained a dream. The condition of the farmer remained much the same. He continued typically to live at the end of a gumbo or red-clay road, which became a morass between highway and house much of the winter. His farmhouse was lighted for the most part by kerosene lamps. His children went to one-room schoolhouses. His wife bought her dress lengths off the shelves of archaic country stores. Yet this was a decade of slow improvement in the production of crops. Fewer acres were farmed, but better crops were gathered off the smaller number of acres. The farmer had not yet the political weight to make this fact count. His life was stagnant.

The life of the coal miner was worse. Very few people in the pleasant twenties who did not live in the coal-mining areas noticed the fact. Coal-mine poverty was taken for granted. Southern miners had always been hungry, poorly paid, and sparely employed, but other miners, those of Pennsylvania, Ohio, Indiana, and Illinois, for a number of decades before the war had slowly pulled up to what seemed a dependable kind of living. Collective bargaining had come to be accepted by the operators of these Northern areas. Wages were relatively high in relation to the wild and untutored coal fields of West Virginia: $7.50 per day compared to $3.00 and $4.00 per day. But in the years during and after the war, owing to the pressure of demand, Southern mining had expanded without improving the conditions of its workers except in the fact that there was more employment. Drastic competition faced the relatively stable, relatively prosperous Northern miners.

Comparative figures, as between 1913 and 1925, show the change:

Coal produced by the Pittsburgh district
1913   71 million tons
1925   48 million tons

Coal produced by the Kentucky and West Virginia district
1913   90 million tons
1925   177 million tons

From the point of view of the Northern miners, the Southern miners produced too much coal too cheaply earned. From the point of view of the consumers north and south, too much coal altogether was produced.

To compete with the voracious Southern operators, the Northern operators now began to reduce the number of days of work offered during the year, or here and there began to reduce the actual wages paid per hour or per day, in spite of previous agreements arrived at in collective bargaining. The operators were losing money because of less and less demand for their soft coal. The Northern miners found themselves cushioning the loss for the owners by working fewer days and taking home fewer dollars.

There was a slight pause in the drop in wages in the North at the time of the 1924 presidential election. It was believed that too much labor unrest would hurt the Republican cause. In 1923 and early 1924 the party victory looked doubtful. Political pressures therefore caused the operators to agree to a certain leveling off and shoring up of wages, below which there was to be no more falling off. This "Jacksonville agreement" was to remain in effect until April 1, 1927.

The Jacksonville scale netted the average miner between $1,200 and $1,500. Out of this amount, an average of $10 a month was paid as rent for the usual four- or five-room house. Two out of one hundred of these houses have bath-tubs, thirteen out of a hundred have running water. The savings through inferior housing standards are largely taken up in higher food costs. The 1922 Coal Commission estimated that an expenditure for food of $800 a year was necessary to provide a healthful living for an average miner's family.[21]

From this ebbed standard in 1927 the general condition sank lower. Families previously assured of $1,200, now received $600 to $750 a year. Miners were laid off, hours and wages reduced, operations curtailed, and the so-called Jacksonville agreement was more and more departed from than held to. Whole towns were hungry. Groups like the Quakers went into these communities to help. Even the National Guard was used in Ohio to open soup kitchens. Squalor unimaginable to the cushioned middle-class American existed. Congressman Fiorello H. La Guardia wrote in a national magazine on April 4, 1928: "The present coal strike is a battle of statistics against human life. It is a test between the theories of a new school of coal economics and every-day living conditions of men and women." He spoke out in the same article against the incidental, but bitterly resented, system of privately owned and operated police forces (the coal operator policing the coal miner): "It becomes necessary for the federal government to intervene and put a permanent stop to these outrageous conditions."[22] His article was entitled "The Government Must Act," but the Federal Government did not act, and for the most part people did not see the necessity.

Such men as La Guardia and Norris were speaking a new language waiting to be translated to find acceptance, not acceptable in 1927 and 1928. La Guardia, a man of infinite gusto and humor and bounce, was aware that he worked for a future day, and he was not in the least downcast by the fact. "He persists in introducing bills that cannot pass for ten years," wrote one interviewer, for La Guardia fascinated; he was beginning to be noticed in the national magazines. " 'They serve educational purposes,' he says, puffing at his two-and-a-half-cent Manila cigar."[23]

The general public did not pay much attention to warnings from such men as La Guardia. It was able to ignore the plight of farmers and miners. Such matters were taken as exceptions, not indications of future trouble for all. Many events seemed marching to conclusions of which the decade might be proud. Disasters such as a hurricane in Florida or a flood along the Mississippi were alleviated by a devoted, intense, volunteer aid. This seemed to show that even the forces of nature might be coped with. The passage of the Flood Control Act was only extra insurance. The frame of government itself in its relations with citizens, in its most intimate relation—the collection of taxes—was adjusted to the private energies of business.

Mellon's tax cuts, a collection of new laws that President Coolidge signed in February, 1926, were understood to benefit the average citizen eventually by benefiting immediately the rich citizen. The wealthy man was to provide a requisite prosperity with his freedom from the tax levy and from other regulations. Business, which was what nearly everybody was engaged in, was most particularly itself when it had its being in large enterprises, and such large enterprises were by 1926 less fettered than they had been for many decades. Those left out of the general nimbus of prosperity that shone around so many great and little heads were looked upon as exceptions who would catch up soon or perhaps deserved to be left out. The public conscience was not bothered.

This was the scene on the glowing surface. This was the general thoughtless concensus, yet below that surface there had gathered much pertinent opposition, some of it already forceful and pointed. There was by this time a sufficient body of support in Congress to overturn the Mellon program of the Harding-Coolidge Republican regime and start a movement in the opposite direction entirely—if these legislators had had in the executive branch someone to agree with them. It wanted only executive leadership; the "new deal" of the next decade was already present in latent form, awaiting only the leadership of a Franklin D. Roosevelt to flower into TVA, banking laws, labor legislation, and the whole paraphernalia of the decade of the thirties.

In disregard of real change beneath the surface, with a kind of esthetic and stubborn purity, the form of the decade hardened more and more into the likeness of itself. Typical settlements of the twenties were reached in the Kellogg-Briand Pact and in the final disposal of the Sacco-Vanzetti case. Solutions at home and abroad reflected the same national temper.

In June, 1927, a writer for a sympathetic magazine went to the Dedham, Massachusetts, jail to pay a visit to Sacco and Vanzetti, who had been in prison since 1920 under sentence of death:

From the cell block they appear, these two most famous prisoners in all the world, walking briskly, side by side. No bars are interposed between them and their visitors; we are introduced, shake hands, sit down on a bench and some chairs, like so many delegates to a convention, meeting for the first time in a hotel lobby. They are in prison garb like the others, they look well, seem in good spirits. Both are of average height, both black-headed, both somewhat bald in front, a baldness which somehow gives them a mild domestic air. Vanzetti wears a big, bristling Italian moustache, Sacco is clean shaven and his hair is clipped rather close on his round Southern skull. Vanzetti is expansive, a glowing friendly temperament, with bright eyes, an expressive face; Sacco is intelligent too, but less emotional.[24]

Earlier in the years, the two men had been somewhat less leniently treated, but as they had become famous, they had received better physical treatment. They had had periods of emotional despair; Vanzetti had seemed at one time on the edge of a crackup; now that the end was near, a kind of tranquillity seemed to have come over them. The year 1927, the last year, was a year of agitation, but nothing in the disposition of their case changed in spite of tentative motions toward review and appeal; for, as in

13. Charles A. Lindbergh standing in front of his plane, the *Spirit of St. Louis:* behind him obscurity; before him fame. Whether hurtful to him or not, his fame was necessary to the twenties.

14. Governor Al Smith of New York. The right man in the wrong time, Smith fought an honorable fight for the presidency in 1928 but was unable to disturb the sense of well being that caused the voter to choose Herbert Hoover.

the Dreyfus affair in France a generation earlier, in disregard of finding truth, opinion divided upon class lines or rather upon a division into "liberal" and "conservative" opinion. Leniency, or commutation of sentence in the face of continuing doubt if not proof of the men's innocence became less and less possible.

On June 22, Bruce Bliven, the journalist, could walk out of Dedham jail into a beautiful day and be free to drive away. Sacco and Vanzetti could not. On August 10, Justice Holmes of the Supreme Court turned down one appeal, and then a second, the first for a writ of habeas corpus, the second for a stay. On August 23, the two men were executed, seven years after arrest, trial and original conviction.

The Sacco and Vanzetti case beginning in 1920 and finished officially by the execution of the two men on August 23, 1927, seared the decade with an intensity of feeling that the world of the flapper and of George Babbitt would have tried to deny or to ignore. One half of the feeling was an illogical hate and fear. The opposing half of this feeling was love or radical sympathy (or sometimes hysterical excitement or cold-blooded exploitation of these qualities) goaded into action—parades, letter-writing, red-hot journalism, fund-raising, committee organization. In the smoothing-out of the level of society after 1922, both qualities of intensity seemed out of keeping, but they held their consistency narrowly but potently across the years. The case became an anomaly in a society devoted to tolerant good times, or at least the middling good life. It was a channel of feeling through which sluiced the passions of the Wilson era, cutting a way straight through to the Franklin D. Roosevelt era. It united one to the other through the twenties.

The decade perfected its form in foreign relations by continuing to be its intensely isolated self. Even an agreement to a pact signed in concert with many other European nations in 1927, a pact entered into with great enthusiasm, was another and triumphant manifestation of isolationism. For in this pact, the Kellogg-Briand Pact, the United States seemed at last to be attaining what it had wished since the war, namely, concord with other nations without any clogging penalties or conditions. The Kellogg-Briand Pact was pure euphoria.

The French Government, through Aristide Briand, its Foreign

Minister, proposed to the United States a pact renouncing re-course to war, in itself an innocuous, harmless proposal. Secretary of State Kellogg suggested expanding it. During 1927 and 1928 Kellogg worked happily, securing signatures to the agreement by all the principal nations with which the United States had diplo-matic relations. On August 27, 1928, when the pact was signed in Paris, he had negotiated agreement with fifteen nations: among them, France, Germany, Italy, Great Britain, Belgium, Japan, Poland, and Czechoslovakia. In signing this treaty, everyone seemed to gain something for nothing. It was painless, toothless, and gutless. But, in the mild glitter of unreality of 1928, it seemed a splendid culmination. Article I "renounced war 'as an instru-ment of national policy.'" Article II "agreed to settle disputes among them only by pacific means."[25] Internal and external trouble securely and finally scotched, the decade sailed into its final phase.

XIII

THE ELECTION
OF HOOVER

THE LIFE OF THE TWENTIES multiplied and thickened. Many lives, many careers, many ways flourished, often knowing nothing about each other. The United States was a country of conflicting and scattered energies and interests, yet all of them were wrapped in the one cocoon of safety from outside invasion or interior defeat.

On August 2, 1927, in the Black Hills, President Coolidge stated precisely and deliberately that he did not choose to run for reelection. This was a repudiation of his expected course of action, since he had been elected in his own right to the presidency but once.

During the year of Coolidge's decision, Al Jolson sang from a screen for the first time and caught the childlike imagination of a whole people. A lonely painter went again and again to the Maine coast and painted yet another picture of what the sea and coast meant to him; John Marin painted in 1927 "Boat and Sea—Deer Isle." In England, a momentous transfer of allegiance took place; the American poet T. S. Eliot became a British citizen. Sinclair Lewis continued to add to his row of novel-portraits of his own land; 1927 was the year of *Elmer Gantry*. Don Marquis wrote some enduring and wise nonsense in *Archy and Mehitabel.* The great, undefined center of America became a little less vague in such books as Sandburg's *American Songbag* and Glenway Wescott's *The Grandmothers.* Ernest Hemingway defined the experiences and attitudes of the special generation of the twenties in *Men Without Women.*

During 1927 the Holland Tunnel between New York and New Jersey was completed, and a preliminary traffic jam accumulated. People were riding in automobiles that were duplications in the millions of a few models. Books were duplicated, too, so that millions could read the same much-discussed book at the same time. The Book-of-the-Month Club was founded in 1926; the Literary Guild, in 1927. Best-seller lists ensured that in 1927 a surfeit of readers read Ludwig's *Napoleon,* T. E. Lawrence's *Revolt in the Desert,* Lindbergh's *We,* Halliburton's *Royal Road to Romance,* Katherine Mayo's *Mother India,* and in 1928, Maurois' *Disraeli,* Wilder's *The Bridge of San Luis Rey,* Byrd's *Skyward.* Not so widely read, but important to 1928, were Yeats' *The Tower* and Pound's *Cantos XVII–XXVII.*

It was an age of gross products, infinitely multiplied, publicly acclaimed, and at the same time of private products carefully crafted and fastidiously discerned by a disdainful minority. The tone of the time lived upon the syncopation of taste. It was the time of the building of gigantic motion-picture palaces with a proliferation of uniformed ushers and usherettes drilled to perform with military smartness, of great pipe organs raised upward from basement levels, of cloud-draped ceilings twinkling with electric stars, of patient multitudes waiting in line to see the star of the year or of the week at Roxy's or the Paramount or the Capitol. Yet the same generation bred dilettantes.

Donald Friede described the typical kind of young, self-conscious, and rather ignorant esthete he and his friends had been: "The basic principle on which we operated, whether we knew it or not, was that if our parents liked anything it could not possibly be good. And, conversely, if they were baffled, angered, or merely bored, then it must be good, and in direct ratio to their unfavorable reactions."[1]

There was superficiality in both the moviegoer and the member of the insistent avant-garde. Yet, in the time of Herbert Hoover and Al Smith's rivalry for the presidency of the United States, the culture thickened. It became rich and idiosyncratic. Peculiarities, differences, small and large accomplishments flourished. For one thing, the regions of the country became visible to each other.

Nineteenth-century literary orthodoxy lost its platitudinous certainty in the rediscovery of Emily Dickinson, Herman Melville, and Henry Thoreau. It semed now, to memory, a landscape of lost and lonely searchers. *The Heart of Thoreau's Journals*, edited by Odell Shepard, was published in 1927. The *American Mercury*, in December, 1928, published Lewis Mumford's article "The Writing of *Moby Dick.*" Melville suddenly seemed a contemporary. More and more of Emily Dickinson appeared and seemed close kin to modern times; in 1929 *Further Poems* was published. What had come to seem authoritative, the New England of Longfellow, Whittier, and Emerson, lost its assurance. In its place was discovered a protesting and odd and individual New England suitable to the dissident, nervous, individual mood of the time.

New England was seen in a new light; the South, also. Out of the South came a new sports hero in Bobby Jones, who won all the golf prizes. Out of the South came also the early novels of William Faulkner. Both *Sartoris* and *The Sound and the Fury* were published in 1929. Out of the mountain South came Thomas Wolfe's *Look Homeward, Angel* (1929). A portion of *The Mind of the South* by W. J. Cash appeared in the *American Mercury* in October, 1929. A new kind of complex American arrived in these books, one who had not been present before. The publication of books by Faulkner, Wolfe, and Cash (although not widely read at first) began to make evident to the rest of the country that the South was not simply a place where things happened or failed to happen, but a territory of the spirit, a rich and terrible foreign land within the continental borders; not George Babbitt's mainland at all, but an area of personal relations, exacerbated and decaying tradition, echoes of greatness, great gulfs of decay, manners, obsessions, and the gift of talk. A new perception grew: that wickedness could be interesting and even entertaining; that perhaps the simple straight version of American progress did not contain all answers, or questions; and that the South's enrichment of human possibilities made America more whole and more

human. Defeat and poverty added a dimension—at least to the
stories that might be told. From a region that had suffered evil
and done evil as well as good, the idea of tragedy crept into
American consciousness.

The upper Midwest, too, became more individual and interesting in Glenway Wescott's stories and first novel: *The Grandmothers* (1927) and *Goodbye, Wisconsin* (1928). Wescott's was
the same geographical territory as in Lewis' novels, but it seemed
inhabited by a different people. The frontier of the time just past
and the human frontier of the present moment in Wescott lost its
raucous satirical edge and became individual, odd, lonely, and
lost. Yet at the same time, Lewis continued from year to year to
assemble cutouts from the same area, books of assured, hard,
bright, sharp outlines, containing recognizable types, giving
names to people, places and states of mind that everyone recognized and adopted: *Elmer Gantry* (1927), *The Man Who Knew
Coolidge* (1928), *Dodsworth* (1929).

The life of the nervous cities found new expression, too, to add
to the solid pictures of Theodore Dreiser. A new kind of fiction
caught the tempo of an underworld that seemed to stretch from
low to high. One of the first of a new type to which the author
and other writers would add titles was Dashiell Hammett's *The
Dain Curse* (1929).

Some people lived not in the region nor in the city but in the
generation as if it were their geography. Their place was defined
by the shapes of new buildings, the pace of sidewalks, the tempo
of jazz and atonal explorations in sound, and most particularly by
the words of certain writers who told them implicitly in stories
and novels how to think and feel. In 1929, Ernest Hemingway
continued to form attitudes; it was the year of *A Farewell to
Arms.* "Grace under pressure" was to be Hemingway's compressed definition of the correct response to life. The "generation"
adopted it. Pressure and cutoff boundaries were assumed by
many who were, however, often pampered by the age in opportunities. Grace was assumed to be an approximation to the vital
wit the novelist's characters assumed, even his boxers and bull-
fighters, in the face of the pressures of organized life or the
assured presence of death.

Another group of Americans lived not in geography nor in the
generation, but were confined by race. For them, or for a small

portion of them, the time of the late twenties was an important crystalization—a stage that lasted but a moment in the succession of decades of Negro history, but a curious and important moment. Suddenly it was a time when certain Negroes were cherished; it was a time when Harlem, the city of the Negro within New York City, bloomed. The prospering of a few careers, the short good time of one urban center—that was all, but it seemed much at the time. It deceived the easily deceived American with hope, and it covered up much unmoved hopelessness below.

Harlem had a short glory in the last years of the twenties.[2] It was clean, it was prosperous, it was law-abiding; these things were true in a relative sense with contradictions around each corner. It was also a unique Negro city, a center of hopeful business enterprise and of remarkably effervescent entertainments. Harlem was shown off, visited, advertised, taken as an example of American democratic success. It became the spoiled darling of dilettantes from downtown who demanded "primitive" dancing and singing. Its jazz bands and its speakeasies became so successful that the patronage of its prosperous "clubs" was nearly altogether a well-heeled white one.

Langston Hughes wrote a wistful "Harlem Night Song" celebrating the place:

> Across
> The Harlem roof-tops
> Moon is shining.
> Night-sky is blue.
> Stars are great drops
> Of golden dew.
> In the cabaret
> The jazz-band's playing . . .

And more familiarly:

> "Me an' ma baby's
> Got two mo' ways,
> Two mo' ways to do de Charleston!
> Da, da,
> Da, da, da!
> Two mo' ways to do de Charleston!"[3]

The time of the self-consciously high-minded taking up of the Negroes by highbrows was also the time of *Saturday Evening Post* stories of Negro life by Octavus Roy Cohen. The stories took it for granted that the ways of Negroes were mildly and necessarily amusing to middle-class white folks. On the other hand, authentic honesty in Negro writers was not welcomed by the newly "nice" middle-class Negroes. They resented Langston Hughes' presentation of the poverty, illiteracy, dirt, and primitive folk attitudes of the Negroes in Harlem. Carl Van Vechten, who was not a Negro, suffered similarly from a fierce Negro reaction against his novel *Nigger Heaven*. Van Vechten was one of the twenties' lordly and aristocratic champions of the mingling of the talents of all races. His parties, famous in his time as a sort of continuing, shifting "salon," integrated all the races in a harmony of gifts. In his work as critic, he leaned toward advocacy of Negro artists. But Harlem had suffered so in climbing a few inches upward that it did not want the route viewed honestly. It wanted to be like its white neighbors, not distinctive.

Harlem was remarkable at this time in that it had achieved for the moment stability, respectability, even grace. Earlier, it had had a history of sliding downward, when the Negroes first moved into what had been a white area of the city; but hoisting itself upward, by 1925 and 1926, Harlem had reached an apparently permanent standard of healthiness and prosperity. No hint of a future slide downward into poverty, disease, dirt, dope, could be imagined in the mid-twenties. Harlem was as blind as the rest of America—doubly blind, for it was in a spiritual straitjacket already, that of artificial separateness, whose hurt would show in the future.

Harlem, the city within the city, in the high twenties seemed to presage success for an entire race moving upward. Individual Negroes had grasped success already: Roland Hayes and Paul Robeson on the concert stage, Florence Mills in nightclubs abroad, Ethel Waters on Broadway at home, James Weldon Johnson, Langston Hughes and Countee Cullen in verse, W. E. B. DuBois in serious prose. Expectation of a transformation of the life of the Negro was extravagant. A special issue of the magazine *Survey* on March 1, 1925, hailed Negro achievement, as embodied in the life of Harlem:

If we were to offer a symbol of what Harlem has come to mean in the short span of twenty years it would be another statue of liberty on the landward side of New York. It stands for a folk-movement which in human significance can be compared only with the pushing back of the western frontier in the first half of the last century, or the waves of immigration which have swept in from overseas in the last half. . . . Harlem represents the Negro's latest thrust towards Democracy.[4]

Harlem's prosperity was so little and so thin. It was a bright, quickening, vivid surface seen as much more than it was, particularly by the sympathetic white observer who did not in his own bones and flesh, like the Negro, feel the lash of prejudice. The twenties, outside of a few favored and special localities, was a time of rigor in the application of the laws of segregation. It was in fact a time of new detailed lawmaking in segregation.

In Virginia a new bill was passed by the House of Delegates "forbidding the sitting together in any gathering within the State of Virginia of white and black people."[5] The cause: whites in the neighborhood of Hampton Institute had attended programs at the school. Even when the Supreme Court ruled in an isolated instance against a Southern state law enforcing segregation, the outcome was not to be a general or extended one. *Outlook,* in the issue of March 30, 1927, reported that the Supreme Court had declared invalid a Louisiana law that "undertook to prohibit a white man from establishing a residence in a preponderantly Negro neighborhood unless he should first secure the consent in writing of a majority of the opposite race. The same prohibition applied to a Negro who might wish to establish residence in a white neighborhood."[6] The conclusion to which *Outlook,* a national magazine, came was characteristic of the halfway reach of change in race relations in the period:

Segregation of the races by law must, it appears, be abandoned. It should be. It does not follow that segregation of the races must be abandoned or that it should be. In some places both races benefit by living separately. In many places the better elements of both races thoroughly recognize the fact. But it is a social rather than a political problem, and is to be solved by other than statutory means.[7]

No mass movement but one concerned itself with the Negro's situation and it was as much a product of ignorance and gullibility as of idealistic yearning. It was the creation of Marcus Garvey, a penniless Jamaican who came to New York unknown during the war years. An observer in 1927 looked back on his amazing ten-year career:

This black John the Baptist with amazing audacity proclaimed the kingdom of Africa was at hand. The negro race throughout the world was called upon to repent or to change its mind, preparatory to the new order of things now about to be set up, which would solve forever the hitherto insoluble problems involved in negro blood. The federation of the black members of the human family into a world empire under self-dominion was a bold dream which no mortal had ever dared dream before.[8]

In the meantime upon the solid ground of Harlem he founded a Universal Negro Improvement Association and the *Negro Journal*. He built a hall, "Liberty Hut," which would hold 6,000 people. He organized grocery stores, laundries, and a steamship line, the Black Star Line. He held meetings and street parades. He polarized the loyalties of frustrated human beings who hardly asked what his aims were, so keenly and surely did his words touch their hurts. It was indifferent to him that educated Negroes scorned him. He deified blackness in counterpart to the worship of whiteness that surrounded the Negro in America. Then suddenly Marcus Garvey dropped out of sight. The Government charged him with violating postal regulations and sent him to the Atlanta penitentiary for five years.

The ache he had assuaged remained. The position of the Negro was not changed fundamentally in law during these years, except that it worsened in the South. Economically he was bettered in only a few places. But after the twenties the Negro could not be what he had been before. Later times would build more solidly upon the gains of the decade, gains made by imperious individual talents. Also, scholarly insights in the work of such men as W. J. Cash and Howard Odum began to make it possible to understand the history and contemporary situation of the Negro in the United States.

The years 1927, 1928, 1929, the ultimate twenties, saw a flowering of literate scholarship. It was a time of a deepening of man's consideration of how man lived, the interest in the Negro and the

South being symptomatic of the trend. At the very same time as the "jazz age" manifested itself, there was taking place a quiet deepening and enriching of the intellectual flavor of American life. The thirties were to owe much to the twenties for preparing for the next decade tools of thought with which to confront the disasters hidden beyond the horizon of 1927. Arthur Holly Compton's work in the physical sciences, for which he received a Nobel Prize in 1927, was related to a somewhat remoter future, but much of the scholarly work of the late twenties was to seem very apt just after the crash. Much of it in words available to the intelligent general reader circled around man's behavior. Margaret Mead's *Coming of Age in Samoa* (1928) was anthropology seeking human likeness and unlikeness in a place a long way off from the United States but bringing back recognitions to that world. Edmund Sapir published his paper "Linguistics" and brought into one focus linguistics proper, anthropology, sociology, and psychology; Ulrich B. Phillips published *Life and Labor in the Old South*, a historian's study of conditioning economic and social facts; Rupert Vance published *Human Factors in Cotton Production;* Howard Odum published *An Introduction to Social Research.* All these were in 1929. Vance and Odum's best work lay just ahead, beyond the jagged break between the decades, but the work of the twenties was laying foundations.

A selection of the earliest Guggenheim fellows chosen (in 1926–27) suggests a multiplying of many kinds of mental activities in the late twenties. Fellows from among a total of only thirty-seven were: Stephen Vincent Benét, Arthur H. Compton, Hallie Flanagan, Marjorie Hope Nicolson, Linus Pauling, Hyder Edward Rollins, Roger Sessions, Norbert Weiner, and Aaron Copland.[9] Two names in music, two in science, one in drama production, one in poetry, two in literary scholarship, one in what was to be called cybernetics: much of the future was here.

In painting, the twenties seemed to compel many American artists to react to and to reflect the common, often dull and vacuous shapes and surfaces of everyday life. Edward Hopper was faithful to reality and infinitely suggestive in overtones of meaning that he saw clinging to old houses, straight streets and railroad tracks, flat bare interiors harshly lighted, and ordinary and casual inhabitants of the scene.[10] The same setting compelled an opposite reaction in Stuart Davis, who used the bright clear colors of the American atmosphere, both those of nature and those of new machine-made things—gas pumps, advertising signs, egg beaters, and other recognizable American angles and curves—to divide the space of his canvas into meaningful yet self-contained abstractions.

Davis understood his sources and his purposes. He went to Paris in May, 1928, for the first time and returned in August, 1929. "Everything about the place [Paris] struck me as being just about right. I had the feeling that this was the best place in the world for an artist to live and work; and at the time it was. The prevalence of the sidewalk cafe was an important factor. It provided easy access to one's friends and gave extra pleasure to long walks through various parts of the city." And he said characteristically and drolly: "It reminded me of Philadelphia."[11] Philadelphia was his place of origin. His father had been art editor of the Philadelphia *Press* and had employed in his art department John Sloan, George Luks, William Glackens, and Everett Shinn. Robert Henri was his father's friend and his own teacher. Past and present and future in American art were present in Stuart Davis' work. After his trip to Paris, he was both affronted and stimulated by his home territory.

I came back to this country in August, 1929 on the maiden voyage of the *Bremen*. On my arrival in New York I was appalled and depressed by its gigantism. Everything in Paris was human size, here everything was inhuman. It was difficult to think of art or oneself as having any significance whatever in the face of this frenetic commercial engine. I thought "Hell, you can't do any painting here." It is partly true. But on the other hand as an American I had the need for the impersonal dynamics of New York City.

He continued in the future, as he looked back a little more objectively, to be articulate about his relationship to his American environment.

They [my pictures] all have their originating impulse in the impact of contemporary American environment. Some of the things that have made me want to paint, outside of other paintings, are: American wood and iron work of the past; Civil War and skyscraper architecture; the brilliant colors on gasoline stations, chain-store fronts, and taxi-cabs; the music of Bach; synthetic chemistry; the poetry of Rimbaud; fast travel by train, auto and aeroplane which has brought new and multiple perspectives; electric signs; the landscape and boats of Gloucester, Massachusetts; 5 and 10 cent store kitchen utensils; movies and radio; Earl Hines' hot piano and Negro jazz music in general, etc. In one way or another, the quality of these things plays a role in determining the character of my painting; not in the sense of prescribing them in graphic images, but by pre-determining an analogous dynamics in the design which becomes a new part of the American environment.[12]

Davis was less easy to understand than his contemporaries who were romantic about the realistic American scene, but he was to wear as well or better. His pictures would hang comfortably side by side twenty years later with the paintings of the "New York School." He reached back to Robert Henri and forward to Jackson Pollock.

It was in this incongruous new America of scholarship and art that the garish, simpleminded political campaign of Herbert Hoover and Al Smith in 1928 was played out. The political life of the nation had deteriorated to a vestigial state. Every other part of its life had become complex and varied. The Government of the great nation, at least in the lesser offices in state, county, and city, was given over to fools, rascals, or good little men of limited imagination. The real interest of the people was turned elsewhere. In business, communicating, transporting, and organizing, in certain kinds of research, in a number of the arts, Americans had a zest for complication, for real questions and real answers. Only in politics they made no effort except sporadically and often in flurries of prejudice, so eventually they did not rule themselves, and the splendid acceleration of effort and enjoyment in which they were wound up slowed down and toppled over.

But a major political campaign stirred up public interest for a few months. On June 12, 1928, the Republican Party opened its national presidential convention in the great Main Street city, Kansas City, and on the first ballot nominated as their candidates for president and vice-president, respectively, Herbert Clark Hoover, Secretary of Commerce under Harding and Coolidge since 1920, and Charles Curtis, Republican Senator from Kansas. The Democratic Party convened in Houston, Texas, on June 26, and on the first ballot nominated Alfred E. Smith, Governor of New York for president, and Senator J. T. Robinson of Arkansas for vice-president. Hoover and Smith represented clear-cut differences, but the campaign as conducted blurred the distinctions.

In general the voter was not ready for a sharp clash of issues. Hoover's political doctrine was orthodox: When business prospered, the rest of the country was assured of prosperity. His statement of these beliefs was lackluster and conventional, but his recent activities during the Mississippi flood lent him an aura of glamor that was foreign to his character but helped his campaign.

Hoover had sat through all the cabinet meetings of Harding from 1920 to 1923 but had never felt compelled to protest any activity of that notorious administration. He had held the same job through the unstirring years of the Coolidge acceptance of the status quo and had never made any attempt to make himself a party center for a more progressive attitude. He had simply run a good Department of Commerce, making it into a bureau to aid business. He was an able man, he was a public-spirited man. He had helped foreign and domestic humanity in trouble. He had been for the end of child labor; for the development of the internal waterways of the states; for the League of Nations, if not vigorously or long; for the World Court, but not to the point of antagonizing anyone about it. Business leaders wanted a sound man, an able man who was neither particularly brilliant nor likely to upset the weekly views aired in such organizations as Chambers of Commerce and Rotary Clubs. The many people who were only middlingly prosperous identified their moderate existences with the more generous ones just above them, and to them Herbert Hoover at this moment seemed their man, larger in fact than he really was.

In the Democratic Party irrelevant issues hurt a man of much more clearly defined ability, a man who had accomplished a great deal, working cleverly in the recalcitrant human material of politics. Alfred E. Smith was a Roman Catholic, he was urban and spoke with a local New York City twang, and he was a "wet." Upon his head, jauntily topped by his famous brown derby, descended the collected prejudices of the decade: the fears loosed by the early Red hunt, by the Scopes trial, by the Ku Klux Klan madness. Middling America too could not find Smith acceptable in his religion, his urban background, or his views on liquor; to them he was not quite "nice." Such half-buried and tortured emotionalism ruined the chances of a qualified man to be president. And yet complacency alone might have had as much to do with his loss as active feeling. The issues in 1928 did not really burn.[13]

As governor of New York State, Alfred E. Smith had concerned himself with three areas of action: "First, the reorganization of the State government; second, the preservation of political, individual, state and legal rights; and third, welfare legislation."[14] Under the goad of the first concern, he had achieved the cutting down of the number of state agencies and a short ballot for elections. Under the second, he had achieved the repeal of a teacher loyalty oath and battled against a state movie-censorship law. He had sponsored, notoriously, the repeal of the state's laws for enforcing the Volstead Act, leaving the federal agents in his state floundering as the sole enforcers of what he thought a foolish law. Under the third of his imperatives, he had extended an existing workmen's compensation act and had tried to have a bill enacted for housing for the poor, wishing to put the state of New York into the revolutionary activity of financing housing for those who could not build otherwise. He was for drastic salary increases for school teachers.

Besides this record of achievement, Smith had another assest. He had a political temperament. He worked well with all kinds of people, including those who differed from him. Hoover, however, was oversensitive to opposition and when faced with it became stiff and obstinate. He had never held an elective office.

Hoover's and Smith's acceptance speeches at their respective Conventions offered a clear-cut choice to the voters. Hoover stood upon the pleasant situation of the average American in the summer of 1928.

But it is not through the recitation of wise policies in government alone that we demonstrate our progress under Republican guidance. To me the test is the security, comfort and opportunity that has been brought to the average American family. . . . The job of every man has been made more secure. Unemployment in the sense of distress is widely disappearing. . . . I especially rejoice in the effect of our increased national efficiency upon the improvement of the American home. That is the sanctuary of our loftiest ideals, the source of the spiritual energy of our people. The bettered home surroundings, the expanded schools and playgrounds, and the enlarged leisure which have come with our economic progress have brought to the average family a fuller life, a wider outlook, a stirred imagination, and a lift in aspiration.[15]

Smith in his acceptance speech rebutted the assurance of well-being.

It [the dominant element in the Republican Party] assumes that a material prosperity, the very existence of which is challenged, is an excuse for political inequality. . . .

The Republican party builds its case upon a myth. When four million men, desirous to work and support their families, are unable to secure employment, there is very little in the picture of prosperity to attract them and the millions dependent upon them. . . .

[About the wet-dry controversy] I personally believe that there should be a change and I shall advise the Congress in accordance with my constitutional duty of whatever changes I deem "necessary and expedient."

Smith opposed interference in the internal affairs of Latin American countries. The immigration law going into effect after a long Congressional delay was wrong: "I am opposed to the principle of restriction based upon the figures of immigration contained in a census thirty-eight years old. I believe this is designed to discriminate against certain nationalities, and is an unwise policy."[16]

In the campaign, Hoover's reputation of respectability and security weighed irresistibly, and about his head played pleasantly the additional glamour of his humanitarian efforts. Hoover, in his shy, sure, undemonstrative presence, straight out of the center of solid worth, seemed the man not to upset things.

He said what people hoped was so: "It is upon a stable economic fabric, upon a solid foundation of orderly, commercial, and industrial sobriety, carefully planned and wrought with forethought for the future, rather than upon any hectic irregularities or momentary booms and slumps that we develop the substantial values of competition and progress."[17]

Smith, however, alleged that the national prosperity was a myth and advanced facts and ideas designed to upset people. He was personally alien to thousands of voters in the South and in the Midwest and Western farm states. His "wetness" was enough to make Carter Glass of Virginia exclaim: "Could Smith be elected? As a Catholic, yes! As a wet, no!"[18] But it was as a Catholic that Smith suffered the most. The attacks upon his religion were not entirely from the ignorant. Charles Marshall, a prominent Episcopal layman and attorney of New York, assailed Smith in an "open letter" in the April, 1927, *Atlantic Monthly*. His thesis strove to prove that Smith as president would be in bondage to the Roman Catholic Church. He carefully avoided any review or discussion of the governor's public career, which had been notable for its defense of personal liberties. A number of churches in the deep rural latitudes of the South displayed photographs of Smith at the dedication of the Holland Tunnel to prove that he had thus prepared his own tunnel to the Vatican, to be used by him as soon as he was elected.

Smith ran the more interesting race. Hoover told people what they wanted to hear. Smith used the radio frequently and marveled that he could address so many people simultaneously. What was remembered was his pronunciation of the word. He pronounced it "rad-dio." He swung west by train, finding the schedule of frequent talks on the observation platform exhausting, but as he went along, drumming up interest. At Omaha he spoke on farm relief. In Oklahoma City he treated the religious question directly. His guards were afraid for his safety. "Without any thought of the consequences I went into it with all the vigor I could command. I referred to the Klan by name, to the Women's Christian Temperance Union . . . [etc.]"[19] Thirty-two years later John F. Kennedy's frontal attack on the same issue would help him. Smith's did not. In Denver he spoke on waterpower development. In Helena he was initiated into the Blackfoot Indian tribe and named Big Chief Leading Star, putting his urban head under a bonnet of feathers. In Louisville, in a hall "protected" by police belonging to the local Republican machine, he spoke on the tariff, and the crowd, not listening, threatened him. Ugly rumor spread the story as he left that Smith was drunk. A troop of newspapermen climbed on the train to see the "wet" in that desirable condition. Smith recalled the futility of the truth, that he had left the hall with his wife upon his arm and had gone straight to the train. The lie followed him.

In Chicago, there was a big reception, and members of the faculty of the University of Chicago presented him with a signed scroll of support. In Boston, he received his biggest ovation of the campaign. "The value of radio for campaigning was further demonstrated in Boston when two halls other than the one where I spoke in person were hooked up on the radio and crowded to the doors."[20] Woodrow Wilson's daughter, Mrs. Francis B. Sayre, presided at Mechanics' Hall, where a group of professors from Harvard presented the candidate with a scroll. It said in part:

In voting for such a man we are glad to express our adherence to the frequently ignored provision of the United States Constitution which made religious tolerance a fundamental part of our government. . . .

Government is something greater than an efficiently administered business corporation with a multitude of inactive shareholders. We support Governor Smith, above all, because of his power to reverse the present trend toward political apathy and arouse in the citizens of the United States an active intelligent interest and participation in the government.[21]

In Newark, Philadelphia, Wilmington, Baltimore, and Brooklyn there were great crowds, but the rest of the country distrusted the support Smith received from the cities of the Northeast and was unmoved by the preference of Chicago and Harvard professors.[22]

In the broader and more open spaces, where tempers were cooler and where, even during a presidential campaign, things went along at a jog on Main Street, it was the familiar reassurance of Herbert Hoover that appealed. Hoover received "a larger popular vote and a larger electoral vote than any president had yet received." The count was:

HOOVER	21,392,190 popular votes	447 electoral votes
SMITH	15,016,443 popular votes	87 electoral votes

Hoover carried all but eight states.

The months between Coolidge's Black Hills statement and Hoover's election were characteristic of the era now fully established. In foreign affairs, the United States played a large role but denied that it was doing so. President Coolidge went to Havana in December, 1927, to open the Sixth Pan American Conference. Flanked by his experts in foreign affairs, Charles Evans Hughes and Dwight Morrow, the President made a speech, "very conciliatory in tone, which made a profound impression."[23] The next spring, in March, 1928, the Government of the United States recognized the new nationalist government of China. In August, 1928, the United States was cosponsor of the Kellogg-Briand Pact.

Thinking that foreign affairs were happily settled, busy multitudes pursued their lives. They lived in a world that was very different from their fathers'. They rode to work and to play in flivvers and Chevvies or in Cadillacs, crossed and recrossed a continent on newly paved national highways, dived under a great river in the new Holland Tunnel, or laboriously pushed their heating cars up a pass over the Rockies. They were in ceaseless motion.

They sent their children in larger and larger numbers to public schools. It ceased to be unusual to be a high-school graduate. Thousands more attended colleges and universities than had done so in earlier decades. It was the time of Joe College and Robert Maynard Hutchins, of young men wearing raccoon coats and carrying banjos and flasks, loading open touring cars with crowds of girl friends whose skirts were short, whose stockings were rolled down, and who were giddy company for the trip to the roadhouse in the next town or the speakeasy in the next block. It was also the time of young men sitting in Harvard classes under Alfred North Whitehead, George Sarton, Arthur Meier Schlesinger, and P. A. Sorokin.

People amused themselves energetically. Thousands saw *Show Boat* on Broadway. Millions saw the first commercial "talking" picture, *The Jazz Singer*. Much of the subtlety of the late silent motion pictures was lost. But the Palace, the Rialto, the Grand of each town across the country attracted larger and larger crowds.

O'Neill's play *Strange Interlude* was published as a book in 1928, as was Allen Tate's book of verse *Mr. Pope and Other Poems*. In the same year, in *Goodbye, Wisconsin*, Glenway Wescott tried to describe his personal Main Street (he called it that, for everyone had adopted Sinclair Lewis' epithet):

Main street down the middle—beef-red brick and faded clapboards; it is lamentably impressive. The new banks, I must admit, are of lighter brick and adorned with brief, reasonably Roman pillars. Dry-goods stores remarkably full of luxury; drug stores which sell everything (at a glance everything seems made of paper), the most expensive cameras and the cheapest books; a windowful of superb apples. Apples are wealth in midwinter; in fact it is all wealth, though it resembles meanest poverty. Branching off Main Street at right angles, up small hills and down gentle slopes, the other streets: short but spacious avenues, noble trees over the snowbanks, lawns under them. Actually it is one lawn, there being no hedges or fences or walls (during the burning summers, no privacy).[24]

A characteristic self-study of the time was Sinclair Lewis' loose episodic story of one citizen's peregrination to the capital city to call upon his president, *The Man Who Knew Coolidge* (1928). It was an elaborate joke. The little man of the story did not really know Coolidge, and he only talked with the secretary in the outer office of the White House, but the story of his going was characteristic of the entire overoptimistic, loquacious, easygoing, mobile, democratic, fraternal, undiscriminating, admiring, likable middle range of the population. Thus, Lewis himself, from 1920 to 1928, had moved from savage satire to a kinder type of fun. He saw the comparative innocence of his readers and conveyed the quality in such descriptions as the stopover of the man who knew Coolidge in a "tourist auto-camp," dirty, tacky, ill equipped, while the traveler made his way toward his capital city and the President, whom he pretended even to himself to know.

More despairing of Main Street and more mystical about its meaning, Paul Rosenfeld wrote in 1928: "Immanent nothing opened directly from the main streets of the towns with their linings of Fords. Roads led blankly north and south toward horizons that secreted no otherwheres beneath their rims and only the unchanging fecund present. Yearning could not breathe, was ridiculous, in this dry ocean."[25]

D. H. Lawrence wondered before he came (though he came, and stayed several years):

> Oh, America
> The sun sets in you.

Are you the grave of our day?
Shall I come to you, the open tomb of my race?

. . .

I confess I am afraid of you.
The catastrophe of your exaggerate love . . .[26]

Another visitor busily and rationally analyzed: "Here [in Detroit, the visitor's favorite city] as often in America, I get the feeling of having been admitted to the private view of a great Exhibition some weeks before its opening. There is the same litter and confusion, the same bustle and hurry, the same visible and intelligent design, if one takes the trouble to look for it."[27]

Yet a tiny crack of apprehension slivered through the wall of surety that buttressed every activity. Stuart Chase reported the findings of *Middletown* and Wesley Mitchell's *Recent Economic Changes in the United States* and asked the unforgivable question: *Prosperity, Fact or Myth?* He likened prosperity to the core of an onion and showed how many outer coverings had to be peeled off to reach that core. The core was there, but it was smaller than people believed.[28] In another perspective, Walter Lippmann, in *A Preface to Morals*, described how a new time was creating a new morality. That he even thought in terms of morality, or used the word, was a sign of the end of the era. In *The Modern Temper* Joseph Wood Krutch seemed consciously to describe the end of a time: "Ours is a lost cause and there is no place for us in the natural universe, but we are not, for all that, sorry to be human. We should rather die as men than live as animals."[29] The happy animals, the Babbitts and the Bohemians in their various habits did not really believe that change was imminent. After all, change was only the progression from Harding to Coolidge to Hoover. More of the same was to come, only it would be better. The date of publication of the three books was 1929.

XIV

THE CRASH

Everything was happily set, everything was secure. Nothing could happen, except a crazy sailing upward of the price of stocks upon the New York Stock Exchange. People who had never put any money into stocks were aware of the way the market soared and took the breath and sense away from many citizens.

Early in 1928, the nature of the boom changed [the boom that dated from 1922]. The mass escape into make-believe, so much a part of the true speculative orgy, started in earnest. . . . While the winter months of 1928 were rather quiet, thereafter the market began to rise, not by slow, steady steps, but by great vaulting leaps. [In 1929 there was a February drop and a March drop, but] . . . after June 1 all hesitation disappeared. Never before or since have so many become so wondrously, so effortlessly and so quickly rich.[1]

Talk about the stock market was widespread. It seemed to many that if they did not know what margin was, or investment trusts, or brokers' loans, or a bull market, their neighbors or friends did, and they were engaged in an exciting, profitable, and mysterious kind of transaction from which it was dull and stupid to be excluded. Sober, after-the-fact analysis shows that not a great proportion of the total population played the market.

The member firms of twenty-nine exchanges in that year [1929] reported themselves as having accounts with a total of 1,548,707 customers. Of these, 1,371,920 were customers of member firms of the New York Stock Exchange. Thus only one and a half million people, out of a population of approximately 120 million and of between 29 and 30 million families, had an active association of any sort with the stock market. And not all of these were speculators.[2]

Probably only 600,000 engaged in margin trading. Yet the infection of the interest was what tinged the tone of the time, not the cold truth of the small number, a situation bearing comparison with the slaveowning of the old South when few were slaveholders but when many shared the psychological attitude of slaveholders. There was a craziness in the air in 1929 in which many more took part than those pouring their money into stocks.

In any case, politics was a conventional necessity in contrast to the entrancing urgencies of making a living or getting rich. A new president was in office and he was expected to make everything right that was possibly wrong. It looked at first as if he were going to do just that. The assumption was that Herbert Hoover was a kind of social engineer, that society was a well-oiled machine, and that any minor repair work required could be performed by him. He was going to make right the enforcement of law and order, which admittedly had suffered in the disorganization brought on by the illegal liquor trade under prohibition; he was going to set right foreign relations, which meant getting the debt-reparations cycle revolving smoothly; he was going to protect American business from foreign business—forced rather urgently into an endorsement of higher tariffs by an eager party of which he was the most popular and publicly approved member and who could, therefore, make the entire country accept this change of direction; he was going to do something for the farmers, but this was to be safely hortatory and advisory, not the "state socialism" that he had deplored during the long length of his recent campaign.

The extravagant expectations surrounding Hoover's early months in office coincided with a season of easy money—at least for a few. It was, during the length of the President's first year in office, until October, 1929, a time of warm, exciting enthusiasm and illusion, a climax to the less hectic but pervasive mood of soft self-congratulation in which many people had lived since 1922. The mood seemed national and unanimous, but it was not. Some intellectuals and artists as well as some political rebels did not believe in the beneficence and goodness of the time. On February 9, 1929, Robert Frost wrote in a characteristic letter to a friend: "Henry Ford says he will save the world by putting it to work for him. What's to forbid my saving it by putting it to work for me. My god I hate to have to listen to Cal and Henry laying it down to us spiritual and aesthetic."[3]

Social workers knew the difference. The poor knew the difference, but if they talked, they were not listened to. Two case workers in settlement houses in Philadelphia and New York City knew the difference and wrote soberly in April, 1929, about the trouble down below:

We like to feel that no neighbor knocks in vain at the settlement door, but these days when Mrs. McNary comes saying, "Could you find me office work? My husband's been laid off three months now," we feel almost as helpless as Mrs. McNary. These knockings reach a crescendo in panic years, but last winter and this winter, years of apparent prosperity, they have been insistent—and the responses we make to them have raised questions that are still unanswered.[4]

September 3, 1929, was the last consistently good day on the New York Stock Exchange. It might be ticketed as the last day when there was an excuse for optimism. Thereafter stocks wavered. "Black Thursday," October 24, was the beginning of a series of spectacular drops in stock prices, of the wiping out of ignorant and knowledgeable investors together, of the suicide of a few (not of many, as it seemed, says J. K. Galbraith, the historian of the crash). Looking back it is curious that not many people recognized that an end had come. The magazines of the nation, of whatever political persuasion, failed to face up to the importance of the crash. It is interesting to turn the pages of October, November, December, 1929, and see how the end of an era was greeted.

The end was not greeted at all in the *Saturday Evening Post*. There was not the echo of a tremor in that magazine in the issues of October 26, November 2, November 9, November 16. On November 23 there was a singularly inappropriate story about "Business Cycles" saying in part: "The relative stability of business in the past few years has encouraged optimists to hope, and even to assert, that the business cycle has been ironed out." Only in one article on November 30 was there a veiled reference to the crash. The article, entitled "Financial Leadership," stated that affairs had been taken over by good conservative leaders and were, therefore, in good hands. A reader, then or today, would never know from the article that anything important had happened. Reassurance came on December 7, in a piece called "Economic Soundness."

The fallacy of identifying prosperity and welfare too closely with the movements of the stock market has been demonstrated more than once.

. . .

The country enjoys a good banking system, and a powerful and liquid supersystem in the Federal Reserve. The people are richer as a whole than ever before. The overwhelming majority can look with equanimity upon convulsions in the market.

The *Literary Digest* completely ignored the crash in its issue of November 2. On November 9 it carried an article, "Wall Street's 'Prosperity Panic,'" attempting jovially to delineate this particular crash as a new and unimportant kind:

Future historians, it is freely predicted, will speak of it as "the prosperity panic of 1929." "The panics of the past were brought about by something fundamentally wrong with finance or business, crop failures, earthquakes, strained international relations, prohibitive rates for money, inflated inventories, and the like," remarks *The Wall Street Journal*. But this October catastrophe on Wall Street was purely a speculative stock-market panic, all authorities agree.

Reassurance was the *Digest*'s tone on November 16, when the lead article of the issue said, "The essential soundness of business is emphasized everywhere." For October, 1929, *The American Magazine* carried one of its inimitable and characteristic interviews with a successful businessman, "How Business Leaders Are Made: As Revealed by the Fine Story of Frederick Beers, New President of the National Biscuit Company." Nothing in November; nothing in December, although that issue did carry an article, "Our Family Pets," by Mrs. Calvin Coolidge. The liberal *New Republic* was just as wrong-headed as the conservative magazines. Its editors were somewhat more alert, however, and mentioned the fact that a financial crash had occurred. On October 30, an editorial read: "The long awaited and often prematurely predicted smash in stock prices seems to have arrived at last. . . . The ultimate result will, of course, be extremely good for business and the country; it will make available more credit and more energy for legitimate productive enterprise."

But the crash was not "extremely good" for the country. Not just the essentially frivolous business of speculation fell apart; the fundamentals of business which were thought to be sound, showed themselves rotten. John K. Galbraith tells how by mid-November, after losses that could not have been worse, stocks stopped falling, for a time. "The low was on November 13 . . . During the rest of November and December the course of the market was moderately up."[5] But the heart was gone out of the great prosperity, and whether the stock market collapse was cause or symptom did not matter greatly to ordinary people who had never gone near the stock market. Symptoms appeared in the financial columns.

Prices of commodities were falling. Freight-car loadings, pig iron and steel production, coal output, and automobile production were also all going down. So, as a result, was the general index of industrial production. Indeed, it was falling much more rapidly than in the sharp postwar depression of 1920–21. There were alarming stories of the drop in consumer buying, especially of more expensive goods. It was said that sales of radio sets in New York had fallen by half since the crash.[6]

Working men and women lost good jobs or could not find jobs if they looked for them. Salaried people found themselves even more vulnerable to notices of job termination. Small independent businesses found themselves with no customers. Large businesses, some of them pyramided precariously upward upon paper structures, collapsed and disappeared. Ford doggedly reduced the price of his cars and kept on selling rather well for a time, but he was an exception. Most businesses experienced a loss of sales, a slump in profits, and a subsequent cut in the working force. An atmosphere of helplessness and fright spread.

This did not all come about at once. There were pockets of prosperity, islands of escape, all through 1929, 1930, 1931. As far as two years into the depression, a musical that contained a keen satire upon the politics of the era was cheerful and jaunty rather than bitter. *Of Thee I Sing* was sharp but light and witty; it belonged to the twenties, not to the thirties, although it was chronologically already past the one decade and into the other. But as the trouble widened and people realized what an extremity they had got into, there was a reaction of bitterness against the party in power and the president just elected. The repudiation of Herbert Hoover was a repudiation of the time ending. His great reputation was murdered publicly, noisily, and painfully—as a thing once loved. In killing the infallibility of Herbert Hoover, the public turned on itself, killing its own optimism, hope, spontaneity, gaiety, killing the inflation of emotion that had kept the twenties afloat. Everything that Hoover had done before the crash, everything that he attempted after the crash, was called into question and fell short of expectation. The disillusionment went far beyond recognizing the simple fact that Hoover was not the man for the job at the time. It was vituperative, despairing, agonized, just because it was an abuse filled with self-recognition. Walter Lippmann brilliantly analyzed the practical weakness of Herbert Hoover. He was a man in political office who did not have a talent for political action.

The weakness Mr. Hoover has displayed as President is a specific, not a general weakness. He is weak in the presence of politics and politicians. Even during the War, when his fame was worldwide and his prestige incalculably great, it was known in Washington that the attack of a relatively obscure man like Senator Reed of Missouri could rattle him for days. . . . He falters only when he has to act in the medium of democracy.[7]

It was not that Hoover, as a sort of chief administrator, had not done or attempted to do many things. On May 20, 1929, the President appointed the Commission on Law Enforcement and Observance. The next July 1, the President made effective one recommendation of the commission ordering the transfer of the Prohibition Bureau from the Treasury to the Justice Department. He saw to it also that, for the first time, prohibition enforcement had a formidable number of agents and that their moral fiber was of first quality. But gangsterism still was widespread in 1929, 1930, and 1931, and there was no longer anything amusing about it. It seemed the monstrous excess of a society that must from the beginning have had something wrong with it. An observer of the tag end of the twenties said (through a character in a novel) that it was worse than Roman excesses, but then, "Rome never saw parties like that. Rome didn't have electric light and champagne and the telephone, thirty-story apartment houses and the view of New York at night, saxaphones and pianos. Here she was [John O'Hara's heroine] just a girl on the town, but about the only thing she had missed was lions and Christians, and she supposed if she hung around long enough she'd have to see that."[8]

The President's busy effort in the farm crisis pleased fewer people than his expense of effort in law enforcement. The farm reformers in Congress made action by the new President necessary. Their bills had been presented over and over again and failed narrowly. Hoover devised a substitute program that, on June 15, 1929, was rescued only at the last minute from the progressives. What it offered the farmers was a new farm board, which was to be an advisory lending agency, having under its control a fund of 500 million dollars. It did not contain the farm bloc's dearest obsession, a system of rebates to farmers on the profits from exports, government supported. The fact that Hoover had gone a certain distance, but only up to a certain point, exacerbated emotions and caused bitterness. During 1930, a drought in the wheatlands caused suffering that no legislation could remedy. In the same year, the President signed the Hawley-Smoot Tariff Bill. Reaction in European countries caused raised tariffs on the other side of the Atlantic and further stoppage of the sale of American farm products abroad. By March, 1931, a real crisis existed in the Farm Board itself.

The board had bought wheat and cotton from 1930's crop. Burdened with this unprecedented kind of governmental responsibility, the board announced on March 23, 1931, that it would be able to buy no more. The new crops were inexorably ripening in the sun and rain in the fields. Despair hit the farmers as the prices of this live and growing crop slid down precipitously. It looked as if the board might well put the old crop on the market in competition with the new one to cut its carrying charges. The board and the President conferred, unsure of themselves, never having been in this situation before, and announced at last that the board would sell only five million bushels of wheat at the time. Wheat prices continued to drop. The board also summoned together the governors of the cotton states on August 12 and appealed to them to ask their farmers in the valleys and upland hills to plow under at least one-third of a bountiful cotton crop, the best in many years. There was no offer of compensation to farmers who would do so. Nothing could prevent always hopeful cotton farmers in small and big farms scattered across the Southeast from enlisting brothers, uncles, children, tenants, in getting in the second-largest crop ever raised. In a desperate move, the board in November agreed to pay for 3,300,000 bales, and private interests cooperated to carry 3,100,000. Prices continued to fall in cotton as in wheat.[9]

The President performed as actively in foreign relations as he did in domestic crises. Abroad, as at home, what became visible was trouble and breakdown. The stage of the world, if Americans looked beyond their own trouble, revealed a new view. The shy prosperity that had brightened the news from overseas in the late twenties faded away into a general malaise. The prosperity of Germany and the Weimar Republic's artistic renaissance began to die away in strange new fanaticism and loyalties. Japan, supposedly democratic and liberal, suddenly seemed far otherwise in its expansion into Manchuria. England, after the momentary misplaced heroism of the general strike, seemed a country spent and done for in its departure from the gold standard. The American scheme of subsidizing the whole circle of the payment of reparations and debts appeared suddenly insane. Hoover's moratorium upon these payments in 1931, a tacit admission that his party's careful management of the whole matter through its Dawes Plan and its Young Plan had been pointless, seemed at first bold and important. The gesture faded into insignificance when nothing new or constructive followed.

Whatever precipitated the fall of stocks in October, 1929, the failure of a speculative enterprise in England, the wrong kind of speech by a public man, the refusal of a state public utilities department to allow a stock split, the ripeness of a plum ready to burst, no one ever discovered.[10] Yet the consequences that followed were irresistible. Whatever the President then undertook to do in the money crisis, which soon became for millions a personal crisis, seemed as wrong as what he was attempting in other fields, domestic and foreign.

Hoover's style was what irritated. It belonged to the time that was dying, not to the time that was being born. Whatever virtues he possessed, and they were many, caused as intense annoyance as they had caused praise before.

The New International Yearbook of 1930, casting a glance backward at the first full year of President Hoover's administration, said with remarkable restraint: "The year was adverse to domestic industry and commerce in almost every branch." The *Yearbook,* close to events, followed keenly but sympathetically the President's balancing between two goals: the spending of public money to "help keep up the incomes of the people in the ordinary ranks of life" and, on the other hand, the holding down of excessive public spending so that the Government might stay solvent and "balanced" and not "leave the Treasury insufficiently supplied and thus compel the imposition of heavier taxation by the December session of Congress." Public works, particularly in Washington, D.C., in the refurbishing of the great stone public buildings of the capital city, were accelerated; the Boulder Dam project was awarded money; appropriations were passed for flood control. There was some boldness here. Yet Hoover was inhibited by long-held ideals. He could not overcome his instinct to hold back in public spending. On April 22, 1930, he wrote a letter to a leading senator and a leading representative, "proposing a close restriction of further appropriations, which he thought likely to cause a deficit, otherwise." In June, 1931, the President made a trip through the coal-mining region of West Virginia, Kentucky, and Ohio and spoke frequently from the platform of the train on which he was traveling, in a manner that anticipated the campaign of the next year. He defended his economic policy, convinced that the American people were grateful that he was "holding fast to the doctrine of individualism."[11]

The suffering people to whom he spoke were not grateful. It was all right to talk of individualism when everyone was either prospering or about to prosper; but when everyone saw a greased slide before him into personal hard times, it seemed a redundant kind of talk. Demands pushed upon the President were no longer polite. Although a special veterans bill had passed only the year before (July, 1930), an American Legion convention in Detroit in September, 1931, called upon the Federal Government to pay in cash the full face value to veterans of the Adjusted Service Compensation certificates. The President spoke to the convention against this demand so authoritatively that for the moment the convention dropped it. But veterans' bonus bills became an element of growing discontent roiling the political scene. People were no longer indifferent to the political leaders they had elected. Of the succession of presidents of the decade, Hoover was the unlucky one.

The once admired President seemed to change, the scenery of American life also changed. Evils that had existed unnoticed suddenly became visible. Harlem, which had been cheerful in its dinginess and hopeful within its marred vitality, seemed a terrible place to a newcomer. Federico García Lorca suffered in his imagination in New York during 1929 and 1930. He wrote:

> You Harlem! You Harlem! You Harlem!
> No anguish to equal your thwarted vermilions,
> your blood-shaken, darkened eclipses,
> your garnet ferocity, deaf and dumb in the shadows,
> your hobbled, great king in the janitor's suit.

Harlem was not what it had seemed; New York was not either:

> Ah, filthy New York,
> New York of cables and death.
> What angel do you carry, concealed in your cheek?
> What ineffable voice will speak the truths of the wheat?
> Who, the terrible dream of your tainted anemones?[12]

This, in García Lorca's "Ode to Walt Whitman," was not Whitman's city, nor was it Scott Fitzgerald's bright and promising city, nor the sacred altar of Hart Crane.

The United States was not Babbitt's country any more either, and he shivered in a blast of fear, anxiety, and uncertainty. Smart, hard, slick honesty, like that of Dashiell Hammett's "private operator" in *The Dain Curse* (1929), *The Maltese Falcon* (1931), and *The Glass Key* (1931), seemed a suitable kind of armor. In life, not fiction, Al Capone's arrest, not for any of the murders he had committed, but for the businessman's crime, tax evasion, was an item in the dying of the twenties.[13] The sick smile upon the pudgy face, the expensive clothes, the white hat, the cigar, all this that made up the Alphonse Capone of the newspapers began to change and to disintegrate as the twenties disintegrated.

The child of the fortunate Lindberghs was kidnapped and senselessly killed. The concentration of attention upon the event was journalism and democracy gone sour. "The Lindbergh kidnapping is not only a harrowing private tragedy; it is also a public event, the effects of which on the public consciousness are likely to be as extensive as those of an earthquake, a flood or even a minor war."[14]

It was a time that heard important news but could not take it in. The newspapers and magazines made sensation of the Gastonia strike, but, except in the words of a humane reporter like Mary Heaton Vorse, failed to state the underlying causes. Strikes had started up simultaneously in many mill towns in the Southeast when in 1929 two things happened. A new system of efficiency was introduced in many of the mills, the Bedaud system, and at the same time, wages were cut. Three years before, a worker had made $19 a week, now he made $17.70. He had tended forty-eight looms then; he tended ninety now.[15]

Such news emphasized the fact that all was not right in the best of all possible American worlds and had not been right for many years. The not-rightness was becoming more and more visible with every day of deepening trouble. Yet desperately, hopefully, people attributed trouble to irrelevant causes or made such sensation out of trouble that it seemed separate from and not the problem of the everyday urban American who read his paper over the breakfast table and so far missed only his orange juice or his bacon.

Much was made of the undoubted Communist Party interference in organizing the workers in Gastonia; little, of the causes of the strike. Police on corners stood by in Gastonia to let well-organized mobs beat up and shoot down strikers. Middle-class inhabitants of the town swore at organizers on the public streets or sat gladly under preachers who preached against the strike. "This outbreak of anarchy rose to a bloody and appalling climax on the afternoon of September 14, when part of a mob which had assembled to prevent a 'Communist' meeting scheduled to take place in South Gastonia pursued a truck full of union members for five miles and murdered one of its occupants, Mrs. Ella May Wiggins, a member of the union and the mother of five children, the eldest eleven years old."[16]

15. Fiorello La Guardia, a progressive Republican from a New York City neighborhood of mixed nationalities, was candid, sharp, an enemy of all stuffed shirts, and a champion of underdogs. He is pictured here examining an example of the fraud of prohibition, a bottle of tonic containing 20 per cent alcohol (February 2, 1929).

16. Stuart Davis, photographed in front of his painting "Summer Landscape" of the year 1930. As a painter, he was one among other creators of the time, self-contained, knowledgeable, persistent, who translated themselves and their time into enduring forms.

The public was as little ready for the "news" in novels published in quick succession by a little-known writer living in a small north Mississippi county seat, Oxford, Mississippi. A new consciousness appeared in William Faulkner's *Sartoris* and *The Sound and the Fury* (1929), *As I Lay Dying* (1930), *Sanctuary* (1931), and *Light in August* (1932). In the minds and actions and emotions of people living in a raw lost land out of the reach of the prosperity of the twenties, the writer brought so much at one time to the public that an indigestion set in. It took years to accommodate Faulkner's insights to the American mind. His best work was born of the life of the South in the twenties and translated into published books in the painful transition between the twenties and the thirties. Yet from this time forth his farmers, planters, bankers, horse traders, washerwomen of Yoknapatawpha County, individuals, and types, had life and meaning in his words.

On a different level of meaning, the insights that were to become *Tobacco Road* and *God's Little Acre* were taking form too, in another region of the deprived South, a deprivation that would loom very large to the rest of the country. Erskine Caldwell as an adolescent boy accompanied his minister father during years of calls on the people of the worn-out farmland near Augusta, Georgia. He saw impressionably the raw material of his heartless farces passing in review in the cluttered yards of the shacks where he waited for his father to complete his calls.

At this inconvenient time the South in various versions burst upon the national mind. Out of generations of experience, but more particularly, out of the hard times of the 1920s, came suddenly a production of books and stories: disturbing, colorful, human. The writers of the previously stricken and silent section asked now questions that had not occurred during the decade before. The dark side of the twenties was now being turned upward. The rich subsoil enriched and fertilized the too bland surface.

The commercial momentum of the twenties did not stop whirring all at once. The twenties' optimism brought into being the new shape of the Empire State Building on Fifth Avenue and Thirty-fourth Street in New York, shining in its new colors against a part of the sky never before 1929 blocked out by a building. It attracted the eyes of a connoisseur of new creations: Edmund Wilson. He wrote appreciatively:

> The first five stories, with their gray façade, silver-framed windows and long rainlike lines in stone, rise graceful and sheer from the street: one feels a sudden relief as one passes them—they do not crowd and overpower Fifth Avenue as most of the newer Fifth Avenue buildings do. And the successive tiers fall back, each just in time not to make too heavy and dull a wall—till the main towering plinth is reached. . . . This plinth, though it is the tallest in the city, has almost always an effect of lightness. . . . On a chilly late afternoon, the mast is like a bright piece of silverware, an old salt-cellar elegantly chased.[17]

He wrote regretfully that the new building was only one-quarter filled and was not likely to be fully occupied at any time soon. It was a shining shell of a purpose somehow lost, and the tens of thousands it was built to hold did not swarm through its halls. Business was shrinking, not growing, and pinched and hungry men haunted the street corners below its soaring height.

The purpose of any institution planned in the twenties and completed in the first days of the depression seemed awry and out of the mood of the new time. The Museum of Modern Art opened its doors in the last days of 1929. An art critic announced its brave purpose: "Just as the great Armory Show of 1913 was the opening gun in the long, bitter struggle for modern art in this country, so the foundation of the new museum marks the final apotheosis of modernism and its acceptance by responsible society."[18] It was many years before the museum (in other quarters) lived up to and found a public for its announced purpose. Another critic in 1931 (Paul Rosenfeld) scolded the museum for a lack of social purpose, for failing to make a vital connection between life and art.[19] But in 1929 the exigencies of life and death crowded the free exercise of art. There were short-lived exceptions. The 1929 Christmas season of the Broadway theater flourished pleasantly. Nothing as vital as Eugene O'Neill, but graceful assurance filled the theaters. *The New Yorker* made a checklist for those who could afford, in December, 1929, to buy theater tickets:

> *Berkeley Square*—"Leslie Howard's performance is superb."
> *Candle-light*—"Gertrude Lawrence as a maid playing lady."

Civic Repertory Theatre, directed by Eva Le Gallienne, "*The Sea Gull*"—"fine production."

Journey's End—"A beautiful and moving play of the war as British officers lived it."

June Moon—"There is a good, honest laugh every two minutes. Ring Lardner and George Kaufman have seen to that."

Street Scene—"Magnificent objective study of a *crime passionel* in a New York tenement."

The Little Show—"Smart, witty, and refreshingly unpretentious revue, in which Clifton Webb, Libby Holman, and Fred Allen figure prominently."

Among the movies of the same week, *The New Yorker* listed:

Disraeli—"George Arliss plays the great minister again, in a screen version that should satisfy the fastidious public."

The Love Parade—"Maurice Chevalier in a picture worthy of his talents. A comedy with music that is really attractive."[20]

The transition time of deepening economic depression was full of the contradiction of accomplishment. Things happened in unrelated, irrelevant fields, which, after the travail of depression, would come together as important elements of a new stage in American civilization. The cyclotron was developed (1931); a new explosion in science was just ahead. The Harvard system of lodging students in residence halls was instituted in 1930–31; a new solidity in the function of the great universities was also ahead, to underly the new scientific and social studies of the next few decades. In scholarly works American self-knowledge deepened in such studies as Walter Prescott Webb's *The Great Plains* (1931), and Constance M. Rourke's *American Humor, A Study of National Character* (1931). In its dying, the twenties contributed its scattered, broken talent to a broader, deeper civilization being born; but in 1930 and 1931, the dying of the old prosperity, the passing away of old heedlessness, the breaking up of the old security (which had seemed so young and free and now looked haggard and worn) were real deaths. Those not affected immediately by the stock-market crash shivered in anticipation. Those who merely watched the spectacle of a New York breadline endured a mortal chill of participation. A visiting Boston newspaperman described the impression that a Times Square breadline made on him when he saw it snaking itself "in long serpentine folds" for over a block in length, so that its members might collect a cup of coffee and two doughnuts. "To see the line for the first time, as I happened to, in a January blizzard was to wonder what on earth it could be. The realization was slow, hardly credible, that this pattern of dark shapes was made up of men, ordinary men, who were hungry enough to stand there in the storm, in the glow of the marvelously irrelevant electric advertising displays, the finest of their kind in the world."[21] The setting was the theatrical district, with unscathed citizens arriving in the early winter night to attend the Broadway shows and being impeded in alighting from their taxis or in crossing Times Square on foot by this double row of fellow human beings waiting in deadly patience for something hot to drink.

It was a time of intense, almost unbearable contradiction. The illusions that had supported the twenties died out gradually in the gaunt light of hard times. The twenties at last no longer existed. The wolves were indeed outside the door. They could be heard snuffling there. And the habit that every generation of Americans had of denying them broke down, at least for a time. What failed, and what killed the twenties in doing so, was the usual easy conjuring up of illusions, "the illusions of eternal strength and health, and of the essential goodness of people; illusions of a nation, the lies of generations of frontier mothers who had to croon falsely that there were no wolves outside the cabin door."[22]

The new time was desperately in need of illusions, but it needed new kinds. Those of the twenties would not serve. Therefore, nothing in the twenties would seem so dead as the feelings and thoughts of the twenties. The thirties would hate the twenties. The forties would find the twenties at best irrelevant and at worst laughable. Only in the fifties and sixties in a cycle of similar illusion in a bigger, richer, and even more vulnerable society, did the twenties seem once more kin.

XV

THE LIBERTARIANS

ON A WIDE AND DUSTY PLAIN a ramshackle new house is going up. Two clowns in the guise of workmen muddle its erection, knocking each other down with boards held awkwardly, falling into pots of paint, chasing each other in sudden, petulant angers around and around the building that they are taking all the time in the world to finish. The road that runs by the house is unfinished and dusty. The landscape surrounding the scene is rough and open, with only a few scattered houses in view. The splendid, unspoiled California light pours down impartially upon their childlike antics. Audiences all over the country laugh sympathetically; this is a Laurel and Hardy movie of the last days of the silent pictures. All the gestures and all the comic conclusions are broad, unsophisticated, irresistible in smirk, grimace, and double take, droll in the unexpected quick timing of the trip-up, the pratfall, the sudden reversal of the chase.

Forty years later, an audience would accept this delicious and nonsensical freedom as typical of the twenties. Something of the lazy space and time available for easygoing comedy to develop had, in the course of time, been identified with the label "the twenties." This is, of course, to oversimplify. The peace of the twenties in the succession of the decades in the American twentieth century would have other meanings. It might be seen as a pause in which materialism swelled and thickened and made certain kinds of opportunities possible and cut off others. It might be seen as a time in which American self-regard became for the first time "modern" and complex, a breeding area for future creativities. It might be seen as a time that completed the "years before" and yet splintered their hopes. It might be seen as the ancestor of the habits of the mid-century in advertising, publicity, communications, transportation, invention, and manufacture.

Yet the quick wit of cartoon and comedy is truer than pedestrian fact. The old movies of Laurel and Hardy tell the truth. There was room enough, there was time enough; life was playful, comic, and even beautiful. It was also erratically obtuse, prejudiced, narrow, self-obsessed, puritanic, and classically conforming. Within the protective barriers of oceans, walled away from the threats hovering over other peoples, behind the barricades of an emotional immunity, for those possessed of a minimum amount of money or talent there was a liberating sense of possibility. It seemed as if an endless margin stretched away, beyond one's own path through life.

A certain kind of person flourished; his beginnings were brilliant; his subsequent career showed no development. John Barrymore played *Hamlet* as it had never been played before on the opening night; through laziness, boredom, inconsequence, he let his performance slide into anticlimax thereafter. Beiderbecke played jazz upon his cornet better than anyone else and allowed the life of the jazz musician in all its indiscipline to kill him. Gutzon Borglum lacked the staying power to complete the carving on Stone Mountain, ending a quarrel with his inartistic sponsors by destroying his models and spoiling as much as he could of the carving upon the mountainface. Thomas Wolfe, whose best book was his first, *Look Homeward, Angel,* drowned his genius in a sea of words that he could not navigate. John Dewey wrote original books about people living together in the new ways of democracy and fathered a system of education that seemed in application like a bastard offspring of a first-rate mind.

There was something meretricious about the ends of many of the talents of the time. Yet there were men who lived in and through the age, not really belonging to it: Robert Frost, Gifford Pinchot, Robert Goddard, Fiorello La Guardia, Stuart Davis. They were its real heroes, not possessed by the time, but enriching it, belonging to themselves and to anyone. They ignored the special false quality of the twenties upon which many gifted individuals relied and that allowed them to practice an easy self-deception. This false quality was simply a foolish confidence in personal and national security. It induced superficiality, heartlessness, and an easy brilliance and spontaneity. It made H. L. Mencken and any Rotarian, brothers under the skin, men unfit to cope with the troubles that after 1929 buried both the graces and the faults of the twenties. After the crash of 1929, both Mencken and his brother Rotarian, whom he so derided, were sadly out of place, unable to help improvise a new age out of poverty, struggle, and the stimulus of insecurity. Yet, they had each contributed something ineffable to the twenties—the hard, superficial satire of the writer; the bland goodwill of the businessman. What was to make the people of the twenties attractive to memory was the relation they had to possibility.

Possibility was something that could be seized hold of quickly and easily. Therefore, the achievements of the twenties, with the exception of the buried lives of men like Goddard and William Carlos Williams, were thin and flashy. They were often brilliant but not enduring, yet the reverse side of the coin was etched in distinction. The achievement of the twenties was a gentlemanly kind of achievement, of individuals freed from censorishness or prudery (these negatives of freedom lurked villainously in the shrubbery of every background).

"We were all Liberals," wrote Joseph Wood Krutch, "but even more conspicuously Libertarians or Libertines—in the Eighteenth Century sense of the term, as well as, frequently at least, in the modern sense also."

Krutch elaborated:

1929 put an end to an epoch and a new generation was soon to dismiss the Twenties as a disgraceful decade during which those who were not hopelessly drunk on bathtub gin were criminally unaware of the various Waves of the Future (good and bad) which were soon to overwhelm them. It is true that to many of us our Bohemianism was a part of what we considered our Liberalism. We attended our own "wild parties" and we inclined to consider sex freedom as by no means the least important of the various freedoms we believed in. Yet in all of these things we did, nevertheless, genuinely believe, and we believed in them with hope. We were not—to use the term now most often applied to the mood of a large segment of present-day intellectuals—"alienated," at least not from man and the universe, though we thought ourselves thoroughly alienated from the United States of Coolidge and Hoover.[1]

The decade in its freedom and cruelty, its "hard heart of a child,"[2] foundered upon the realities of the consequences that its blindness had engendered. The thirties came into being out of a reaction against the twenties and killed the spontaneities that had preceded it. After October 24, 1929, the "Black Thursday" of the stock market, there could be nothing of the twenties left but a relentless running down into decline. The time, the place, the tone would no longer exist. Yet to the steady and sympathetic gaze of a later age the twenties seems a time that contained traits recognizable as human. It would remain a time irresistibly appealing to other eras perhaps more honest but less happy.

NOTES

I. IDENTITY OF A DECADE

1. Robert Frost, *In the Clearing* (New York, Holt, Rinehart & Winston, Inc., 1962), p. 20. By permission of the publisher.
2. C. Vann Woodward, *The Strange Career of Jim Crow* (New York, Oxford University Press, 1960), p. viii.

II. THE YEARS BEFORE

1. Any study of the period is illuminated by Henry F. May, *The End of American Innocence: A Study of the First Years of Our Own Time, 1912–1917* (New York, Alfred A. Knopf, Inc., 1959).
2. From 1910–20, 840; from 1920–27, 304; from 1918–27, 454; from 1900–10, 921; from 1890–1900, 1,665. See Walter White, *Rope and Faggot* (New York, Alfred A. Knopf, Inc., 1929).
3. John R. Bolling, comp., *Chronology of Woodrow Wilson: Together With His Most Notable Addresses* (New York, Frederick A. Stokes Co., 1927), p. 37.
4. August Heckscher, ed., *The Politics of Woodrow Wilson: Selections from His Speeches and Writings* (New York, Harper & Bros., 1956), p. 229.
5. Bolling, *op.cit.*, p. 26.
6. *Ibid.*, p. 43.
7. Mary Antin, *The Promised Land* (Boston, Houghton Mifflin Co., 1912), p. 182.
8. Madison Grant, *The Passing of the Great Race* (New York, Charles Scribner's Sons, 1916), p. 14.

9. For a vivid picture of this kind of hope and disappointment, see Theodore Dreiser, *Sister Carrie* (printed but not sold by the publisher Doubleday, Page, New York, 1900; published, London, Wm. Heinemann, 1901).

10. Ralph Chaplin, *Wobbly: the Rough-and-Tumble Story of an American Radical* (Chicago, The University of Chicago Press, 1948), pp. 133–34.

11. *Ibid.*, p. 189.

12. *Ibid.*, p. 125.

13. The recollections of many men who took part in perfecting the assembly line have been collected in Allan Nevins and Frank E. Hill, *Ford: the Times, the Man, the Company* (New York, Charles Scribner's Sons, 1954), Vol. I, Chapts. XVIII–XXII.

14. Some 78,000 were produced in 1911–12; 168,000 in 1912–13; and 248,000 in 1913–14; by 1916–17 production was up to 730,000. *Ibid.*

15. Gifford Pinchot, *Breaking New Ground* (New York, Harcourt, Brace & Co., Inc., 1947), p. 324.

16. Watson's "behaviorism" was a viewpoint and a discipline that was to be sophisticated and made respectable by a later generation of scholars, but in 1912 Watson's new idea (not original with him, but popularized by him) was confident, sweeping, and vulgar. "In 1912 the behaviorists reached the conclusion that they could no longer be content to work with intangibles and unapproachables. They decided either to give up psychology or else to make it a natural science." And: "The interest of the behaviorist in man's doings is more than the interest of the spectator—he wants to control man's reactions as physical scientists want to control and manipulate other natural phenomena." Watson published in 1925 the lectures delivered in 1912. *Behaviorism* (New York, The People's Inst. Publishing Co., 1924, 1925), pp. 6, 11.

17. Margaret Anderson, ed., *The Little Review Anthology* (New York, Hermitage House, Inc., 1953), p. 13.

18. Frederick J. Hoffman, *et. al.*, eds., *The Little Magazine: A History and a Bibliography* (Princeton, N.J., Princeton University Press, 1946), p. 87.

19. Van Wyck Brooks, *America's Coming of Age* (New York, B. W. Huebsch, 1915), pp. 14, 16.

20. Walter Pach's recollection in Hedley H. Rhys, *Maurice Prendergast* (Cambridge, Mass., Harvard University Press, 1960), p. 50.

21. Morton G. White's phrase for this change in the direction of thought, *Social Thought in America* (New York, The Viking Press, 1949).

22. *Ibid.*, p. 63.

23. *Ibid.*, p. 96.

24. Bolling, *op. cit.*, pp. 44–45.

25. Avery Craven and Walter Johnson, eds., *Documentary History of the American People* (Boston, Ginn & Co., 1951), p. 654.

III. THE EXPERIENCE OF THE WAR

1. Bernard Baruch, *Baruch, op. cit.*, Vol. II, p. 34.

2. *Selected Literary and Political Papers and Addresses of Woodrow Wilson,* (largely drawn from *The Public Papers of Woodrow Wilson,* ed. by Ray Stannard Baker and William E. Dodd). Preface, Ida M. Tarbell, (New York, Grosset & Dunlap Publ., 1926, 1927), Vol. II, pp. 238, 244.

3. *Ibid.*, p. 236.

4. From speech of April 4, 1917, quoted in George Norris, *Fighting Liberal* (New York, The Macmillan Co., 1945), p. 197.

5. Worthington C. Ford, ed., *Letters of Henry Adams* (Boston, Houghton Mifflin Co., 1930), Vol. II, p. 643.

6. "The War Chest Plan in Practice," *Survey,* Vol. 40 (Sept. 7, 1918), pp. 642–43.

7. "The Chart of Household Economies," *Outlook,* Vol. 116 (Jan. 18, 1917), p. 439.

8. Dudley Glass, "How's Atlanta Now?" *Forum,* Vol. 60 (Nov., 1918), pp. 605–6.

9. Percy Lubbock, ed., *Letters of Henry James* (New York, Charles Scribner's Sons, 1920), Vol. II, p. 480.

10. Ben Hecht, "How's Chicago Now?" *Forum,* Vol. 60 (Aug., 1918), pp. 180–82.

11. Lawrence Stallings and Maxwell Anderson recalled what their editor, Frank I. Cobb, told them that the President said this to him the night before the declaration of war, in John L. Heaton, *Cobb of "The World": A Compilation from his Editorial Articles and Public Addresses* (New York, E. P. Dutton & Co., Inc., 1924), pp. 268–70.

12. George Soule, *Prosperity Decade* (New York, Rinehart & Co., 1947), p. 8.

13. Pierce G. Fredericks, *The Great Adventure: America in the First World War* (New York, E. P. Dutton & Co., Inc., 1960), p. 79.

14. Baruch, *op. cit.*, pp. 43, 52.

15. *Ibid.*, p. 17.

16. Story and quotes in *ibid.*, pp. 60–61.

17. Arthur S. Link, *American Epoch* (New York, Alfred A. Knopf, Inc., 1955), p. 216.

18. Preston W. Slosson, *The Great Crusade and After, 1914–1928*, Vol. XII, *A History of American Life* (New York, The Macmillan Co., 1930), p. 67.

19. Oliver Wendell Holmes and Frederick Pollock, *Holmes-Pollock Letters, 1874–1932* (Cambridge, Mass., Harvard University Press, 1941), Vol. II, pp. 31–32.

20. Oswald G. Villard, *Fighting Years: Memoirs of a Liberal Editor* (New York, Harcourt, Brace & Co., Inc., 1939), p. 354.

21. Speech to Knights of Columbus meeting, Oct. 12, 1915.

22. Dwight L. Dumond, *Roosevelt to Roosevelt: the United States in the Twentieth Century* (New York, Henry Holt & Co., 1937), pp. 226–27.

23. Chaplin, *op. cit.*, pp. 226, 233, 246.

24. George Creel, *How We Advertised America* (New York, Harper and Bros., 1920), pp. 4, 5.

25. For a summary of the life, see Louis Filler, *Randolph Bourne* (Washington, D. C., American Council on Public Affairs, 1943).

26. Randolph Bourne, *War and the Intellectuals: Collected Essays, 1915–19*, Carl Resek, ed. (New York, Harper & Row, Publ., 1964), p. 61.

27. *Ibid.*, p. 46.

28. *Ibid.*, p. 45.

29. *Ibid.*, pp. 63–64.

IV.   THE UNRESOLVED PEACE

1. E. E. Cummings, *The Enormous Room* (New York, Jonathan Cape & Harrison Smith, 1922), p. 286.

2. Eunice Tietjens, *The World at my Shoulder* (New York, The Macmillan Co., 1938), p. 2.

3. *The Letters of Robert Frost to Louis Untermeyer*, with commentary by Louis Untermeyer (New York, Holt, Rinehart & Winston, 1963), p. 78.

4. *Felix Frankfurter Reminisces*, recorded talks with Harlan B. Phillips (New York, Reynal & Hitchcock, 1960), p. 161.

5. *Selected . . . Addresses of Woodrow Wilson, op. cit.*, pp. 318–21.

6. Gerald Johnson, *Incredible Tale: the Odyssey of the Average American in the Last Half Century* (New York, Harper & Bros., 1950), pp. 71, 78, 81.

7. Harold Nicolson, *Peacemaking, 1919: Being Reminiscences of the Paris Peace Conference* (Boston, Houghton Mifflin Co., 1933), pp. 41–42.

8. A paraphrase of Nicolson's reactions and reflections.

9. William Z. Foster, *The Great Steel Strike and Its Lessons* (New York, B. W. Huebsch, 1920), p. 71.

10. Compare *ibid.*, p. 14, and Interchurch World Movement, *Report on the Steel Strike of 1919*, by the Commission of Inquiry (New York, Harcourt, Brace & Howe, 1920), p. 5.

11. Foster, *op. cit.*, p. 77.

12. Mary Heaton Vorse, "Behind the Picket Line: The Story of a Slovak Steel-Striker—How He Lives and Thinks," *Outlook*, Vol. 124 (1920), p. 108.

13. *The New York Times*, Jan. 22, 1919.

14. Stanley Coben, *A. Mitchell Palmer: Politician* (New York, Columbia University Press, 1963), p. 208.

15. *Ibid.*, p. 207.

16. Quoted in *ibid.*, p. 217.

17. *Ibid.*, p. 218.

18. Frederick R. Barkley, "Jailing Radicals in Detroit," *The Nation*, Vol. 110 (1920), p. 136.

19. *Ibid.*

20. The account of Post's conduct, from Coben, *op. cit.*, pp. 231–35.

21. See account in Harold Nicolson, *op. cit.*

22. Nov. 19, 1919. Text published in pamphlet, Washington, D.C., 1919, and collected in *European War, 1914–18* (Pamphlets), No. XVII, Emory University Library.

23. Dec. 21, 1918, *European War, 1914–18*, Emory University Library.

24. John Dewey, "Our National Dilemma," *The New Republic* Vol. XXII, p. 118, March 24, 1920.

25. Sept. 25, 1919, in *Selected . . . Addresses of Woodrow Wilson, op. cit.*, p. 370.

26. *Ibid.*, pp. 374–90.

27. Edith B. Wilson, *My Memoir* (Indianapolis, 1938, 1939), pp. 284, 286–87; Cary T. Grayson, *Woodrow Wilson: An Intimate Memoir* (New York, The Bobbs-Merrill Co., 1960), p. 100. Both state very precisely that, although the President became ill on the train leaving Pueblo, he suffered his paralytic stroke three days after he returned to Washington. Tumulty states that the President was stricken with paralysis in Pueblo, and it is so stated in many secondary writings.

28. Joseph P. Tumulty, *Woodrow Wilson as I Know Him* (New York, Doubleday, Page & Co., 1921), pp. 509–10.

V. SYMPTOMS OF THE NEW

1. Lee Allan, *100 Years of Baseball* (New York, Bartholomew House, 1950), 202.

2. U.S. Census, 1920, *Historical Statistics of the United States, Colonial Times to 1957* (Washington, D.C., U.S. Bureau of the Census, 1960), p. 91.

3. Howard Mumford Jones, ed., *The Letters of Sherwood Anderson* (Boston, Little, Brown & Co., 1953), p. 48 (to Waldo Frank).

4. Preface to the 1st ed., *The American Language* (New York, Alfred A. Knopf, Inc., 1919), p. viii.

5. *The Letters of Robert Frost to Louis Untermeyer, op. cit.*, (Jan. 4, 1919), p. 80.

6. Sherwood Anderson, Preface, *Winesburg, Ohio* (New York, B. W. Huebsch, 1919).

7. Sinclair Lewis, *Main Street*, c. 1920 (Harcourt, Brace & Co., Inc., 1961 reprint), pp. 27, 29, 39.

8. James died in 1917. In 1918 Pound jibed at his fellow countrymen in an essay in *The Little Review:* "They do not even know what they lost." *Make It New* (New Haven, Conn., Yale University Press, 1935), p. 252.

9. Blanche A. Price, ed., *The Ideal Reader: Selected Essays* by Jacques Rivière (New York, Meridian Books, Inc., 1960), p. 94. Rivière was editor of the *Nouvelle Revue Française*, 1910–25.

10. Carl Sandburg, "Jazz Fantasia," *Smoke and Steel* (New York, Harcourt, Brace & Co., 1920), collected in *Harvest Poems, 1910–60* (New York, Harcourt, Brace & World, Inc., 1960), p. 59. By permission of the publisher.

11. *The American Language, op. cit.*, p. 190.

VI. HARDING'S TIME

1. James E. Pollard, *The Presidents and the Press* (New York, The Macmillan Co., 1947), p. 699.

2. Karl Schriftgiesser, *This Was Normalcy: An Account of Party Politics During Twelve Republican Years: 1920–1932* (Boston, Little, Brown & Co., 1948), p. 9.

3. Pollard, *op. cit.*, p. 700.

4. Nevins and Hill, *Ford, op. cit.*, Vol. II, p. 158.

5. Robert G. Albion, "Washington Naval Conference (1921–22)," *Encyclopedia Americana* (Americana Corp., 1964).

6. Herbert C. Hoover, *Memoirs* (New York, The Macmillan Co., 1951–52), Vol. II, p. 48.

7. Edmund W. Starling (as told to Thomas Sugrue), *Starling of the White House* (New York, Simon & Schuster, Inc., 1946), p. 167.

8. *Ibid.*, p. 166.

9. *Ibid.*, p. 174.

10. Jane Addams, *The Second Twenty Years at Hull-House* (New York, The Macmillan Co., 1930), pp. 240–41.

11. Quoted in Kenneth Allsop, *The Bootleggers and Their Era* (New York, Doubleday & Co., 1961), p. 31.

12. Herbert Asbury, "The Noble Experiment of Izzie and Moe," in Isabel Leighton, ed., *The Aspirin Age, 1919–1941* (New York, Simon & Schuster, Inc., 1949), pp. 39, 41.

13. Ralph McGill, *The South and the Southerner* (Boston, Little, Brown & Co., 1964), p. 86.

14. Allsop, *op. cit.*, p. 35.

15. *Ibid.*, p. 181.

16. Henrik Henriksen, jazz scholar and collector of Minneapolis, in a letter, May 8, 1965.

17. Discussion of this mixture of strains in Allsop, *op. cit.*

18. Nevins and Hill, *op. cit.*, Vol. II, pp. 200–2, describes and has maps.

19. *Ibid.*, pp. 140–41.

20. *Ibid.*, p. 145.

21. *Ibid.*, p. 124.

22. McGill, *op. cit.*, pp. 131–34, on the genesis of the twentieth-century Klan.

23. Francis B. Simkins, "Ku Klux Klan," *Encyclopedia Americana.* He summarizes the growth, manipulation, appeal, power, numbers, and decline of the organization.

24. Robert Coughlin, "Konklave in Kokomo," in Leighton, *op. cit.*, pp. 105–6. ("Kigy" means "Klansman, I greet you," and "Itsub" means "In the sacred, unfailing bond.")

25. *Main Street*, p. 113.

26. T. S. Eliot, "The Waste Land," *Collected Poems* (New York, Harcourt Brace & Co., 1936), p. 86.

27. *Ibid.*, p. 75. Both quotations from "The Waste Land" by permission of the publisher.

28. *The Dial*, Vol. 73 (Dec., 1922), p. 616.

29. Brom Weber, ed., *The Letters of Hart Crane, 1916–1932* (New York, Heritage House, 1952), p. 129 (Mar. 2, 1923).

30. *Ibid.*, p. 134 (May 9, 1923).

31. *Ibid.*, p. 129.

32. *Ibid.*, p. 110 (Dec. 24, 1922).

33. Hoover, *op. cit.*, p. 49.

VII. SURFACE SOLUTIONS

1. Burton K. Wheeler, with Paul F. Healy, *Yankee from the West* (New York, Doubleday & Co., Inc., 1962), p. 102.

2. *Ibid.*, p. 212.

3. Quotation and description, Kenneth C. McKay, *The Progressive Movement of 1924* (New York, Columbia University Press, 1947), pp. 115, 110–17.

4. *Ibid.*, p. 213.

5. Wheeler, *op. cit.*, p. 259.

6. McKay, *op. cit.*, p. 205.

7. *The Nation*, Vol. 117, p. 153.

8. William Allen White, *A Puritan in Babylon: the Story of Calvin Coolidge* (New York, The Macmillan Co., 1938), p. 145 (the salaries of policemen); p. 166 (quotation).

9. Wheeler, *op. cit.*, pp. 233–34.

10. "Who Then Are the Traitors," *The New Republic*, Vol. 38 (Apr. 9, 1924), pp. 166–67.

11. "Punishing the Guilty Without Admitting the Guilt," *ibid.*, Vol. 38, pp. 165–66.

12. *Ibid.*, p. 166.

13. White, *op. cit.*, p. 335.

14. John H. McKee, comp., *Coolidge Wit and Wisdom: 125 Short Stories about "Cal"* (New York, Frederick A. Stokes Co., 1933), p. 42.

15. *Ibid.*, p. 66.

16. Arthur Meier Schlesinger, Sr., *Political and Social Growth of the American People, 1852–1933* (New York, The Macmillan Co., 1934), p. 454. The period of nonanswering was the first six months.

17. Baruch, *op. cit.*, p. 109.

18. *Ibid.*, p. 108.

VIII. A SUFFICIENT FREEDOM

1. F. Scott Fitzgerald, "My Lost City," *The Crack-Up* (New York, New Directions Paperback, 1956), p. 24.

2. Andrew Turnbull, ed., *The Letters of F. Scott Fitzgerald* (New York, Charles Scribner's Sons, 1963), p. 163.

3. Louis Sullivan, *The Testament of Stone* (Evanston, Ill., Northwestern University Press, 1963), p. 134.

4. He visited the United States in the fall and winter of 1927–28. John A. Spender, *The America of Today* (London, Ernest Benn, Ltd., 1928), pp. 22, 73.

5. *Ibid.*, p. 29.

6. D. H. Lawrence, *Studies in Classic American Literature* (New York, The Viking Press, 1964 ed.), p. 65.

7. Figures from *Historical Statistics of the United States, op. cit.*

8. U. C. Loftin, "Living with the Boll Weevil for Fifty Years," in *Annual Report of the Smithsonian Institution, 1945* (Washington, D.C., Gov't Printing Office, 1946), pp. 275, 276.

9. Andrew W. Mellon, *Taxation: the People's Business* (New York, The Macmillan Co., 1924), pp. 93–95.

10. Harvey O'Conner, *Mellon's Millions: the Biography of a Fortune, the Life and Times of Andrew W. Mellon* (New York, The John Day Co., 1933), p. 140 (the result of the 1926 tax program summarized); pp. 128, 131, 135 (comparative surtax figures for 1921, 1924, 1926).

11. Allan Nevins, "Andrew Mellon," *Dictionary of American Biography* (New York, Charles Scribner's Sons, 1932).

12. Facts about the beginning of the Wilderness System from statements on floor of the House of Representatives by Wayne N. Aspinwall, reprinted in *The Living Wilderness* (Spring–Summer 1964), p. 7.

13. Editor's summary of the case, collected with introductory notes by Alfred Lief, *The Social and Economic Views of Mr. Justice Brandeis* (New York, The Vanguard Press, 1930), p. 232.

14. Brandeis, dissenting opinion, *Gilbert v. State of Minnesota*, 1920, *ibid.*, pp. 233–40.

15. *Federal Trade Commission v. Winsted*, 1922, *ibid.*, pp. 86–87.

16. *Ibid.*, p. 98.

17. Lawrence Elliott, "Beyond Fame and Fortune: The Story of George Washington Carver," *Reader's Digest*, Vol. 86 (May, 1965), pp. 259–62.

18. Dale Nelson, AP story, Atlanta *Journal and Constitution*, Sept. 27, 1964.

IX.   THE EVOLUTION OF THE FLAPPER

1. Cyril H. Bretherton, *Midas, or the United States and the Future* (London, K. Paul, Trench, Trubner & Co., 1926), p. 66.

2. For instance, in the pages of the *Saturday Evening Post*, a product of the popular culture, in illustrations, advertisements, cover

drawings, from 1921 to 1926, the flapper evolved until she finally existed.

3. *The New Republic*, Sept. 9, 1925.

4. Allsop, *op. cit.*, p. 98.

5. *Ibid.*, p. 57.

6. *Ibid.*, p. 199.

7. *Ibid.*, p. 64.

8. *The New Republic*, Vol. 44, p. 124.

9. *The New Republic*, Sept. 9, 1925.

10. *The Dial*, Nov., 1921.

11. *The Dial*, "Comment," unsigned, July, 1920.

X.   THE YEAR NOTHING HAPPENED

1. *New International Yearbook, 1925* (New York, Dodd, Mead & Co., 1926), pp. 721, 723.

2. Starling, *op. cit.*, p. 207.

3. *Historical Statistics of the United States, op. cit.* Series Y 254-57, p. 711.

4. "It Seems to Me," New York *World*, Jan. 27, 1925.

5. *Historical Statistics of the United States, op. cit.*

6. Margaret Sanger, *My Fight for Birth Control* (New York, Farrar & Rinehart, 1931), p. 292.

7. *New International Yearbook, 1925, op. cit.*, p. 399.

8. Quotes and general line of argument of this paragraph from Selig Adler, *The Isolationist Impulse: Its Twentieth-Century Reaction* (London and New York, Abelard-Schuman Ltd., 1957), pp. 176, 177.

9. "Aeronautics," *New International Yearbook, 1925, op. cit.*, pp. 5-7.

10. *Ibid.*, p. 5.

11. *The New Yorker*, Vol. I (incomplete), May 16, 1925–Jan. 30, 1926, in New York Public Library collection. This untitled poem by P. G. Wylie was published without attribution, in *The New Yorker* of Jan. 2, 1926 and is reprinted by permission; copyright © 1926, 1954. The New Yorker Magazine, Inc. (Published just beyond the end of "the year nothing happened," but in the spirit of 1925.)

12. *Ibid.*

13. *The New Yorker*, Aug. 21, 1926.

14. "Darrow vs. Bryan," *The Nation*, Vol. 121 (Jan. 29, 1925), p. 136.

15. *The Nation*, Vol. 121, p. 137.

16. James W. Quigley, "The Defeated Farmer," in *ibid.*, pp. 140-41.

17. Two quotes from Tugwell in "The Problems of Agriculture," *Political Science Quarterly* (1924), pp. 39–40, 549–91.

18. Quotes on the cooperative movement, Lloyd S. Tenny, "The New Cooperative Marketing Law," *Review of Reviews,* Vol. 74 (Sept., 1926), p. 304.

19. J. Harvey Young, from the manuscript of *The Medical Messiahs,* a history of American medical quackery in the twentieth century.

20. Quote and line of reasoning of previous paragraph from Adler, *op. cit.,* pp. 163–64.

21. See C. Herman Pritchett, *The Tennessee Valley Authority: A Study in Public Administration* (Chapel Hill, N.C., The University of North Carolina Press, 1943), Chap. I.

22. Full page ad, New York *World,* Oct. 30, 1925.

23. About new air mail service, "Aeronautics," *New International Yearbook, 1925, op. cit.*

24. H. S. Gorman, New York *World,* Oct. 18, 1925.

25. E. F. Edgett, Boston *Transcript,* Jan. 9, 1926.

26. *Independent,* May 2, 1925.

27. Isabel Paterson, New York *Tribune,* Apr. 19, 1925.

28. *The New York Times,* Oct. 18, 1925.

29. *The Nation,* Feb. 10, 1926.

30. *The Dial,* Aug., 1925.

XI.   HOW SOME PEOPLE LIVED

1. Robert S. and Helen M. Lynd, *Middletown* (New York, Harcourt, Brace & Co., Inc., 1929).

2. *Ibid.,* p. 499.

3. Harold Nicolson, *Dwight Morrow* (New York, Harcourt, Brace & Co., Inc., 1935), pp. 48–49.

4. John Merriman Gaus, "The Issues at Amherst," *The Nation,* Vol. 117 (Jan. 4, 1923), p. 12.

5. "American life, with its attempt to live beautifully, sweetly, honestly, and courageously is a glorious, mad, intoxicating thing," from President Meiklejohn's address at his last Amherst alumni dinner, Nicolson, *Dwight Morrow, op. cit.,* p. 256.

6. *Ibid.,* pp. 280 f.

7. *Ibid.,* pp. 309–10.

8. Raymond Schuessler, "How America Muffed Space Supremacy," *American Mercury,* Vol. 90 (May, 1960), pp. 25–30.

9. The impression of Ernest Hemingway as a young writer is drawn from *A Moveable Feast* (New York, Charles Scribner's Sons, 1964), p. 211.

10. Edmund Wilson, "15 Beech Street," *The New Republic,* Vol. 51 (June 29, 1927), p. 150.

11. *The Autobiography of William Carlos Williams* (New York, New Directions, copyright 1948, 1949, 1951 by William Carlos Williams, reprinted by permission of the publisher, New Directions Publishing Corp.), p. 158.

12. *Ibid.,* p. 175.

13. *Ibid.,* p. 190.

14. *The Selected Letters of William Carlos Williams* (New York, McDowell, Obolensky, 1957), p. 88.

15. The first two quotations from *Spring and All,* 1923, the third from *An Early Martyr,* 1935; in *The Complete Collected Poems of William Carlos Williams* (Norfolk, 1938), 122, 127, 213. ("The Red Wheelbarrow" and "To A Poor Old Woman," William Carlos Williams, *The Collected Earlier Poems of William Carlos Williams,* copyright 1938, 1951 by William Carlos Williams; reprinted by permission of the publisher, New Directions Publishing Corp.)

16. *In the American Grain* (New York, copyright 1925 by James Laughlin, 1933 by William Carlos Williams; reprinted by permission of the publisher, New Directions Publishing Corp.), p. 63.

17. *Ibid.,* pp. 130, 136.

18. Quotation lifted from, and sense of passage about "Hatrack" case paraphrased from, Edgar Kemler, *The Irreverent Mr. Mencken* (Boston, Little, Brown & Co., 1950), pp. 190–204.

19. Although Mencken won the case in the Boston court, Mr. Chase appealed to the U.S. Post Office Department immediately and succeeded in moving that agency, still clothed in wartime censorship powers, to ban the entire April issue of the *Mercury* from the mails. The issue was all out, but the threat hung over future issues. Mencken was deserted by the press, with few exceptions, and denounced all across the country as "a salacious, publicity-seeking editor who deserved all the punishment that the courts or the Post Office could administer to him." *Ibid.,* p. 208.

20. Donald Friede, *The Mechanical Angel, His Adventures and Enterprises in the Glittering 1920's* (New York, Alfred A. Knopf, Inc., 1948), p. 225.

21. *Ibid.,* pp. 47, 58–59.

22. Frankfurter, *op. cit.,* p. 202.

23. G. Louis Joughin and Edmund M. Morgan, *The Legacy of Sacco and Vanzetti* (New York, Harcourt, Brace & Co., Inc. 1948); Robert H. Montgomery, *Sacco-Vanzetti: The Murder and The Myth* (New York, The Devin-Adair Co., 1960).

24. Marion D. Frankfurter and Gardner Jackson, eds., *The Letters of Sacco and Vanzetti* (New York, E. P. Dutton & Co., Inc., 1960), p. 70.

25. *Ibid.*, pp. 81, 377, 379.

26. George Jean Nathan, "The World in Paleface," in *The Magic Mirror: Selected Writings on the Theatre* (New York, Alfred A. Knopf, Inc., 1960), p. 4.

XII.   HIGH TWENTIES

1. An editorial in the *Saturday Evening Post* of Apr. 10, 1926, commended Italy as contrasted with France and said, "There are indications that in many ways Italy is not doing so badly."

2. Nevins and Hill, *op. cit.*, Vol II, p. 437.

3. Paul Gallico, *Farewell to Sport* (New York, Alfred A. Knopf, Inc., 1938), p. 41.

4. The three quotations about Ruth's personal attributes (appearance, speech, habits) in *ibid.*, pp. 31, 32–33, 38.

5. Charles Lindbergh has characterized himself and his preparations for the flight, *The Spirit of St. Louis* (New York, Charles Scribner's Sons, 1953), pp. 3–133.

6. Heywood Broun, "It Seems to Me," *The Nation*, Vol. 126 (Feb. 1, 1928), p. 116.

7. The two quotations from "The Bridge," *The Collected Poems of Hart Crane*. By permission of Liveright Publishers, New York. Copyright © renewed, 1961 by Liveright Publishing Corp., 1933 ed., p. 4.

8. Bruce Bliven, "The Hall-Press-Mills Case," *The New Republic*, Vol. 49 (Dec. 1, 1926), pp. 39–40.

9. Lindbergh, *op. cit.*, pp. 190, 191–92.

10. Gertrude M. Shelby, "Florida Frenzy," *Harper's Magazine*, Vol. 152 (Jan., 1926), p. 176.

11. Stella Crossley, "Florida Cashes in Her Chips," *The Nation*, Vol. 123 (Jan. 7, 1926), p. 11.

12. Henry S. Villard, "Florida Aftermath," *The Nation*, Vol. 126 (June 6, 1928), p. 636.

13. Statistics, "The Florida Disaster," *Survey*, Vol. 57 (Dec. 15, 1926), pp. 396–97.

14. Hamilton Basso, "Flood-water," *The New Republic*, Vol. 51 (June 22, 1927), p. 123.

15. Helen Murphy, "Overflow Notes," *Atlantic Monthly*, Vol. 140 (Aug., 1927), p. 228.

16. Basso, *op. cit.*, p. 123.

17. Hoover, *op. cit.*, pp. 125–26.

18. *New International Yearbook, 1928* (New York, Dodd, Mead & Co., 1929), pp. 769, 771.

19. Gifford Pinchot, "Prevention First," *Survey*, Vol. 58 (Jan. 1, 1927), p. 368.

20. Voting figures on two measures and quotation, *New International Yearbook, 1928, op. cit.*, pp. 774, 775.

21. Colston E. Warne, "The Coal War," *The Nation*, Vol. 126 (Apr. 4, 1928), p. 370. The general description of the worsening of the northern miner's situation from the same.

22. Fiorello La Guardia, "The Government Must Act," *The Nation*, Vol. 126, p. 378.

23. Duff Gilfond, "Americans We Like: Congressman La Guardia," *The Nation*, Vol. 126 (Mar. 21, 1928), p. 319.

24. Bruce Bliven, "In Dedham Jail: A Visit to Sacco and Vanzetti," *The New Republic*, Vol. 51 (June 22, 1927), p. 120.

25. *New International Yearbook, 1928, op. cit.*, p. 770.

XIII.   THE ELECTION OF HOOVER

1. Friede, *op. cit.*, p. 224.

2. See special issue on Harlem, *Survey*, 53 (March 1, 1925), James Weldon Johnson, Alain Locke, *et. al.* Johnson, pp. 635, 639: "It is not a slum or a fringe, it is located in the heart of Manhattan and occupies one of the most beautiful and healthful sections of the city. It is not a 'quarter' of dilapidated tenements, but is made up of new-law apartments and handsome dwellings, with well-paved and well-lighted streets. It has its own churches, social and civic centers, shops, theatres, and other places of amusement. Nor is there any unusual record of crime. I once heard a captain of the 38th Police Precinct (the Harlem Precinct) say that on the whole it was the most law-abiding precinct in the city."

3. Langston Hughes, "Harlem Night Song," *The Weary Blues* (New York, Alfred A. Knopf, Inc., 1926), pp. 62, 26. By permission of the publisher.

4. Alain Locke, "Harlem," *Survey*, Vol. 53 (Mar. 1, 1925), p. 629.

5. The Hampton Institute story (along with other instances) in "The Rising Tide of Prejudice," *The Nation*, Vol. 122 (Mar. 10, 1926), p. 247.

6. "Statutory Segregation Illegal," *Outlook*, Vol. 145 (Mar. 30, 1927), p. 388.

7. *Ibid.*

8. Kelly Miller, "After Marcus Garvey—What of the Negro?" *Contemporary Review*, Vol. 131 (Apr., 1927), p. 492.

9. The list in "Reports: the Guggenheim Memorial Fellowships," *School and Society*, Vol. 23 (Apr. 24, 1926), pp. 525–26.

10. Sam Hunter, *Modern American Painting and Sculpture* (New York, Dell, Laurel Ed., 1964 ed., copyright 1959), pp. 108–9, 112–16.

11. Quoted in James Johnson Sweeney, *Stuart Davis* (New York, Museum of Modern Art, 1945), p. 19.

12. *Ibid.*, pp. 22, 34.

13. "Do the Issues Burn?" *Outlook*, Vol. 149 (Jan. 11, 1928), p. 411.

14. Alfred E. Smith, *Up to Now: An Autobiography* (New York, The Viking Press, 1929), p. 253.

15. From Hoover's acceptance speech in the Stanford University stadium at Palo Alto on Aug. 11, 1928, in Stewart Beach, "The Story of the Week," *Independent*, Vol. 121 (Aug. 18, 1928), pp. 166–67.

16. Excerpts from Smith's acceptance speech, *Congressional Digest*, Vol. 7 (Aug.–Sept., 1928), pp. 236–37, 247, 250.

17. See Herbert Hoover, "Backing Up Business," *Review of Reviews*, Vol. 78 (Sept., 1928), p. 278.

18. *Review of Reviews*, Vol. 75 (May, 1927), pp. 477–79.

19. Smith, *op. cit.*, p. 396.

20. *Ibid.*, p. 403; the entire campaign, pp. 382–414.

21. *Ibid.*, p. 404.

22. College and university professors were not favored citizens of the twenties. Harvard University full professors averaged $9,000 in 1928. In Samuel Eliot Morison, *Three Centuries of Harvard, 1636-1936* (Cambridge, Mass., Harvard University Press, 1936), p. 460.

23. Claude M. Fuess, *Calvin Coolidge, The Man from Vermont* (Boston, Little, Brown & Co., 1940), p. 417.

24. Glenway Wescott, *Goodbye, Wisconsin* (New York, Harper & Bros., Publ., 1928), pp. 14–15.

25. Paul Rosenfeld, "Midwest," *By Way of Art* (New York, Coward-McCann, Inc., 1928), p. 218.

26. "The Evening Land," from *The Complete Poems of D. H. Lawrence*, ed. by Vivian de Sora Pinto & F. Warren Roberts, copyright 1923, 1950 by Frieda Lawrence. Reprinted by permission of The Viking Press, Inc., New York, Vol I, p. 289–90.

27. Spender, *op. cit.*, p. 19.

28. Stuart Chase, *Prosperity, Fact or Myth?* (New York, Charles

Boni Paper Books, 1929), pp. 173–76. Written before the October, 1929, crash.

29. Joseph Wood Krutch, *The Modern Temper* (New York, Harcourt, Brace & Co., Inc., 1956 ed., copyright 1929), p. 169.

XIV. THE CRASH

1. John K. Galbraith, *The Great Crash, 1929* (Boston, Houghton Mifflin Co., 1961 ed., copyright 1954, 1955), pp. 16–17, 47.

2. *Ibid.*, p. 83.

3. Lawrance Thompson, ed., *Selected Letters of Robert Frost,* (New York, Holt, Rinehart & Winston, 1964), pp. 353–54 (to Frederick G. Melcher).

4. Irene Hall and Irene H. Nelson, "How Unemployment Strikes Home," *Survey,* Vol. 62 (Apr. 1, 1929), p. 51.

5. Galbraith, *op. cit.*, pp. 140–41.

6. *Ibid.*, pp. 141–42.

7. "The Peculiar Weakness of Mr. Hoover," *Harper's Magazine,* Vol. 161 (Jan. 1930), p. 6.

8. John O'Hara, *Butterfield 8* (New York, Harcourt, Brace & Co., Inc., 1935), pp. 268–69. (Copyright 1935, but strongly smelling of the late prohibition era.)

9. The general farm situation, *New International Yearbook, 1931* (New York, Dodd, Mead & Co., 1932), p. 808.

10. Galbraith, *op. cit.*, p. 96.

11. *New International Yearbook, 1930* (New York, Dodd, Mead & Co., 1931), pp. 768, 771, 806.

12. Federico García Lorca, *Poet in New York,* complete Spanish text with a new translation by Ben Belitt, published by Grove Press, Inc., New York. Spanish text copyright © 1940 by Francisco García Lorca. This English translation copyright © 1955 by Ben Belitt, pp. 21, 119.

13. "The Capone Indictment is Just an Incident," *Outlook,* Vol. 158 (June 17, 1931), p. 196.

14. Editorial, unsigned, *The New Republic,* Vol. 70 (Mar. 16, 1932), p. 110.

15. "Gastonia," *Harper's Magazine,* Vol. 159 (Nov., 1929), p. 700–1.

16. Nell Battle Lewis, "Anarchy vs. Communism in Gastonia," *The Nation,* Vol. 129 (Sept. 25, 1929), p. 321.

17. "Progress and Poverty," *The New Republic,* Vol. 67 (May 20, 1931), p. 13.

18. Lloyd Goodrich, "A Museum of Modern Art," *The Nation,* Vol. 129 (Dec. 4, 1929), p. 664.

19. "Breadlines and A Museum," *The Nation,* Vol. 132 (Feb. 11, 1931), pp. 160–63.

20. Stage and movie listings from the week of Dec. 21, 1929.

21. "Lean Times in Boston, Depression and the Drys," *Atlantic Monthly,* Vol. 211 (Feb., 1963), p. 49.

22. From *Tender Is the Night,* New York, copyright 1934, Charles Scribner's Sons, in *The Portable F. Scott Fitzgerald* (New York, The Viking Press, 1945), pp. 307–8.

XV. THE LIBERTARIANS

1. Joseph Wood Krutch, *More Lives Than One* (New York, Wm. Sloane Associates, 1962), pp. 173, 178.

2. Elinor Wylie, the last line of "Beauty," in *Nets to Catch the Wind,* 1921, in *Collected Poems* (New York, Alfred A. Knopf, Inc., 1938), p. 3. By permission of the publisher.

SELECTIVE BIBLIOGRAPHY

I. TOOLS FOR FACT-FINDING

REFERENCE, STATISTICAL, BIBLIOGRAPHICAL

While encyclopedias principally used—*Dictionary of American Biography* (New York, Charles Scribner's Sons, 1928–36), *The Encyclopaedia Britannica* (Chicago, London, Encyclopaedia Britannica, Inc., William Benton Publ., 1965), *The Encyclopedia Americana* (New York, Americana Corp., 1964)—may be taken for granted, other more special aids should be cited.

A Guide to the Study of the United States of America, prepared under the direction of Roy P. Basler, by Donald H. Mugridge and Blanche P. McCrum (Washington, The Library of Congress, 1960).

Alice P. Hackett, *Sixty Years of Best Sellers, 1895–1945* (New York, R. R. Bowker Co., 1945).

Howard Mumford Jones, *Guide to American Literature and Its Backgrounds since 1890,* 2nd ed. rev. (Cambridge, Mass., Harvard University Press, 1959).

The New International Yearbook, 1925–1931 (New York, Dodd, Mead & Co., 1926–32).

Robert E. Spiller, *et al.,* eds., *Literary History of the United States: Bibliography* (New York, The Macmillan Co., 1946–48).

U.S. Bureau of the Census, *Historical Statistics of the United States, Colonial Times to 1957* (Washington, 1960).

II. PERIODICALS

The periodicals listed below were used intensively. The kinds of writers, stories, and articles featured, the advertisements, illustrations, and emphases, sustained across the decade in several different kinds of magazines, reveal the blindness or the wisdom of the time. The sampling includes publications superficial and thoughtful, conservative and liberal, popular and special.

American Magazine, The: 1920, 1921, 1924, 1929.
American Mercury: 1924–29.
Dial, The: 1920–25, 1929.
Literary Digest: 1919, 1920, 1922, 1924, 1926, 1929.
New Republic, The: 1920–29.
New Yorker, The: 1925, 1926, 1929.
New York Times, The: 1918, 1919, 1921.
New York *World:* 1919, 1925, 1926.
Saturday Evening Post: 1921–30.

III. CONTEMPORARY WITNESS
A. *In Letters, Memoirs, Speeches*

The kinds of people reflected in the autobiographical writings are of the most incongruous range, important and unimportant, pleasant and unpleasant, who write well and write poorly. Their words, taken together, give a texture of the time.

Adams, Henry, *Letters of Henry Adams,* Worthington C. Ford, ed., 2 vols. (Boston, Houghton Mifflin Co., 1930).

Addams, Jane, *The Second Twenty Years at Hull-House* (New York, The Macmillan Co., 1930).

Anderson, Sherwood, *The Letters of Sherwood Anderson,* Howard M. Jones, ed. (Boston, Little, Brown & Co., 1953).

Antheil, George, *Bad Boy of Music* (Garden City, N. Y., Doubleday, Doran & Co., 1945).

Antin, Mary, *The Promised Land* (Boston, Houghton Mifflin Co., 1912).

Bankhead, Tallulah, *Tallulah: My Autobiography* (New York, Harper & Brothers, 1952).

Baruch, Bernard, *Baruch,* 2 vols. (New York, Henry Holt & Co., 1957–60).

Beach, Sylvia, *Shakespeare & Co.* (New York, Harcourt, Brace & Co., Inc., 1959).

Benn, John Andrews, *Columbus—Undergraduate* (Philadelphia, J. B. Lippincott & Co., 1928).

Borah, William E., *Closing Speech . . . on the League of Nations,*

Nov. 19, 1919 Speech in the Senate of the United States (Washington, 1919). Pamphlet, European War, 1914–18, pamphlets, Vol. XVII, Emory University Library.

Bourne, Randolph, *History of a Literary Radical and Other Papers* (New York, S. A. Russell, 1956. Copyright 1920).

Brooks, Van Wyck, *Days of the Phoenix: The 1920s I Remember* (New York, E. P. Dutton & Co., Inc., 1957).

Caldwell, Erskine, *Call It Experience* (New York, Duell, Sloan & Pearce, 1951).

Callaghan, Morley, *That Summer in Paris* (New York, Coward-McCann, Inc., 1963).

Chaplin, Ralph, *Wobbly: The Rough-and-Tumble Story of an American Radical* (Chicago, The University of Chicago Press, 1948).

Cobb, Frank I., *Cobb of "The World,"* John L. Heaton, comp. (New York, E. P. Dutton & Co., Inc., 1924).

Coolidge, Calvin, *The Autobiography of Calvin Coolidge* (New York, Cosmopolitan Book Corp., 1929).

——, *Coolidge Wit and Wisdom: 125 Short Stories about "Cal,"* John H. McKee, comp. (New York, Frederick A. Stokes Co., 1933).

Cowley, Malcom, *Exile's Return* (New York, W. W. Norton & Co., Inc., 1934).

Cox, James M., *Journey Through My Years* (New York, Simon & Schuster, Inc., 1946).

Crane, Hart, *The Letters of Hart Crane, 1916–1932*, Brom Weber, ed. (N. Y., Hermitage House, 1952).

Cummings, E. E., *The Enormous Room* (New York, Jonathan Cape & Harrison Smith, 1922).

Darrow, Clarence, *Attorney for the Damned*, Arthur Weinberg, ed. (New York, Simon & Schuster, Inc., 1957).

Debs, Eugene Victor, *Walls and Bars* (Chicago, The Socialist Party, 1927).

Dreiser, Helen P., *My Life with Dreiser* (Cleveland, World Publishing Co., 1951).

Dreiser, Theodore, *Letters of Theodore Dreiser: A Selection*, Vol. II, Robert H. Elias, ed. (Philadelphia, University of Pennsylvania Press, 1959).

Edge, Walter E., *A Jerseyman's Journal* (Princeton, Princeton University Press, 1948).

Fitzgerald, F. Scott, *The Crack-Up* (New York, New Directions Paperback, 1956).

——, *The Letters of F. Scott Fitzgerald*, Andrew Turnbull, ed. (New York, Charles Scribner's Sons, 1963).

Fletcher, John Gould, *Life Is My Song: The Autobiography of John Gould Fletcher* (New York, Farrar & Rinehart, Inc., 1937).

Foster, William Z., *Pages from a Worker's Life* (New York, International Publishers, 1939).

Fowler, Gene, *Skyline: A Reporter's Reminiscence of the 1920s* (New York, The Viking Press, 1961).

Frank, Waldo, *The Rediscovery of America* (New York, Duell, Sloan & Pearce, 1947, copyright 1929).

Frankfurter, Felix, *Felix Frankfurter Reminisces,* recorded talks with Harlan B. Phillips (New York, Reynal & Hitchcock, 1960).

Friede, Donald, *The Mechanical Angel, His Adventures and Enterprises in the Glittering 1920's* (New York, Alfred A. Knopf, Inc., 1948).

Frost, Robert, *The Letters of Robert Frost to Louis Untermeyer* (New York, Holt, Rinehart & Winston, 1963).

———, *Selected Letters of Robert Frost,* Lawrence Thompson, ed. (New York, Holt, Rinehart & Winston, 1964).

Garnett, David, *The Golden Echo* (New York, Harcourt, Brace & Co., Inc., 1954).

Grayson, Cary T., *Woodrow Wilson: An Intimate Memoir* (New York, Holt, Rinehart & Winston, 1960).

Harriman, Margaret Case, *The Vicious Circle, The Story of the Algonquin Round Table* (New York, Rinehart & Co., 1951).

Hemingway, Ernest, *A Moveable Feast* (New York, Charles Scribner's Sons, 1964).

Holmes, Oliver Wendell, *Holmes-Pollock Letters, 1874–1932,* Vol. II (Cambridge, Mass., Harvard University Press, 1941).

Hoover, Herbert C., *Memoirs* (New York, The Macmillan Co., 1951–52.)

Hughes, Langston, *The Big Sea* (New York, Alfred A. Knopf, Inc., 1940).

Hull, Cordell, *The Memoirs of Cordell Hull,* Vol. I (New York, The Macmillan Co., 1948).

James, Henry, *The Letters of Henry James,* 2 vols., Percy Lubbock, ed. (New York, Charles Scribner's Sons, 1920).

Johnson, James Weldon, *Along This Way* (New York, The Viking Press, 1933).

Krutch, Joseph Wood, *More Lives than One* (New York, William Sloane Associates, 1962).

Lindbergh, Charles A., *The Spirit of St. Louis* (New York, Charles Scribner's Sons, 1953).

Lodge, Henry Cabot, *The Coming Treaty of Peace:* Speech of Hon. Henry Cabot Lodge of Massachusetts in the Senate of the United States, Saturday, Dec. 21, 1918 (Washington, 1918). In European War, 1914–1918. Pamphlets, Vol. XLVI, Emory University Library.

Lomax, John A., *Adventures of a Ballad Hunter* (New York, The Macmillan Co., 1947).

McAdoo, William G., *Crowded Years: The Reminiscences of William G. McAdoo* (Boston, Houghton Mifflin Co., 1931).

McGill, Ralph, *The South and the Southerner* (Boston, Little, Brown & Co., 1964, copyright 1959 and 1963).

Morris, Lloyd, *Not So Long Ago* (New York, Random House, Inc., 1949).

Norris, George W., *Fighting Liberal: The Autobiography of George William Norris* (New York, The Macmillan Co., 1945).

Pinchot, Gifford, *Breaking New Ground* (New York, Harcourt, Brace & Co., Inc., 1947).

Porter, Katherine Anne, *The Days Before* (New York, Harcourt, Brace & Co., Inc., 1926–52).

Rascoe, Burton, *We Were Interrupted* (New York, Doubleday & Co., Inc., 1947).

Sacco, Nicola, and Vanzetti, Bartolomeo, *The Letters of Sacco and Vanzetti,* Marion D. Frankfurter and Gardner Jackson, eds. (New York, E. P. Dutton & Co., Inc., 1960).

Sanger, Margaret, *My Fight for Birth Control* (New York, Farrar & Rinehart, Inc., 1931).

Sitwell, Osbert, *Laughter in the Next Room* (Boston, Little, Brown & Co., 1948).

Smith, Alfred E., *Up to Now: An Autobiography* (New York, The Viking Press, 1929).

Starling, Edmund W., as told to Thomas Sugrue, *Starling of the White House* (New York, Simon & Schuster, Inc., 1946).

Tietjens, Eunice, *The World at My Shoulder* (New York, The Macmillan Co., 1938).

Villard, Oswald G., *Fighting Years: Memoirs of a Liberal Editor* (New York, Harcourt, Brace & Co., Inc., 1939).

Walker, Stanley, "New York in the 20s," New York *Herald Tribune,* The Lively Arts, April 2, 1961.

Wescott, Glenway, *Images of Truth: Remembrances and Criticism* (New York, Harper & Row, 1962).

Wheeler, Burton K., with Paul F. Healy, *Yankee from the West* (New York, Doubleday & Co., Inc., 1962).

White, William Allen, *Selected Letters of William Allen White*, W. Johnson, ed. (New York, Henry Holt & Co., Inc., 1947).

Williams, William Carlos, *Autobiography* (New York, Random House, Inc., 1951).

———, *The Selected Letters of William Carlos Williams* (New York, McDowell, Obolensky, 1957).

Wilson, Edith Bolling, *My Memoir* (Indianapolis, The Bobbs-Merrill Co., 1938, 1939).

Wilson, Woodrow, *Chronology of Woodrow Wilson: Together with His Most Notable Addresses*, compiled by John Randolph Bolling and others (New York, Frederick A. Stokes Co., 1927).

———, *The Politics of Woodrow Wilson: Selections from his Speeches and Writings*, August Heckscher, ed. (New York, Harper & Bros., 1956).

———, *Selected Literary and Political Papers and Addresses of Woodrow Wilson*, Vol. II (New York, Grosset & Dunlap Pubs., 1926, 1927).

B. In Journalism

"Al Capone's Victory," *The New Republic*, Vol. 67 (Jan. 1, 1931), p. 167.

Amory, Cleveland, and Bradlee, Frederic, eds., *Vanity Fair: A Cavalcade of the 1920s and 1930s* (New York, The Viking Press, 1960).

Angly, Edward, *Oh Yeah?* compiled from newspapers and public records (New York, The Viking Press, 1931).

Allen, Robert S., and Pearson, Drew, *Washington Merry-Go-Round* (New York, H. Liveright, Inc., 1931).

Barkley, Frederick R., "Jailing Radicals in Detroit," *The Nation*, Vol. 110 (1920), pp. 136–37.

Basso, Hamilton, "Flood-water," *The New Republic*, Vol. 51 (June 22, 1927), pp. 123–24.

Beach, Stewart, "The Story of the Week," *Independent*, Vol. 121 (Aug. 18, 1928), pp. 166–67.

Bliven, Bruce, "The Hall-Press-Mills Case," *The New Republic*, Vol. 49 (Dec. 1, 1926), pp. 39–40.

———, "In Dedham Jail: A Visit to Sacco and Vanzetti," *The New Republic*, Vol. 51 (June 22, 1927), pp. 120–21.

Broun, Heywood, *It Seems to Me, 1925–1935* (New York, Harcourt, Brace & Co., Inc., 1935).

———, "It Seems to Heywood Broun," *The Nation*, Vol. 126 (Feb. 1, 1928), p. 116.

Cabot, Philip, "Judge Gary's Opportunity," *Atlantic Monthly*, Vol. 127 (May, 1921), pp. 599–606.

"Calvin Coolidge: Made by a Myth," *The Nation*, Vol. 117 (Aug. 15, 1923), p. 153.

"Capone Indicted," *Outlook and Independent*, Vol. 158 (June 17, 1931), pp. 196–97.

"Chart of Household Economics, The," *Outlook*, Vol. 116 (July 18, 1917), p. 439.

Crossley, Stella, "Florida Cashes in her Chips," *The Nation*, Vol. 123 (July 7, 1926), p. 11.

Denny, Harold Norman, "Mr. Babbitt Draws a Queen," *Forum*, Vol. 77 (Mar., 1927), pp. 344–53.

"Do the Issues Burn?" *Outlook*, Vol. 149 (July 11, 1928), p. 411.

Duff, Gilfond, "Americans We Like: Congressman La Guardia," *The Nation*, Vol. 126 (Mar. 21, 1928), p. 319.

"Florida Disaster, The" *Survey*, Vol. 57 (Dec. 15, 1926), pp. 396–97.

"Floyd Collins Tragedy," *Literary Digest*, Vol. 84 (Feb. 28, 1925), pp. 84–88.

Frankfurter, Felix, "The Case of Sacco and Vanzetti," *Atlantic Monthly*, Vol. 139 (Mar., 1927), pp. 409–32.

Gaus, John Merriman, "Issues at Amherst," *The Nation*, Vol. 117 (July 4, 1923), p. 12.

"Girl Who Wouldn't Quit, The," *Saturday Evening Post*, Vol. 199 (Sept. 11, 1926), p. 38.

Glass, Carter, "Could Smith Be Elected? As a Catholic, Yes! As a Wet, No!" *Review of Reviews*, Vol. 75 (May, 1927), pp. 477–79.

Hall, Irene, and Nelson, Irene H., "How Unemployment Strikes Home," *Survey*, Vol. 62 (Apr. 1, 1929), pp. 50–53, 84–86.

Hoover, Herbert, "Backing Up Business," *Review of Reviews*, Vol. 78 (Sept. 1928), p. 278.

Irwin, Will, "The Aftermath—Mud and Money," *Survey*, Vol. 58 (July 1, 1927), p. 358.

Key, Ellen, "War and the Sexes," *Atlantic Monthly*, Vol. 117 (July, 1916), pp. 837–44.

Krutch, Joseph Wood, "Darrow vs. Bryan," *The Nation*, Vol. 121 (July 29, 1925), pp. 136–37.

La Guardia, Fiorello H., "The Government Must Act," *The Nation*,

"Lesson of the Scandals, The," *The Nation*, Vol. 118, pp. 332–33.

Lewis, Nell Battle, "Anarchy vs. Communism in Gastonia," *The Nation*, Vol. 129 (Sept. 25, 1929), pp. 321–22.

Vol. 126 (Apr. 4, 1928), pp. 378–79.

"Lindbergh Kidnapping, The," *The New Republic,* Vol. 70 (Mar. 16, 1932), p. 110.

Linderman, Frank B., "Charles Russell—Cowboy Artist," *Outlook,* 145 (Apr. 13, 1927), pp. 466–68.

Lippmann, Walter, "The Peculiar Weakness of Mr. Hoover," *Harper's Magazine,* Vol. 161 (June, 1930), pp. 1–7.

Lovett, Robert Morss, "Meiklejohn of Amherst," *The New Republic,* Vol. 35 (July 4, 1923), pp. 146–48.

"Man Out of Work," by his wife, *Harper's Magazine,* Vol. 161 (July, 1903), pp. 195–201.

Merz, Charles, "Bigger and Better Murders," *Harper's Magazine,* Vol. 155 (Aug., 1927), pp. 338–43.

Miller, Kelly, "After Marcus Garvey—What of the Negro?" *Contemporary Review,* Vol. 131 (Apr., 1927), pp. 492–500.

"Minnesota, the Nonpartisan League, and the Future," *The Nation,* Vol. 117 (Aug. 1, 1923), p. 102.

Morgan, Arthur E., "The Mississippi: Meeting a Mighty Problem," *Atlantic Monthly,* Vol. 140 (Nov., 1927), pp. 661–74.

Murphy, Helen, "Overflow Notes," *Atlantic Monthly,* Vol. 140 (Aug., 1927), pp. 223–30.

"No One Is Starving," *The Nation,* Vol. 134 (Mar. 30, 1932), p. 356.

Parker, John M., "After the Flood," *Outlook,* Vol. 146 (June 1, 1927), pp. 148–49.

Pinchot, Gifford, "Prevention First," *Survey,* Vol. 58 (July 1, 1927), pp. 367–69.

———, "The State, the Nation, and the People's Needs," part of address given at Governors' Conference at Cheyenne, Wyo., July 26, 1926, *Annals of the American Academy of Political and Social Science,* Vol. 129 (Jan., 1927), pp. 72–76.

Pound, Ezra, "Henry James and Remy de Gourmont," *The Little Review,* Aug., 1918; in *Make It New* (New Haven, 1935).

"Punishing the Guilty Without Admitting the Guilt," *The New Republic,* Vol. 38 (Apr. 9, 1924), pp. 165–66.

Quigley, James W., "The Defeated Farmer," *The Nation,* Vol. 121 (July 29, 1925), pp. 140–41.

Rascoe, Burton, *A Bookman's Daybook,* ed. C. Hartley Grattan (N. Y., Horace Liveright, 1929).

"Reports: the Guggenheim Memorial Fellowships," *School and Country,* Vol. 23 (Apr. 24, 1926), pp. 525–26.

"Rising Tide of Prejudice, The," *The Nation,* Vol. 122 (Mar. 10, 1926), p. 247.

Rogers, Will, "Bacon and Beans and Limousines," *Survey*, Vol. 67 (Nov. 15, 1931), pp. 185, 219.

Rosenfeld, Paul, "After the O'Keefe Show," *The Nation*, Vol. 132 (Apr. 8, 1931), pp. 388–89.

Ryder, D. W., "Aimee Semple McPherson," *The Nation*, Vol. 123 (July 28, 1926), pp. 81–82.

Shelby, Gertrude M., "Florida Frenzy," *Harper's Magazine*, Vol. 152 (Jan., 1926), p. 176.

"Snyder Murder Mystery, The," *Outlook*, Vol. 146 (May 18, 1927), pp. 74–75.

Springer, Gertrude, "Ragged White Collars," *Survey*, Vol. 67 (Nov. 15, 1931), pp. 183–84.

"Statutory Segregation Illegal," *Outlook*, Vol. 145 (Mar. 30, 1927), p. 388.

Tenny, Lloyd S., "The New Cooperative Marketing Law," *Review of Reviews*, Vol. 74 (Sept., 1926), pp. 304–6.

"Third Party Is Born, The," *The Nation*, Vol. 115 (Nov. 22, 1922), p. 541.

Tugwell, Rexford Guy, "The Problem of Agriculture," *Political Science Quarterly*, Vol. 39–40 (1924), pp. 549–91.

"Unemployment Disaster, The," *The Nation*, Vol. 132 (Apr. 1, 1931), p. 342.

Villard, Henry S., "Florida Aftermath," *The Nation*, Vol. 126 (June 6, 1928), pp. 635–36.

Vorse, Mary Heaton, "Behind the Picket Line: The Story of a Slovak Steel-Striker—How He Lives and Thinks," *Outlook*, Vol. 124 (1920), pp. 107–9.

———, "Gastonia," *Harper's Magazine*, Vol. 159 (Nov., 1929), pp. 700–10.

"War Chest Plan in Practice, The," *Survey*, Vol. 40 (Sept. 7, 1918), pp. 642–43.

Warne, Colston E., "The Coal War," *The Nation*, Vol. 126 (Apr. 4, 1928), pp. 369–70.

"Who Then Are the Traitors?" *The New Republic*, Vol. 38 (Apr. 9, 1924), pp. 166–67.

Wilson, Edmund, "15 Beech St.," *The New Republic*, Vol. 51 (June 29, 1927), pp. 150–51.

———, "A Great Magician," *The New Republic*, Vol. 56 (Oct. 17, 1928), pp. 248–50.

IV. BIOGRAPHY

Adams, Samuel Hopkins, *Incredible Era: The Life and Times of Warren Gamaliel Harding* (Boston, Houghton Mifflin Co., 1939).

Angoff, Charles, *H. L. Mencken: A Portrait from Memory* (New York, Thomas Yoseloff, Inc., 1956).

Bennett, Harry Herbert, *We Never Called Him Henry* (New York, Fawcett Publishers, 1951).

Brinnin, John Malcolm, *The Third Rose: Gertrude Stein and Her World* (Boston, Little, Brown & Co., 1959).

Burlingame, Roger, *Don't Let Them Scare You: The Life and Times of Elmer Davis* (Philadelphia, J. B. Lippincott & Co., 1961).

Coben, Stanley, *A. Mitchell Palmer: Politician* (New York, Columbia University Press, 1963).

Filler, Louis, *Randolph Bourne* (Washington, D.C., American Council on Public Affairs, 1943).

Flanner, Janet, *Men and Monuments* (New York, Harper & Bros., 1947–57).

Gallico, Paul, *Farewell to Sport* (New York, Alfred A. Knopf, Inc., 1938).

Johnson, Gerald W., *Woodrow Wilson: The Unforgettable Figure Who Has Returned to Haunt Us* (New York, Harper & Bros., 1944).

Kemler, Edgar, *The Irreverent Mr. Mencken* (Boston, Little, Brown & Co., 1950).

La Follette, Belle C. and Fola, *Robert M. La Follette*, 2 vols. (New York, The Macmillan Co., 1953).

Lippmann, Walter, *Men of Destiny* (New York, The Macmillan Co., 1927).

Lueders, Edward, *Carl Van Vechten and the Twenties* (Albuquerque, N. M., University of New Mexico Press, 1955).

Madison, Charles A., *Leaders and Liberals in Twentieth Century America* (New York, Frederick Ungar Pub. Co., 1961).

Manchester, William, *Disturber of the Peace: The Life of H. L. Mencken* (New York, Harper & Bros., 1950, 1951).

Miller, Perry, "The Incorruptible Sinclair Lewis," *Jubilee: 100 Years of the Atlantic* (Boston, Little, Brown & Co., 1957).

Mizener, Arthur, *The Far Side of Paradise: A Biography of F. Scott Fitzgerald* (Boston, Houghton Mifflin Co., 1951).

Nevins, Allan, with the collaboration of Frank Ernest Hill, *Ford*, Vols. I and II (New York, Charles Scribner's Sons, 1954 and 1957).

Nicolson, Harold, *Dwight Morrow* (New York, Harcourt, Brace & Co., Inc., 1935).

O'Connor, Harvey, *Mellon's Millions: The Biography of a Fortune, the Life and Times of Andrew W. Mellon* (New York, The John Day Co., 1933).

"Rocket Dreamer," *Time*, Vol. 76 (Aug. 15, 1960), pp. 18–19.

Schuessler, Raymond, "How America Muffed Space Supremacy," *American Mercury*, Vol. 90 (May, 1960), pp. 25–30.

Tumulty, Joseph P., *Woodrow Wilson as I Know Him* (New York, Doubleday, Page & Co., 1921).

Turnbull, Andrew, *Scott Fitzgerald* (New York, Charles Scribner's Sons, 1962).

White, William Allen, *A Puritan in Babylon: The Story of Calvin Coolidge* (New York, The Macmillan Co., 1938).

———, *Woodrow Wilson: The Man, His Times, and His Task* (Boston, Houghton Mifflin Co., 1924).

Wilson, Edmund, "Justice Oliver Wendell Holmes," *Patriotic Gore* (New York, Oxford University Press, 1962).

Zinn, Howard, *La Guardia in Congress* (Ithaca, N.Y., Cornell University Press, 1959).

V.   HISTORY: GENERAL AND SPECIAL

History here is taken in its broadest sense, to include political, social, and cultural works, and also stretched to include, as historians, both professionals and amateurs.

Adams, James Trustlow, *Our Business Civilization: Some Aspects of American Culture* (New York, A. & C. Boni, 1929).

Adler, Selig, *The Isolationist Impulse: Its Twentieth-Century Reaction* (London and New York, Abelard-Schuman, Ltd., 1957).

Allen, Frederick Lewis, *The Big Change* (New York, Harper & Bros., 1952).

———, *The Lords of Creation* (New York, Harper & Bros., 1935).

———, *Only Yesterday: An Informal History of the Nineteen-Twenties* (New York, Harper & Bros., 1931).

Allen, H. C., and Hill, C. P., *British Essays in American History* (New York, St. Martin's Press, Inc., 1957).

Allen, Lee, *One Hundred Years of Baseball* (New York, Bartholomew House, 1950).

Allsop, Kenneth, *The Bootleggers and Their Era* (New York, Doubleday & Co., Inc., 1961).

American Heritage, Special Issue, "The 20's," Vol. 16, No. 5, Aug., 1965.

Asbury, Herbert, *The Great Illusion: An Informal History of Prohibition* (Garden City, N.Y., Doubleday & Co., Inc., 1950).

Beard, Charles A. and Mary R., *A Basic History of the United States* (New York, The New Home Library, 1944).

Binkley, Wilfred E., *President and Congress* (New York, Alfred A. Knopf, Inc., 1947).

Blum, Daniel C., *A Pictorial History of the American Theatre* (New York, Greenberg, 1950).

Cochran, Thomas C., and Miller, William, *The Age of Enterprise: A Social History of Industrial America* (New York, The Macmillan Co., 1942).

Craven, Avery, Johnson, Walter, and Dunn, F. Roger, *A Documentary History of the American People* (Boston, Ginn & Co., 1951).

Cunliffe, Marcus, *The Literature of the United States* (Baltimore, Penguin Books, 1954).

Dumond, Dwight Lowell, *Roosevelt to Roosevelt: The United States in the Twentieth Century* (New York, Henry Holt & Co., 1937).

Ekirch, Arthur A., *The Decline of American Liberalism* (New York, Longmans, Green & Co., 1955).

Falconer, Robert Alexander, *The United States as a Neighbour from a Canadian Point of View* (London, Cambridge University Press, 1925).

Faulkner, Harold U., *From Versailles to the New Deal* (New Haven, Yale University Press, 1950).

Feis, Herbert, *The Diplomacy of the Dollar* (Baltimore, The Johns Hopkins Press, 1950).

Fitch, James Marston, *American Building: The Forces that Shape It* (Boston, Houghton Mifflin Co., 1948).

Foster, William Z., *The Great Steel Strike and Its Lessons* (New York, B. W. Huebsch, 1920).

Fredericks, Pierce G., *The Great Adventure: America in the First World War* (New York, E. P. Dutton & Co., Inc., 1960).

Furniss, Norman F., *The Fundamentalist Controversy, 1918–1931* (New Haven, Yale University Press, 1954).

Galbraith, John K., *The Great Crash, 1929* (Boston, Houghton Mifflin Co., 1954, 1955).

Goldman, Eric F., *Rendezvous with Destiny: A History of American Reform* (New York, Alfred A. Knopf, Inc., 1952).

Graebner, Norman A., ed., *An Uncertain Tradition: American Secretaries of State in the Twentieth Century* (New York, McGraw-Hill Book Co., Inc., 1961).

Haynes, William, *Men, Money and Molecules* (Garden City, N.Y., Doubleday, Doran & Co., Inc., 1936).

Hicks, John D., "Opportunities for Historical Research on the 1920's" (unpublished paper).

———, *Republican Ascendancy: 1921–1933* (New York, Harper & Bros., 1960).

Higham, John, *Strangers in the Land: Patterns of American Nativism, 1860–1925* (New Brunswick, N.J., Rutgers University Press, 1955).

Hoffman, Frederick J., Allen, C., and Ulrich, C. F., *The Little Magazine: A History and a Bibliography* (Princeton, N.J., Princeton University Press, 1946).

Hofstadter, Richard, *Great Issues in American History,* Vol. II, 1864–1957 (New York, Vintage Books, 1958).

Holbrook, Stewart H., *Lost Men of American History* (New York, The Macmillan Co., 1946).

Hollingsworth, J. Rogers, "Consensus and Continuity in Recent American Historical Writing," *South Atlantic Quarterly,* Vol. 61, No. 1 (winter, 1962).

Hugh-Jones, E. M., *Woodrow Wilson and American Liberalism* (New York, The Macmillan Co., 1948).

Hughes, H. Stuart, "Is Contemporary History Real History?" *American Scholar,* Vol. 32, No. 4 (autumn, 1963), pp. 516–25.

Hunter, Sam, *Modern American Painting and Sculpture* (New York, Dell, 1959).

Hutchens, John K., ed., *The American Twenties: A Literary Panorama* (Philadephia, J. B. Lippincott Co., 1952).

I Remember Distinctly: A Family Album of the American People, 1918–1941, assembled by Agnes Rogers, comment by Frederick Lewis Allen (New York, Harper & Bros., 1947).

Jacobs, Lewis, *Rise of the American Film: A Critical History* (New York, Harcourt, Brace & Co., Inc., 1939).

Johnson, Gerald, *Incredible Tale: The Odyssey of the Average American in the Last Half Century* (New York, Harper & Bros., 1950).

Kennan, George F., *American Diplomacy, 1900–1950* (Chicago, The University of Chicago Press, 1951).

———, "Russia and the Versailles Conference," *American Scholar,* Vol. 30, No. 1 (winter 1960–61).

Keynes, John M., *The Economic Consequences of the Peace* (New York, Harcourt, Brace & Co., Inc., 1920).

Kootz, Samuel M., *Modern American Painters* (New York, Brewer & Warren, Inc., 1930).

Krutch, Joseph Wood, *The American Drama since 1918: An Informal History* (New York, Random House, 1939).

Larkin, Oliver W., *Art and Life in America* (New York, Rinehart & Winston, copyright 1949, 1960).

Leighton, Isabel, ed., *The Aspirin Age, 1919–1941* (New York, Simon & Schuster, Inc., 1949).

Leuchtenburg, William E., *Perils of Prosperity: 1914–1932* (Chicago, The University of Chicago Press, 1958).

Link, Arthur S., *American Epoch* (New York, Alfred A. Knopf, Inc., 1955).

———, Langer, William L., and Goldman, Eric F., *Woodrow Wilson and the World of Today* (Philadelphia, University of Pennsylvania Press, 1957).

Loftin, U. C., "Living with the Boll Weevil," *Annual Report of the Smithsonian Institution*, 1945 (Washington, D.C., U.S. Government Printing Office, 1946).

MacKay, Kenneth C., *The Progressive Movement of 1924* (New York, Columbia University Press, 1947).

May, Henry F., *The End of American Innocence: A Study of the First Years of Our Own Time, 1912–1917* (New York, Alfred A. Knopf, Inc., 1959).

Mitgang, Herbert, "The Downfall of Jimmy Walker," *Atlantic Monthly*, Oct., 1962, pp. 97–116.

Morison, Samuel Eliot, *Three Centuries of Harvard, 1636–1936* (Cambridge, Mass., Harvard University Press, 1936).

Morris, Lloyd R., *Postscript to Yesterday: America, the Last Fifty Years* (New York, Random House, 1947).

Murray, Robert K., *Red Scare* (Minneapolis, University of Minnesota Press, 1955).

Murrell, William, *History of American Graphic Humor: 1865–1938* (New York, The Macmillan Co., 1938).

Nevins, Allan, *The United States in a Chaotic World: A Chronicle of International Affairs, 1918–1933* (New Haven, Yale University Press, 1950).

Nicolson, Harold, *Peacemaking 1919: Being Reminiscences of the Paris Peace Conference* (Boston, Houghton Mifflin Co., 1933).

Perkins, Dexter, *The Evolution of American Foreign Policy* (New York, Oxford University Press, 1948).

Pollard, James E., *The Presidents and the Press* (New York, The Macmillan Co., 1947).

Potter, David M., "Explicit Data and Implicit Assumptions in Historical Study," *Generalization in the Writing of History:* A Report of the Committee on Historical Analysis of the Social Science Research Council, Louis Gottschalk, ed. (Chicago, The University of Chicago Press, 1963).

———, *People of Plenty: Economic Abundance and the American Character* (Chicago, The University of Chicago Press, 1954).

Pritchett, C. Herman, *The Tennessee Valley Authority: A Study in Public Administration* (Chapel Hill, The University of North Carolina Press, 1943).

Schlesinger, Sr., Arthur Meier, *Political and Social Growth of the American People, 1852–1933*, rev. ed. (New York, The Macmillan Co., 1934).

Schriftgiesser, Karl, *This Was Normalcy: An Account of Party Politics during Twelve Republican Years, 1920–1932* (Boston, Little, Brown & Co., 1948).

Seldes, Gilbert, *The Years of the Locust* (Boston, Little, Brown & Co., 1933).

Slosson, Preston William, *The Great Crusade and After, 1914–1928* (New York, The Macmillan Co., 1930).

Smith, Charles Edward, introductory essay, *Riverside History of Classic Jazz* (New York, Bonanza Books, a Division of Crown Publishers, Inc., 1956).

Soule, George, *Prosperity Decade: From War to Depression, 1917–1929* (New York, Rinehart & Co., 1947).

Sullivan, Mark, *Our Times: The United States, 1900–1925*, Vol. VI, *The Twenties* (New York, Charles Scribner's Sons, 1935).

Trevelyan, G. M., *History of England*, Vol. III (New York, Doubleday & Co., Inc., 1953).

Tuchman, Barbara W., "The Anarchists," *Atlantic Monthly*, May, 1963, pp. 91–110.

Webb, Walter Prescott, "How the Republican Party Lost Its Future," *An Honest Preface and Other Essays* (Boston, Houghton Mifflin Co., 1959).

Wecter, Dixon, *The Age of the Great Depression* (New York, The Macmillan Co., 1948).

Werner, Morris R., and Starr, John, *Teapot Dome* (New York, The Viking Press, 1959).

Wiebe, Robert, "Dissent and the Twenties," unpublished.

Woodward, C. Vann, *The Strange Career of Jim Crow* (New York, Oxford University Press, 1955).

Young, J. Harvey, "The Myth of Prosperity in the 1920's," *Emory University Quarterly*, Vol. 13, No. 2 (June, 1957).

———, " 'Truth in Advertising,' " and "The New Muckrakers," Chaps. 6 and 7, in *The Medical Messiahs* (in manuscript), a history of medical quackery in the United States in the twentieth century.

VI. OBSERVATION AND COMMENT

Addams, Jane, "Social Consequences of Depression," *Survey*, Vol. 67 (Jan. 1, 1932), pp. 370–71.

Angoff, Charles, "The Tone of the Twenties," *The Literary Review*, Vol. 4, No. 1 (autumn, 1960).

Beard, Charles A., ed., *Whither Mankind: A Panorama of Modern Civilization* (New York, Longmans, Green & Co., 1928).

Becker, Carl, *Everyman His Own Historian* (New York, Appleton-Century-Crofts, Inc., 1935).

Birnbaum, Lucille, "Behaviorism in the 1920's," *American Quarterly*, Vol. 7 (spring, 1955), pp. 15–30.

Blackmur, R. P., "The American Literary Expatriate," in David F. Bowers, *Foreign Influences in American Life* (Princeton, Princeton University Press, 1944).

Brandeis, Louis, *The Social and Economic Views of Mr. Justice Brandeis*, collected, Alfred Lief (New York, The Vanguard Press, 1930).

———, *The Words of Justice Brandeis*, Solomon Goldman, ed. (New York, Henry Schuman, 1953).

Bretherton, Cyril H., *Midas, or the United States and the Future* (London, Trench, Trubner & Co., 1926).

Chase, Stuart, *Prosperity: Fact or Myth* (New York, Charles Boni Paper Books, 1929).

Cohen, Morris R., *American Thought: A Critical Sketch* (Glencoe, Ill., The Free Press, 1954).

Cowley, Malcolm, *After the Genteel Tradition: American Writers Since 1910* (New York, W. W. Norton & Co., Inc., 1937).

Davidson, Donald, *The Attack on Leviathan: Regionalism and Nationalism in the United States* (Chapel Hill, The University of North Carolina Press, 1938).

Felix, David, "Apotheosis in Boston: Sacco and Vanzetti, from Case to Legend," *Columbia University Forum* (fall, 1963), pp. 33–38.

Galbraith, John K., *The Liberal Hour* (Boston, Houghton Mifflin Co., 1960).

Hofstadter, Richard, *Anti-Intellectualism in American Life* (New York, Alfred A. Knopf, Inc., 1963).

Hunt, Edward Eyre, *An Audit of America: A Summary of Recent Economic Changes in the United States* (New York, McGraw-Hill Book Co., Inc., 1930).

Interchurch World Movement, *Report on the Steel Strike of 1919*, by the Commission of Inquiry (New York, Harcourt, Brace & Howe, 1920).

Joad, C. E. M., *The Babbitt Warren* (New York, Harper & Bros., 1927).

Joughin, G. Louis, and Morgan, Edmund M., *The Legacy of Sacco and Vanzetti* (New York, Harcourt, Brace & Co., Inc., 1948).

Kirchwey, Freda, ed., *Our Changing Morality: A Symposium* (New York, A. & C. Boni, 1924).

Knoles, George Harmon, *The Jazz Age Revisited: British Criticism of American Civilization During the 1920's* (Stanford, Stanford University Press, 1955).

Laidler, Harry W., and Thomas, Norman, eds., *Prosperity? Symposium* . . . (New York, Vanguard Press, 1927).

Lerner, Max, "The Social Thought of Mr. Justice Brandeis," in *Mr. Justice Brandeis: Essays*, by Charles E. Hughes and others (New Haven, Yale University Press, 1932).

Lippmann, Walter, *American Inquisitors, a Commentary on Dayton and Chicago* (New York, The Macmillan Co., 1928).

———, *Liberty and the News* (New York, Harcourt, Brace & Co., Inc., 1920).

Luthin, Reinhard H., *American Demagogues: Twentieth Century* (Boston, The Beacon Press, 1954).

Mellon, Andrew W., *Taxation: The People's Business* (New York, The Macmillan Co., 1924).

Montgomery, Robert H., *Sacco-Vanzetti: The Murder and the Myth* (New York, The Devin-Adair Co., 1960).

Morton, Charles W., "Lean Times in Boston: Depression and the Drys," *Atlantic Monthly*, Vol. 211, No. 2 (Feb., 1963).

Munson, Gorham, "The Birthday of the Twenties," *Literary Review* (autumn, 1961).

Porter, Katherine Anne, "Paris: A Little Incident in the Rue de l'Odéon," *Ladies Home Journal* (Aug., 1964).

Pritchett, V. S., "That Time and that Wilderness," *New Statesman*, Vol. 64, No. 1646 (Sept. 28, 1962), pp. 405–6.

Rosenberg, Harold, "The Armory Show: Revolution Re-enacted," *The New Yorker*, Apr. 6, 1963.

Rosenfeld, Paul, *By Way of Art* (New York, Coward-McCann, Inc., 1928).

———, *Men Seen: 24 Modern Authors* (New York, The Dial Press, 1925).

Siegfried, André, *America Comes of Age* (New York, Harcourt, Brace & Co., Inc., 1927).

Sitwell, Osbert, "New York in the Twenties," *Atlantic Monthly* (Feb., 1962, pp. 38–43).

Spender, John Alfred, *The America of Today* (London, Ernest Benn Ltd., 1928).

Tippett, Tom, *When Southern Labor Stirs* (New York, Jonathan Cape & Harrison Smith, 1931).

Tomkins, Calvin, "Living Well Is the Best Revenge," *The New Yorker*, July 28, 1962.

Ward, John William, "The Man, or the Machine?" *University: A Princeton Magazine* (winter, 1961, No. 7).

White, Morton G., *Social Thought in America* (New York, The Viking Press, 1949).

White, Walter, *Rope and Faggot: A Biography of Judge Lynch* (New York, Alfred A. Knopf, Inc., 1929).

VII. A SAMPLING IN BOOKS OF CREATIONS, PRODUCTS, ATTITUDES

Anderson, Sherwood, *Winesburg, Ohio* (New York, B. W. Huebsch, 1919).

Barton, Bruce, *The Man Nobody Knows: A Discovery of the Real Jesus* (Indianapolis, The Bobbs-Merrill Co., 1924, 1925).

Bernays, Edward L., *Crystallizing Public Opinion* (New York, Boni & Liveright, Publishers, 1923).

Bishop, John Peale, *Collected Essays*, Edmund Wilson, ed. (New York, Charles Scribner's Sons, 1948).

Bourne, Randolph, *War and the Intellectuals: Collected Essays, 1915–19*, Carl Resek, ed. (New York, Harper & Row, 1964).

Brooks, Van Wyck, *America's Coming-of-Age* (New York, B. W. Huebsch, 1915).

Caldwell, Erskine, *Tobacco Road* (New York, Charles Scribner's Sons, 1932).

Crane, Hart, "White Buildings," (1926) and "The Bridge," (1930), in *The Collected Poems of Hart Crane*, Waldo Frank, ed., (New York, Liveright Pub. Corp., 1933).

Creel, George, *How We Advertised America* (New York, Harper & Bros., 1920).

Cummings, E. E. "Tulips and Chimneys," (1923): "XLI–Poems," (1925); "Is 5" (1926); in *Collected Poems* (New York, Harcourt, Brace & Co., Inc. 1938).

Dreiser, Theodore, *An American Tragedy* (New York, Horace Liveright, 1925).

————, *Sister Carrie*, Printed but not sold, New York, Doubleday, Page, 1900.

Du Bois, Guy Pène, *Edward Hopper* (New York, Whitney Museum of American Art, 1931).

Dunne, Finley Peter, *Mr. Dooley at His Best* (New York, Charles Scribner's Sons, 1938).

Eliot, T. S. "Poems," (1920); "The Waste Land," (1922); "The Hollow Men," (1925); "Ash Wednesday," (1930); in *Collected Poems, 1909–1935* (New York, Harcourt, Brace & Co., 1930, 1934, 1936).

Faulkner, William, *As I Lay Dying* (New York, Harrison Smith & Robert Haas, 1930).

————, *Sartoris* (New York, Harcourt, Brace & Co., Inc., 1929).

————, *The Sound and the Fury* (New York, Jonathan Cape & Harrison Smith, 1929).

Fitzgerald, F. Scott, *The Great Gatsby* (New York, Charles Scribner's Sons, 1925).

————, *The Stories of F. Scott Fitzgerald: A Selection of 28 Stories*, introd. Malcolm Cowley (New York, Charles Scribner's Sons, 1958).

————, *Tender Is the Night* (New York, Charles Scribner's Sons, 1934).

Frost, Robert, "New Hampshire" (1923) and "West-Running Brook" (1928) in *Collected Poems* (New York, Halcyon House, 1940).

Goossen, E. C., *Stuart Davis* (New York, George Braziller, Inc., 1959).

Hammett, Dashiell, *The Dain Curse* (New York, Alfred A. Knopf, Inc., 1928, 1929).

————, *The Maltese Falcon* (New York, Alfred A. Knopf, Inc., 1930).

Hemingway, Ernest, *A Farewell to Arms* (New York, Charles Scribner's Sons, 1929).

————, *The Sun Also Rises* (New York, Charles Scribner's Sons, 1926).

————, *Men Without Women* (New York, Charles Scribner's Sons, 1927).

————, *In Our Time: Stories* (New York, Charles Scribner's Sons, 1924).

Hughes, Langston, *The Weary Blues* (New York, Alfred A. Knopf, Inc., 1926).

I'll Take My Stand: The South and the Agrarian Tradition, by twelve Southerners (New York, Harper & Bros., 1930).

John Sloan, American Artists Group: Monograph No. 1 (New York, American Artists Group, 1945).

Krutch, Joseph Wood, *The Modern Temper* (New York, Harcourt, Brace & Co., Inc., 1929).

Lawrence, D. H., *The Complete Poems of D. H. Lawrence,* 2 vols. (New York, The Viking Press, 1964).

———, *Studies in Classic American Literature* (New York, The Viking Press, 1923).

Sinclair Lewis, *Arrowsmith* (New York, 1925).

———, *Babbitt* (New York, Harcourt, Brace & Co., Inc., 1922).

———, *Dodsworth* (New York, Harcourt, Brace & Co., Inc., 1929).

———, *Elmer Gantry* (New York, Harcourt, Brace & Co., Inc., 1927).

———, *Main Street* (New York, Harcourt, Brace & Co., Inc., 1920).

———, *The Man Who Knew Coolidge* (New York, Harcourt, Brace & Co., Inc., 1928).

Lippmann, Walter, *A Preface to Morals* (New York, The Macmillan Co., 1929).

Little Review Anthology, The, Margaret Anderson, ed. (New York, Hermitage House, 1953).

Lorca, Federico García, *Poet in New York,* Ben Belitt, trans. (New York, Grove Press, 1955, copyright 1940).

Lynd, Robert S. and Helen M., *Middletown* (New York, Harcourt, Brace & Co., Inc., 1929).

Mencken, H. L., *The American Language* (New York, Alfred A. Knopf, Inc., 1919).

———, *Notes on Democracy* (New York, Alfred A. Knopf, Inc., 1926).

———, *Prejudices,* first, second, third, and sixth series (New York, Alfred A. Knopf, Inc., 1919, 1920, 1922, 1927).

Munsterberg, Hugo, *Psychology and Industrial Efficiency* (Boston, Houghton Mifflin Co., 1913).

Murrell, William, *Charles Demuth,* American Artists Series (New York, Whitney Museum of American Art, n.d.).

Nathan, George Jean, *The Magic Mirror: Selected Writings on the Theatre,* Thomas Quinn Curtiss, ed. (New York, Alfred A. Knopf, Inc., 1960).

O'Hara, John, *Appointment in Samarra* (New York, Harcourt, Brace & Co., Inc., 1934).

———, *Butterfield 8* (New York, Harcourt, Brace & Co., Inc., 1935).

Ransom, John Crowe, "Chills and Fevers" (1924) and "Two Gentlemen in Bonds" (1927) in *Selected Poems* (New York, Alfred A. Knopf, Inc., 1952).

Rhys, Hedley Howell, *Maurice Prendergast, 1859–1924* (Cambridge, Harvard University Press, 1960).

Rivière, Jacques, *The Ideal Reader: Selected Essays*, Blanche A. Price, ed. (New York, Meridian Books, Inc., 1960).

Rourke, Constance, *American Humor: A Study of National Character* (New York, Doubleday & Co., Inc., 1931).

Sandburg, Carl, "Chicago Poems," (1916); "Cornhuskers," (1918); "Smoke and Steel," (1920); "Slabs of the Sunburst West," (1922); "Good Morning, America," (1928) in *Harvest Poems, 1910–1960* (New York, Harcourt, Brace & Co., Inc., 1960).

Sapir, Edward, *Culture, Language and Personality: Selected Essays*, David G. Mandelbaum, ed. (Berkeley and Los Angeles, University of California Press, 1962).

Stein, Gertrude, *Three Lives* (New York, New Directions, 1933, copyright 1909).

Stevens, Wallace, *Harmonium* (New York, 1953, Alfred A. Knopf, Inc., c. 1923, 1931).

Sullivan, Louis, *The Testament of Stone*, Maurice English, ed. (Evanston, Ill., Northwestern University Press, 1963).

Sweeney, James Johnson, *Stuart Davis* (New York, Museum of Modern Art, 1945).

Watson, John B., *Behaviorism* (New York, The People's Institute Pub. Co., 1924, 1925).

Webb, Walter Prescott, *The Great Plains* (New York, Ginn & Co., 1931).

Wescott, Glenway, *Goodbye, Wisconsin* (New York, Harper & Bros., 1928).

———, *The Grandmothers: A Family Portrait* (New York, Harper & Bros., 1927).

Williams, William Carlos, *The Complete Collected Poems of William Carlos Williams* (Norfolk, Conn., New Directions, 1938).

———, *In the American Grain* (Norfolk, Conn., New Directions, 1925, 1933).

———, and others, *John Marin* (Berkeley, Calif., University of California Press, 1956).

Wilson, Edmund, *The American Earthquake: A Documentary of the Twenties and Thirties* (New York, Doubleday & Co., Inc., 1958).

———, *The Shores of Light: A Literary Chronicle of the 20's and 30's* (New York, Farrar, Straus & Young, Inc., 1952).

Wylie, Elinor, *Collected Poems* (New York, Alfred A. Knopf, Inc., c. 1921–32, 1938).

INDEX

Millay, Edna St. Vincent: *A Few Figs from Thistles*, 75; and Ralph McGill, 90-91
Miller, Alice Duer: in *Saturday Evening Post*, 140
Mills, Florence, 214
Mississippi River flood (1927), 198, 199-202
Mississippi River Flood Commission, 201
Mitchell, General William D. (Billy): fight for air power, 157-58, 176
Mitchell, Wesley: *Recent Economic Changes in the United States*, 227
Model T Ford: style of, 20
Money-making, 138
Montana: Walsh and Wheeler's, 105
Moore, Marianne: "Two Poems" in *The Dial*, 79; *Observations*, 168
Morgan, J. P., 16, 36
Morrow, Dwight: character and career of, 174-78; at Sixth Pan American Conference, 225
Mother's Day: first national celebration of, 19
"Mother" Jones, 19
Mount Pisgah (North Carolina): and the birth of American forestry, 21
Munsterberg, Hugo: *Psychology and Industrial Efficiency*, 23
Muscle Shoals, 132
Museum of Modern Art: opened, 240
Mussolini, Benito: seized power, 189

Nashville *Banner*: Ralph McGill, reporter for, 90
Nathan, George Jean: twenties mood of, 188
Nation, The: censored, 38; on the methods of the Red Scare, 60-61; on Calvin Coolidge, 113; on farming, 162
NEP (in Russia), 82
Neutrality: American, 28-29
Nevins, Allan: on Henry Ford, 191

New Deal: latent in the late twenties, 206; foreshadowed, 112
New England writers: reassessed, 136
New Republic, The: on Calvin Coolidge, 116-17; and Dwight Morrow, 175; mentioned, 43
New York City: center for the arts, 79; viewed by García Lorca, 237
New York port: described by E. E. Cummings, 47
New York Times, The: on Prohibition, 56; on the bomb plot, 57; on Attorney General Palmer, 59
New York *Tribune*: critical of wartime government, 39
New Yorker, The: early history of, 159-61
Nicolson, Harold: on Woodrow Wilson, 52; on Dwight Morrow, 174-75, 177-78
Nicolson, Marjorie Hope: early Guggenheim Fellow, 217
Nine-Power Treaty, 84
Non-Partisan League, 110
Norris, Senator George: his style, 8; opposed to war, 30; and the bankers, 36; in 1924 Progressive Party campaign, 110; and public power, 132; prevented sale of Muscle Shoals, 166; speaking for the future, 205

Oberholtzer, Madge, 156
Odum, Howard: scholarly contribution, 216, 217; *An Introduction to Social Research*, 217
Oil: discovered in Montana, 100-101
Of Thee I Sing: political satire, 233
Oliver, King Joe, 93
Olmsted, Frederick Law, 21
O'Neill, Eugene: *Bound East for Cardiff*, 26; *Desire Under the Elms*, 136; *Strange Interlude*, 225; mentioned, 240
Oppenheim, James: editor of *The Seven Arts*, 25

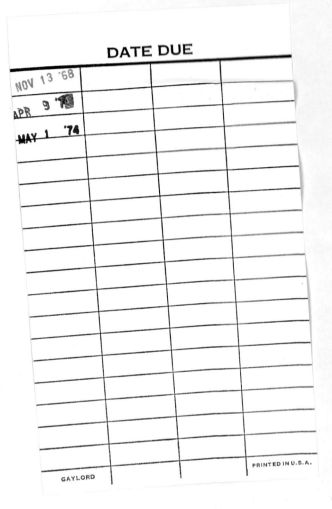

DATE DUE

NOV 13 '68			
APR 9 '7			
MAY 1 '74			
GAYLORD			PRINTED IN U.S.A.